# The
# Magic of
# Australia

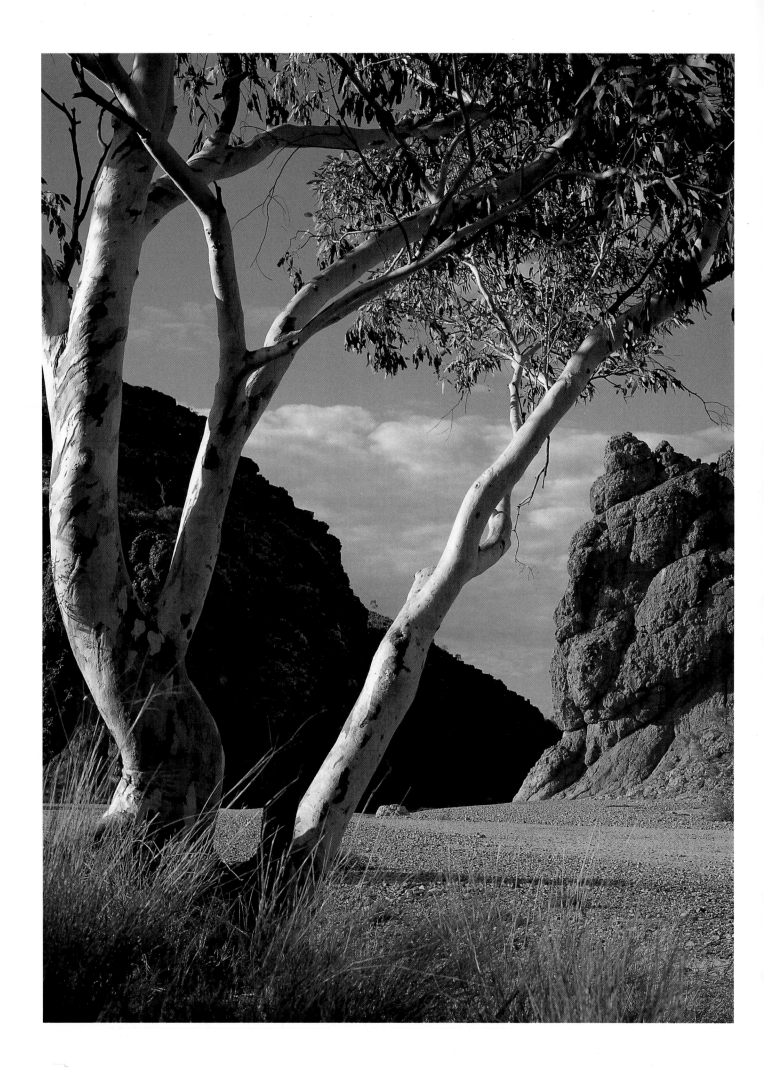

# The
# Magic of
# Australia

## Text by Bruce Elder
### Colour photographs by Geoff Higgins and Ken Stepnell

Beaut BOOKS
AUSTRALIA

This edition distributed by
Beaut Books Australia Pty Ltd
Unit 13, E2 No 6–8 Byfield Street
North Ryde, NSW, 2113

First published in 1995 by
National Book Distributors Pty Ltd
3/2 Aquatic Drive, Frenchs Forest, NSW 2086

Devised and produced by
Murray Child and Company Pty Ltd, 64 Suffolk Avenue,
Collaroy, NSW, 2097
Reproduction by Hirt & Carter (Pty) Ltd, Cape Town, South
Africa
Printed and bound by Tien Wah Press

National Library of Australia Cataloguing-in-Publication data

Elder, Bruce
  The magic of Australia

  Includes index
  ISBN 1 86436 073 9.


  1. Australia - History. 2. Australia - Pictorial works.
  3. Australia - History -Pictorial works. I. Title.

994

Halftitle: *Sunrise at Nuriootpa, South Australia.*
Frontispiece: *Glen Helen Gorge, Northern Territory.*
Title page: *Sunrise at Bluff Beach, Devonport, Tasmania.*
Left: *Weano Gorge, Hamersley Range National Park, Western
Australia.*
Contents page: *Sleepy Bay, Freycinet National Park, Tasmania.*
Pages 6-7: *The Olgas, Northern Territory.*

# Contents

# Australia: THE HERITAGE

The history of Australia is deceptively simple and uncomplicated. With no internal struggles and no serious external threats the country has evolved in a series of neatly defined periods of change.

The country's original inhabitants probably arrived about 50 000 years ago. These early residents, ancestors of modern-day Australian Aborigines, spread throughout the country over the next 30 000 years. They continued their uncomplicated lives, spending most of their waking hours engaged in hunting and gathering, until the late eighteenth century when Britain decided that Australia would make an ideal penal colony for the detritus of London's prisons.

The arrival of convicts at Port Jackson in 1788 was followed by a fifty-year period when settlements were established around the coastline and large tracts of fertile land were settled by sheep and cattle graziers.

By the 1840s the concept of Australia as a penal colony was being seriously questioned by liberals and reformers. The 'convict' period of Australian history came to an abrupt end with the discovery of gold. For the next thirty years miners from all over the world arrived in Australia. The goldfields in New South Wales, Victoria, Western Australia and Queensland yielded rich harvests.

The end of the nineteenth century saw the colonies, which had all become autonomous states, drawing together to create a unified federation. A country with a clear identity.

Australia in the twentieth century has slowly emerged from an unconfident ex-colony trying to assert its independence to a confident nation actively involved in the development and prosperity of its own region and committed to the broader international community through such agencies as the United Nations.

The search for identity has been unceasing. Throughout the century images of Australia have ranged from bronzed Anzacs to urbane city dwellers. The enduring images have always contained elements of sturdy independence, a refusal to respect authority, a genuine sense of egalitarianism, a dislike of pretentiousness and a sense of energy and exuberance. No matter whether Australians live in cities (as most people do) or work in the 'outback' these qualities endure. The result is a sense of identity which emphasises informality and independence. These qualities seem so natural whenever anyone takes an overview of the country's development.

## Aboriginal settlement before the arrival of Europeans

Modern understanding of early Aboriginal settlement is based on careful analysis of scarce, and often ambiguous, archaeological data. It is now accepted that the ancestors of modern Aborigines arrived on the continent at least 40 000 years ago. This is supported by the evidence of camp sites in New South Wales and Perth which date from that period.

Some archaeologists believe that the first Aborigines arrived as early as 50–55 000 years ago.

They claim that it took 10 000 years for Aborigines to move from the northern coast to south-western and south-eastern Australia. They also argue that 50 000 years ago the world's sea level was 150 metres lower and consequently the journey through the Indonesian archipelago would have been a relatively easy combination of walking and short boat trips.

The first inhabitants could not have realised that they had arrived on a continent, not just another island. In fact at that time it is likely that Australia, Papua New Guinea and Tasmania were all joined.

For the next 55 000 years the Aborigines moved right across the continent actively hunting and gathering and establishing themselves in semi-permanent settlements in areas where the food was rich and plentiful. Recent archaeological work has provided a number of hints as to the progress the people made across the continent.

The oldest known tools to be discovered probably date from around 38 000 years ago. These were located in the upper reaches of the Swan River in Western Australia. It would seem that at this point Aborigines had moved down through Western Australia and were living in areas where the winters would have been much colder than they are today.

One of the most significant of all early Aboriginal archaeological sites is that at Lake Mungo in far western New South Wales. This dates from around 30–32 000 years ago. The significance of this site is that it suggests a range of complex social behaviour. There is evidence of the use of ochre in ritual burial at the site. In the book *Bruising the Red Earth*, Antonia Sagona writes: 'At Lake Mungo, New South Wales, a male skeleton (Mungo III) of delicate build was found stained red with haemetite. The skeleton was found in a shallow grave, placed on its back and turned slightly to the right so that its head rested on the shoulder; the hands were clasped resting on the pelvis, and the legs were slightly bent at the knees. Dated to 30 000 BP (Before Present), the Mungo interment attests the only known use of ochre in mortuary practice from a Pleistocene site in Australia.'

Malangerr in the Northern Territory has also been the source of a major archaeological discovery. Stone axe heads dating back to 24 000 BP have been found there. These are some of the oldest axe heads found on earth.

Discoveries at a number of other sites have given an indication of the spread of Aborigines throughout the Australian continent. Archaeologists have found evidence of stone tools at Keilor in Victoria which date back to 32 000 BP. Around 28 000 BP there is evidence at Devils Lair in Western Australia that Abori-

*Torres on the northern coast of Australia.*

gines were living off the flora and fauna of the area. By 26 000 BP Aborigines were fishing for yabbies and other fresh-water life on the shores of Tandou Lake in New South Wales and there is evidence of Aboriginal settlement in Tasmania.

Around 20 000 BP archaeological finds suggest that most of the continent was inhabited and that the Aborigines were actively using the local resources in creative ways. There is evidence of settlement in Tasmania (Kutinkina Cave in Tasmania is reputedly the southern-most ice age site in the world), on the Nullarbor Plain, at Mount Newman in Western Australia, in northern Queensland and in Arnhem Land. In these widely varying sites evidence has been found of flint mining, the use of ochre for artistic purposes and the first finger painting on cave walls. It seems from the walls of Koonalda Cave on the Nullarbor Plain that the local Aborigines were painting on the walls.

If this dating is accurate, it means that the Australian Aborigines were expressing themselves artistically 5000 years before Europeans crept into caves in southern France and Spain to draw crude images of animals on walls.

By 18 000 BP Aborigines had devised a method of collecting and grinding wild seeds (a technique which survives to the present day). The continent seems to have been well settled by this time. Settlement sites range from the Murray River in western New South Wales to the Ord River in far northern Western Australia.

Over the next 18 000 years stone tools became increasing sophisticated and by 1000 BP hook and line fishing, probably learnt from the trepang fishermen and traders from Timor and Indonesia, became commonplace around the coast.

It was also during this period that the narrow land corridor between Australia and New Guinea was cut off by the rising level of the ocean (around 8000 BP) and the Aborigines in Tasmania were no longer capable of moving back to the mainland (6000 BP).

During this time the dingo arrived on the Australian mainland (around 4000 BP) and the remarkable X-ray art which is such a feature of the caves in Kakadu National Park, became a common feature of Aboriginal art.

By 1788 there were somewhere between 300 000 and one million Aborigines living in Australia. Population densities varied according to the richness of the areas. It is thought that at the time of the arrival of the first Europeans there were about 3000

*The* Duyfken *in the Gulf of Carpentaria.*

people living in the Sydney basin (about 1500 on the coast and about the same number on the Cumberland Plain), 4000 in Gippsland, 3500 in Tasmania and as many as 5000 in the south-western corner of Western Australia. They were essentially hunters and gatherers but their lifestyle varied according to the availability of food. The inhabitants of the Sydney basin and the north and south coasts of New South Wales were quite sedentary, while the Wiradjuri, who occupied the south-western slopes of New South Wales from the Blue Mountains to the edges of the Snowy Mountains, led an extremely active life.

*Tasman's carpenter landing at Storm Bay.*

### Early exploration of the Australian coastline

For most of the nineteenth and twentieth centuries a very Eurocentric view of Australian history prevailed. This view argued that the first explorers to reach Australia were the Portuguese in the sixteenth century. This conveniently ignored the fact that the Chinese had been exploring the area some centuries before the Europeans rounded the Cape of Good Hope. It seems most likely that the first explorer to reach Australia was the Chinese navigator Cheng Ho, who in the early years of the fifteenth century ventured into the Indian Ocean. It is probable that

a statue found near the present-day site of Darwin in 1879 was left by Cheng Ho.

A century later, as a result of Bartholomew Diaz rounding the Cape of Good Hope in 1488, European explorers were venturing across the Indian Ocean. In 1514 Antonio de Abreu reached Timor to the north of Australia and there is some evidence that in 1522 Christo de Mendonça reached the north-west coast of Australia.

By 1531 the words *Terra Australis* were appearing on European maps and by 1536 it was commonplace for these maps to indicate the presence of a major landmass to the south of the East Indies. Throughout the sixteenth century, although there is no evidence of any European charting the coasts of Australia, it was widely accepted by cartographers that south of Java there was a substantial landmass.

There seems to be little doubt that the first European to sight Australia was Luis Vaez de Torres who saw Cape York at the northern tip of Queensland in July 1606. The irony of this discovery was that for over a century the Portuguese had been searching for *Terra Australis Incognito* but Torres assumed it (Cape York) was another island and did not investigate further. Later that year when the Dutch explorer Willem Janszoon sailed the *Duyfken* down the west coast of Cape York he did not realise that he was charting *Terra Australis* he believed that he was still exploring the coast of New Guinea. Remarkably, one of groups of Aborigines on Cape York still have a story about a strange vessel with sails which moved down the coast.

The first extensive and detailed exploration of the Australian coastline was a mixture of accident and expediency. By 1619 the Dutch had captured the main centre on the island of Java, renamed it Batavia, and established it as the centre of Dutch influence in the East Indies. Seeking an easier route to the East Indies, Dutch sailors decided to let themselves be pushed across the Indian Ocean by the Roaring Forties and when they hit the coast of New Holland all they had to do was turn north and head for Batavia. The inevitable happened: some ships sailed too far east and crashed into the coast of what is now Western Australia.

It was Henderik Brouwer who, in 1610, discovered that the best route from the Cape of Good Hope to Batavia was via the Roaring Forties. Brouwer achieved the crossing of the Indian Ocean and successfully sailed up the coast of Western Australia.

# *The March of Time:* **1780s and 1790s**

| 1788–9 | 1790–2 | 1793–4 | 1795–7 | 1798–1800 |
|---|---|---|---|---|

## EVENTS

**1788** In January the First Fleet arrives at Botany Bay and six days later moves to Port Jackson.

**1789** The Hawkesbury River, the Nepean River and the Blue Mountains, NSW, are discovered by an expedition led by Watkin Tench.

**1790** First circumnavigation of the continent by Henry Lidgbird Ball in storeship *Supply.* The colony is threatened with famine; Government House is built at Parramatta and in June the first free immigrant, Philip Schaeffer, arrives in Sydney.

**1791** The first Irish convicts arrive in Australia.

**1792** The British government allows free settlers to take up land in NSW.

**1793** Elizabeth Farm is built by John Macarthur. It is now the oldest extant building in Australia.

**1794** The Reverend Samuel Marsden arrives in Sydney.

**1795** George Bass and Matthew Flinders explore the Georges River and Botany Bay in the *Tom Thumb.*

**1796** Port Hacking, Lake Illawarra and Port Kembla are discovered and explored by Bass and Flinders.

**1797** Coal deposits are found south of Botany Bay and Captain John Shortland discovers coal in his exploration of the Hunter River area.

**1798** Bass and Flinders begin journey to discover if Van Diemens Land is an island.

**1799** Aborigines opposing the settlements at Parramatta and in the Hawkesbury River area suffer severe reprisals.

**1800** A Customs House opens in Sydney and the first taxes are levied on beer, wine and spirit imports.

## GOVERNMENT AND FOREIGN AFFAIRS

**1788** In January Captain Arthur Phillip becomes the first Governor of the colony of NSW and in February the Colony of NSW is officially proclaimed by Judge Advocate David Collins.

**1789** The colony establishes its first police force.

**1790** A ticket-of-leave system is introduced by Governor Phillip.

**1791** The Third Fleet arrives carrying 1763 convicts.

**1792** In December Governor Phillip is forced to return to England because of ill health. Francis Grose becomes Acting Governor and replaces civil magistrates with military officers.

**1793** The NSW Corps earns the name 'Rum Corps' by their illegal trading in liquor.

**1794** Francis Grose is replaced by Captain William Paterson as

administrator of colony and head of NSW Corps.

**1795** John Hunter, who captained the *Sirius* in the First Fleet, becomes Governor of NSW.

**1796** John Macarthur and the Rum Corps constantly oppose John Hunter.

**1797** The first merino sheep are imported into the colony.

**1798** Richard Dore succeeds David Collins as Deputy Judge-Advocate.

**1799** Coal is exported to India from Newcastle.

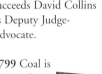

**1800** Philip Gidley King is appointed Governor with instructions to end the monopoly of the Rum Corps.

## LEISURE AND LIFESTYLE

**1788** 'The Rogue's March' becomes the first musical piece to be performed in public in the colony.

**1789** A book entitled *Narrative of the Expedition to Botany Bay* by Watkin Tench is published in London.

**1790** *Journal of a Voyage to New South Wales* by John White is published in London.

**1791** James Ruse becomes the first self-sufficient farmer in the colony after receiving the first official land grant.

**1792** White population is estimated at 3120.

**1793** The Reverend Richard Johnson establishes the first church in the colony in what is now Hunter Street, Sydney. It is destroyed by fire in 1798.

**1793** John and Elizabeth Macarthur receive a land grant of 100 acres near Parramatta and establish a sheep-breeding farm.

**1794** A settlement is established at Windsor.

**1795** The first brewery in the colony is established by John Squires near Parramatta.

**1796** The colony's first full-time playhouse and theatre opens in Bligh St, Sydney.

**1797** First recorded sighting by Europeans of the platypus.

**1798** *An Account of the English Colony in New South Wales* by former Judge-Advocate David Collins is published in London.

**1799** Whaling and sealing are becoming major industries.

**1800** George Caley, naturalist and botanist, arrives to study Australian marsupials. John Lewin arrives and is the first professional artist and engraver.

Six years later Dirk Hartog sailed too far and landed at Cape Inscription on 26 October 1616. It was here that Hartog left his famous pewter plate inscribed (in Dutch): '1616. On 25th October there arrived here the ship *Eendraght* of Amsterdam. Supercargo Gilles Miebais of Liege; skipper Dirck Hatichs of Amsterdam. On 27th do. she set sail again for Bantam. Subcargo Jan Stins; upper steersman Pieter Doores of Bil. In the year 1616.'

Two years later both van Hillegom, Captain of the *Zeewolf*, and Jacobsz, Captain of the *Mauritius*, accidentally landed on the coast. In 1619 Commander Frederik de Houtman sighted Rottnest Island.

In 1623 Dutch ships *Pera* and *Arnhem*, under the commands of Dirk Meliszoon and Wellem van Coolsteerdt respectively, charted the west coast of Cape York and the northern coasts of Arnhem Land. The Gulf of Carpentaria was named after Pieter de Carpentier, Governor-General of the Dutch East Indies.

Four years later Pieter Nuyts sailed along most of the coast of the Great Australian Bight, and in 1629, the survivors of the shipwrecked *Batavia*, which had literally struck the Houtman Abrolhos islands, sailed for 800 kilometres up the Western Australian coast before heading for Java.

The most revered of all the Dutch explorers was Abel Tasman who, on two voyages in 1642 and 1644, discovered Van Diemen's Land and explored large sections of the northern coastline of the continent. Tasman is credited with the discovery that Australia was not connected to Papua New Guinea and with giving the continent the name 'New Holland'.

The Dutch continued to explore the Western Australian coastline for the next century but they made no attempt to establish an outpost there. The numerous Dutch shipwrecks led to many important voyages of exploration. After the sinking of the *De Ridderschap van Holland* in 1694, Willem de Vlamingh went in search of survivors and discovered Rottnest Island, explored up to 80 kilometres inland, and found Dirk Hartog's pewter plate.

The first Englishmen to set foot on Australian soil was the pirate William Dampier who landed on the Western Australian coast in 1688 and 1699. His best-selling account of his first voyage, *A New Voyage Round the World*, had little to say in Australia's favour and probably dissuaded the British from further exploration of the country. He described the Aborigines as 'the miserablest people on earth' and his description of the climate and terrain 'we Anchor'd at three several Places, and stay'd at the first of them (on the W. side of the Bay) till the 11th. During which time we searched about, as I said, for fresh Water, digging Wells, but to no purpose.' These were hardly descriptions to encourage further exploration or possible settlement.

The final act in the early exploration of Australia started in 1768 when Captain James Cook, commanding HM Barque *Endeavour*, was sent to the South Seas to observe the transit of Venus and explore the 'Great South Land'. On 20 April 1770 Zachary Hicks, the First Lieutenant on the ship, sighted the coast of Australia. Cook sailed up the coast for the next four months and on 22 August 1770, on Possession Island, he claimed all the eastern coast for King George III and named it New South Wales.

Nine years later Sir Joseph banks recommended Botany Bay as a suitable site for a penal colony and in 1786 the British Government authorised the sending of convicts to New South Wales.

*Cook landing at Botany Bay.*

## The first settlement at Sydney Cove

King George had no doubt about the function of the first European colony on Australian soil. In his speech to the British Parliament in January 1787 he referred to the proposal to send an expedition to Botany Bay as another attempt to 'remove the inconvenience which arose from the crowded state of the gaols in different parts of the Kingdom'. It was hardly the kind of fulsome and enthusiastic description which would bring hope to those who, on 13 May 1787, set sail from Portsmouth. The first fleet consisted of eleven ships: two escorts, HMS *Sirius*, commanded by Governor Arthur Phillip, and HMS *Supply*; six transport ships, *Alexander, Friendship, Scarborough, Charlotte, Lady Penrhyn* and *Prince of Wales*; and three storeships, *Fishburn, Borrowdale* and *Golden Grove.* They carried 759 convicts, twenty-three of them died during the voyage and six children were born. After a journey of nine months, 1030 people landed, 736 of them were convicts.

The site for the settlement was to be Botany Bay. On 18 January Governor Phillip reached the bay on HMS *Supply.* The lack of good, fresh water made the site unsuitable and Phillip proceeded immediately to examine Port Jackson, a short distance to the north. It was, in Phillip's famous expression, 'the finest harbour in the world' and so, by 26 January the entire fleet had moved north and the colony of Sydney had begun.

The early sequence of events was a mixture of decorum and necessity. On 26 January the British flag was raised at Sydney Cove and a few days later the official documents formally appointing Phillip as Governor and formally establishing the colony of New South Wales were read to all members of the expedition. Phillip spoke to the convicts and told them that he hoped the new colony would bring them 'reformation, happiness, and prosperity'.

The first problem, and the one that would come to obsess the early governors, was food. By nineteenth-century standards the convicts had been well fed on the journey to Australia. They had been given 3 quarts (3.4 litres) of water per day and their weekly food rations included 7 pounds (3 kilograms) of biscuit, 2 pounds (1 kilogram) of salt pork, 4 pounds (2 kilograms) of salt beef, 2 pounds (1 kilogram) of peas, 3 pounds (1.5 kilograms) of oatmeal, 6 ounces (170 grams) of butter, 12 ounces (340 grams) of cheese and ½ pint (284 millilitres) of vinegar per week.

While this was adequate it was hardly a healthy diet and consequently there was an urgent need to produce fresh foodstuffs so that the diet of everyone in the colony could be improved.

To compound the problem the authorities in England had badly underestimated the difficulty of agricultural activity in the area around Sydney Cove. Not only were there few tools but most of the convicts had been urban dwellers and their agricultural ability was restricted. The British authorities had omitted to ensure that skilled labour was on the ships.

Determined to give the new colony every opportunity to succeed, Phillip quickly established other colonies in the area and on 14 February Lieutenant Philip Gidley King, accompanied by fifteen convicts and six soldiers, sailed to Norfolk Island with a view to growing crops and harvesting native flax.

Necessity drove the early colony. By July a number of crudely made huts and storehouses had been completed and a Government House (a cottage rather than a gracious dwelling) was being constructed on the hill above the cove. By this time a brick kiln had been built and bricks were being made.

Nothing went smoothly for the early colony. On 30 May two convicts, William Okey and Samuel Davis, were killed by Aborigines while gathering rushes at Rushcutters Bay. While it was an isolated incident it did indicate a certain level of friction between the new settlers and the estimated population of 3000 Aborigines who were living in the Sydney basin at the time.

By July the rations in the colony were running low. In a despatch to the British Under-Secretary of State, Phillip recorded the rations which were being fed to both marines and male convicts—the women were getting two-thirds of these rations: 'Each received 7 pounds of bread or in lieu thereof 7 pounds of flour, 7 pounds of beef or in lieu thereof pork, 3 pints of pease, 6 ounces of butter.'

# *The March of Time:* **1800s and 1810s**

| | 1801–2 | 1803–4 | 1805–6 | 1807–8 | 1809–10 |
|---|---|---|---|---|---|

## EVENTS

**1801** Matthew Flinders begins two-year journey to circumnavigate and chart the entire continent.

**1802** John Macarthur convinces Privy Council in London to establish an Australian wool industry to overcome shortages in Europe. He is granted 10 000 acres and stock from King George III's flock.

**1803** Matthew Flinders returns from his complete circumnavigation of the continent

**1804** The first bale of colonial wool is sold in London by John Macarthur (above).

**1805** Macarthur chooses to take up his 10 000 acre land grant in the Cowpastures area and establishes his Camden Park Estate.

**1806** Both flood and drought destroy crops and lead to a reduction in rations and increased costs.

**1807** Wool export trade begins with the shipment of a large consignment of wool to England.

**1808** Governor Bligh forcibly removed from office and imprisoned by Major Johnson and NSW Corps in what was later known as the 'Rum Rebellion'.

**1809** An official Post Office is established in Sydney.

**1810** Governor Macquarie and his wife undertake a journey during which he plans and names the five 'Macquarie Towns': Richmond, Wilberforce, Pitt Town, Windsor and Castlereagh.

## GOVERNMENT AND FOREIGN AFFAIRS

**1801** John Macarthur is sent to England for court-martial following duel with Colonel Paterson, Commanding Officer of NSW Corps.

**1802** Lieutenant Charles Robbins is sent to Van Diemens Land to proclaim it a British possession when the French are suspected of planning to claim it for themselves.

**1803** The first settlement is established in Van Diemens Land, at Risdon Cove.

**1804** An uprising by Irish convicts at Castle Hill is quickly put down by Major George Johnson and his Rum Corps but fifteen convicts are killed.

**1805** A merchant, Robert Campbell, attempts to break the trade monopoly of the East India Co. by exporting seal oil and skins directly to London instead of China.

**1806** New Governor, William Bligh (below), outlaws the use of rum for currency making enemies of the Rum Corps and John Macarthur.

**1807** John Macarthur and Captain Edward Abbott illegally import two rum stills. Governor Bligh prohibits their use.

**1808** After the removal of Governor Bligh, Major Johnson administers the colony for seven months until Lieutenant-Colonel Joseph Foveaux arrives.

**1809** Lachlan Macquarie arrives to take up post of Governor bringing with him a battalion of the 73rd Regiment to replace the recalled NSW Corps.

**1810** Macquarie is sworn in on New Year's Day, promising justice for all.

## LEISURE AND LIFESTYLE

**1801** Two Female Orphan Schools open.

**1802** The first book is published in the colony, *New South Wales General Standing Orders: Selected from the General Orders Issued by Former Governors.*

**1803** The first suggestion of using the name 'Australia' (from *Terra Australis*. meaning 'Southland') is made by Matthew Flinders.
  The first newspaper is published, the *Sydney Gazette and New South Wales Advertiser,* by George Howe.

**1804** 26 January is first celebrated as the colony's foundation day.

**1805** In August a cockfight near Sydney attracts large crowds of spectators and gamblers.

**1806** The first triplets are born in the colony.
  The term 'bushranger' is used for first time, in the *Sydney Gazette.*

**1807** An emancipated surveyor, James Meehan, surveys and draws a map of Sydney Town.

Successful Scottish merchant Robert Campbell (above) begins building ships in Sydney.

**1808** Stock and crops are damaged when the Hawkesbury River floods.

**1809** The colony's first Presbyterian church is built at Ebenezer.

**1810** The first government-approved horse race is held in Sydney. It is organised by the 73rd Regiment.

| 1811–12 | 1813–14 | 1815–16 | 1817–18 | 1819–20 |
|---|---|---|---|---|

## EVENTS

**1811** Macquarie visits Van Diemens Land and plans Hobart Town.

**1812** For the first time a ship, the *Indefatigable*, brings convicts directly to Van Diemens Land from England.

**1813** The Blue Mountains are finally crossed by Gregory Blaxland, William Wentworth and William Lawson.

**1814** A road from Sydney to Liverpool via Parramatta opens and shortly after a coach service begins—the first public transport in the colony.

**1815** William Cox and thirty convicts take just six months to complete a road across the Blue Mountains. Cox is rewarded with a land grant and the convicts with their freedom.

**1816** The 'Rum Hospital' opens in Sydney.

**1817** The Bank of NSW opens in Macquarie Place, Sydney. It is the first trading bank and public company in Australia.

**1818** The Great Western Road linking Sydney and Parramatta to the Blue Mountains is opened, and the Hobart to Launceston road is finished.

**1819** A new barracks for male convicts is opened at Hyde Park, The building still stands in Macquarie Street.

**1820** St James Church of England in Sydney and Lancer Military Barracks in Parramatta, both designed by Francis Greenaway, are completed.

## GOVERNMENT AND FOREIGN AFFAIRS

**1811** In London, Macarthur is reprimanded and Johnson is cashiered for their actions during the 'Rum Rebellion'.

**1812** Henry Bathurst is appointed Secretary of State for the Colonies and  John Oxley (left) is appointed Surveyor-General of NSW.

**1813** Currency shortages force Macquarie to use imported dollar coins as 'holey dollars' and 'dumps' (valued at five shillings and fifteen pence respectively), until 1824.

**1814** The British government appoints Jeffrey Bent as first judge of the Supreme Court.

**1815** White population is estimated at almost 15 000.

**1816** A convict, Francis Greenaway, is appointed Civil Architect and Assistant Engineer by Macquarie, despite not having completed his fourteen-year sentence for forgery.

**1817** John Macarthur returns to Sydney but is barred from public affairs.

**1818** Justices of the Peace are empowered to hear complaints from employees as well as employers and to direct payment of wages.

**1819** John Thomas Bigge is sent to Australia by British Parliament to head a Commission of Inquiry into the state of affairs in NSW and Van Diemens Land.

**1820** Sydney is visited by four Russian ships. The Russians set up a temporary observatory on Kirrabilli Point.

## LEISURE AND LIFESTYLE

**1811** A stone arch bridge over the Tank Stream connects east and west Sydney.

**1812** The first recorded hunt using hounds is held by the newly established Sydney Hunt Club.

**1813** Hoping to improve morality in the colony, Governor Macquarie decrees that part of each Sunday is to be devoted to religious duties.

**1814** In a book published in London the day before his death, Matthew Flinders (right) advocates the name Australia for the continent rather than New Holland.

**1815** A school for Aboriginal children is established at Parramatta.

**1816** The first Botanical Gardens are established in Sydney.

**1817** Governor Macquarie uses name 'Australia' in official correspondence to England.

**1818** The first biography is published—a pamphlet by Thomas Wells based on the life of Michael Howe entitled *The Last and Worst of the Bushrangers of Van Diemens Land.*

**1819** The 'Landholders, Merchants and other Respectable Inhabitants of the Colony' draw attention to social and economic grievances during a meeting in Sydney.

**1820** The Roman Catholic church is established; the first Methodist service is held in Van Diemens Land; the first Jewish service is held and the first Australian Masonic Lodge is founded.

*Sydney Cove in 1788.*

By September the situation was so bad that the last cow had been killed for meat and the HMS *Sirius* had been despatched to Cape Town to bring back any food they could get. The following May it returned with 6.5 tonnes of flour. It had circumnavigated the world in the Roaring Forties.

On 2 November, in another attempt to secure the future of the colony, Phillip sent a party of marines and ten convicts to develop a farm at Rose Hill near the present-day site of Parramatta.

In spite of this tentative start the colony slowly began to take root. Phillip was an enthusiastic explorer and, in the space of a year, he had carried out expeditions to the foothills of the Blue Mountains, to the shores of Broken Bay in the north, and to Botany Bay where he explored the Cook's, George's and the Woronora rivers.

The quality of life in the colony began to improve in 1789. Government House was completed; on 4 June some convicts performed George Farquhar's comedy *The Recruiting Officer;* and in October a boat was built to carry supplies up the Parramatta River from Sydney Cove to the settlement at Rose Hill.

In spite of this apparent optimism food was still the colony's grand obsession. In November 1789 supplies were so low that everyone had their limited rations reduced to two-thirds.

Mercifully, on 21 November, Phillip gave the convict James Ruse 2 acres (3.8 hectares) at Rose Hill. He also supplied him with seed, livestock and suitable farming equipment. By December the farms at Rose Hill had produced 200 bushels of wheat and 60 bushels of barley. However, this was only a temporary relief and by January the colony's food supply was so small that everyone was put on half rations.

By April the food situation was so bad that Phillip told his officers and administrators that only six weeks rations remained. Rations were reduced even more and the whole colony focussed on catching fish in the harbour and trying to trap kangaroos and wallabies in the hinterland. Convicts who stole food were being sentenced to 2000 lashes.

On 3 June, after one convict had died from starvation, the Second Fleet sailed through the heads. There were a number of store ships and thus adequate supplies to save the colony from starvation. With the Second Fleet came instructions to settle the land as quickly as possible and to produce food to feed the colony by any possible means.

The first two years had been extremely difficult but the colony had survived. On 25 February 1791, a little over two years after Phillip had raised the flag in Sydney Cove, James Ruse announced that his small farm at Rose Hill was producing enough food to feed himself and his wife, proving that it was possible to survive in the Sydney basin. The colony now had some genuine hope.

## Exploration and expansion of the new continent

It would seem that Australia's first European settlers were a curious and adventurous lot. From the moment they arrived at Botany Bay and Sydney Cove they were eager to push into the hinterland and explore the vast unknown which lay beyond the shoreline and the sand dunes.

On one level they were riding a wave of European exploration which had started in the fifteenth century and which had effectively crossed every ocean and explored every continent. On another level, with the journey from England taking up to six months, there was an urgent need to find fertile soils and verdant pastures so the colony could become self-sufficient.

It was inevitable that Arthur Phillip, his soldiers and convicts would wonder what lay beyond the horizon. Some convicts, driven more by optimism than reality, believed that they could walk from Sydney to Batavia. Some even believed that a white settlement existed beyond the mountains. They escaped from Sydney Cove only to die in the foothills of the Blue Mountains or to be befriended by local Aborigines.

In March 1788 Phillip and a small party had reached the Pittwater area of Broken Bay and by April the northern shore of Sydney Harbour had been explored. But the real source of fascination were the mountains to the west of the settlement which, on a clear day, looked remarkably blue.

The first twenty-five years of settlement saw only small-scale, land-based explorations. In 1789 expeditions led by Phillip and Watkin Tench discovered the Hawkesbury and Nepean river system on the edge of the Sydney basin. In 1797 a group of shipwreck survivors walked 640 kilometres up the coast towards Sydney from Bass Strait. In the same year Lieutenant John Shortland discovered the Hunter River north of Port Jackson. Later in the decade two parties headed south-west from Sydney and reached as far as the present site of Goulburn.

The real journeys of exploration occurred after 1813 when Blaxland, Wentworth and Lawson crossed the Blue Mountains. Their successful expedition was the culmination of attempts to cross the range which had started as early as 1789.

*The Hawkesbury River at Wisemans Ferry.*

In the next decade a series of expeditions left Sydney to explore the lands beyond the mountains. In 1815 a road over the Blue Mountains was built and George Evans, who had been exploring beyond the mountains, headed south from the village of Bathurst and reached the Lachlan River.

In 1817 and 1818 John Oxley pushed south and nearly reached the Murrumbidgee River, then headed north and reached the present site of Port Macquarie. In 1819 John Howe successfully travelled overland to the Hunter Valley and in 1823 Captain Mark Currie explored the Lake George area near present-day Canberra and pushed on until he reached the Murrumbidgee River.

If the 1810s had seen explorers stay relatively close to Port Jackson the 1820s and 1830s saw them

*Hume and Hovell Expedition.*

# *The March of Time:* **1820s and 1830s**

| 1821–2 | 1823–4 | 1825–6 | 1827–8 | 1829–30 |
|---|---|---|---|---|

## EVENTS

**1821** Port Macquarie penal settlement is opened.

**1822** John Macarthur's wool sells for high prices in London and he is presented with two gold medals in recognition of its high quality.

A penal settlement for difficult convicts is established at Macquarie Harbour, Van Diemens Land.

**1823** The first alluvial gold is discovered on the Fish River in NSW by James McBrien.

**1824** Hamilton Hume and William Hovell set out on a journey of exploration to Spencer Gulf.

**1825** Richmond Bridge in Van Diemens Land is completed. It is now the oldest extant bridge in Australia.

**1826** In an effort to forestall colonisation by the French, Governor Darling sends Major Edmund Lockyer to King George Sound to establish a settlement. It is the first settlement in Western Australia and the present site of Albany.

**1827** Allan Cunningham leads an expedition to Moreton Bay. He discovers the Darling Downs and a gap through the Great Dividing Range which will provide access to the Darling Downs from Moreton Bay.

**1828** An expedition led by Charles Sturt sets out to search for an inland sea by tracing the Macquarie River.

**1829** Charles Sturt's expedition discovers the Darling River and explores the Bogan and Castlereagh rivers.

**1830** A penal settlement, a place of severe punishment for repeat offenders, is established at Port Arthur, south-east of Hobart.

## GOVERNMENT AND FOREIGN AFFAIRS

**1821** Macquarie resigns and Major General Sir Thomas Makdougall Brisbane (above) becomes Governor.

**1822** John Thomas Bigge's report is completed and published in London.

**1823** An Act of Parliament is passed in London making NSW and Van Diemens Land separate colonies with each having an appointed Legislative Council.

**1824** Governor Brisbane is forced to place the area around Bathurst under martial law after serious conflicts between whites and Aborigines.

**1825** Ralph Darling becomes Governor.

**1826** Governor Darling decides to make an example of two disgraced soldiers which leads to the Sudds and Thompson Case. Darling's bungling of the affair eventually leads to his departure from the colony.

**1827** Governor Darling is prevented by the Chief Justice from passing a law to stifle press criticism of his administration.

**1828** Sir Thomas Mitchell is appointed Surveyor-General, a position he holds for twenty-seven years.

**1829** Governor James Stirling formally makes the entire continent of New Holland British Territory when he proclaims the settlement of Western Australia.

**1830** Lieutenant-Governor George Arthur makes a disastrous attempt to round up all the remaining Aborigines in Van Diemens Land and force them to resettle on Flinders Island. However, his infamous 'Black Line' catches only one woman and a young boy.

## LEISURE AND LIFESTYLE

**1821** *Michael Howe, The Terror of Van Diemen's Land* by J. Amherst becomes the first Australian play to be performed on the London stage.

**1822** Thirty-four bushrangers are sentenced to hang in Sydney as bushranging becomes a serious problem.

**1823** Dr William Sherwin becomes the first Australian member of the Royal College of Physicians in London and Dr Henry Cowper, who first uses quinine to treat fever in Queensland, becomes the first Australian-born member of the Royal College of Surgeons.

**1824** William Charles Wentworth and Robert Wardell begin the *Australian,* Australia's first privately-owned daily newspaper, just one day before the rigid censorship of the press is abolished.

**1825** Augustus Earle, portrait painter and topographical artist, arrives in Australia.

**1826** The first oil lamp in an Australian street is lit in Macquarie Place, Sydney, and a Sydney shop records the first use of gaslight.

**1827** The Colonial Museum (later the Australian Museum) is founded in Sydney.

**1828** George Wyndham plants a vineyard on his property, Dalwood, in the Hunter Valley, which still produces wine today.

**1829** One of the first notable industrial actions occurs in Australia when newspaper compositors in Sydney strike over wage reductions.

**1830** Ex-convict John Savery's novel, *Quintus Serviton,* becomes the first novel to be written, printed and published in Australia.

# *The March of Time:* **1820s and 1830s**

| 1831–2 | 1833–4 | 1835–6 | 1837–8 | 1839–40 |
|---|---|---|---|---|

## EVENTS

**1831** The steamer *Sophia Jane* arrives from England to begin a regular service between Sydney and Parramatta.

**1832** A road down the Victoria Pass in the Blue Mountains of NSW is completed under the supervision of Sir Thomas Mitchell, who then goes on to supervise the Sydney–Goulburn road.

**1833** Australia's main exports are whale and seal products but as wool sales increase it begins to replace these as the country's primary industry.

**1834** First (unauthorised) settlement at Portland, Victoria, by Edward Henty.

**1835** John Batman, after exploring the area around Geelong, makes a treaty with local Aborigines to 'purchase' 600 000 acres of land. The treaty is later disallowed by Governor Bourke.

**1836** Major Thomas Mitchell's expedition explores the Murrumbidgee, Lachlan, Murray and Lodden rivers discovering rich grazing land. He refers to the land as 'Australia Felix'.

**1837** Elizabeth Bay House in Sydney is completed and construction begins on St Andrews Cathedral.

**1838** A settlement is established at Port Essington to provide a northern trading station.

**1839** Angus McMillan enters East Gippsland and opens up land for agricultural purposes.

Exploration of the Australian Alps is begun by Paul Edmund de Strzelecki, a Polish explorer and scientist.

**1840** Paul Strzelecki climbs and names Australia's highest mountain, Mt Kosciusko.

## GOVERNMENT AND FOREIGN AFFAIRS

**1831** The practice of giving free land grants to settlers is abolished and a system of land auctions is introduced.

**1832** Assisted immigration begins when a shipload of female immigrants leaves England, their fares having been subsidised by the government.

**1833** The House of Commons in London is petitioned for more representative government following a large public meeting in Sydney.

**1834** The *South Australian Act* is passed in British Parliament to establish a new, non-convict, 'planned' settlement in South Australia.

**1835** The last of the Aborigines from Van Diemens Land is captured and sent to Flinders Island. George Robinson is appointed Protector of the 300 surviving Aborigines now living on the island.

**1836** Surveyor-General of South Australia, Colonel William Light, chooses an inland site for the settlement against recommendations for a coastal port site.

**1837** The total white population is estimated to be 132 819.

**1838** Twenty-eight Aboriginal men, women and children are massacred at Myall Creek. Seven white men are later hanged for the crime.

**1839** The British government claims New Zealand and it becomes part of New South Wales. A year later it becomes a separate colony.

**1840** Transportation of convicts from England to NSW ceases but will continue to Van Diemens Land and Norfolk Island.

## LEISURE AND LIFESTYLE

**1831** A four-page newspaper, the *Sydney Herald*, begins production in April. In 1842 it was renamed the *Sydney Morning Herald* and is now the oldest extant newspaper in the Southern Hemisphere.

**1832** Two Anglican Kings Schools open, one in Sydney and one at Parramatta (above), to bring higher education to the sons of wealthy colonists.

**1833** The first School of Arts and Mechanics Institute is founded in Sydney.

**1834** A NSW Temperance Society is formed in Sydney.

**1835** The 'Wild White Man', William Buckley, an escaped convict, surrenders after living with Aborigines for thirty-two years in the Port Phillip Bay area. He is granted a free pardon.

**1836** The naturalist Charles Darwin visits Sydney on HMS *Beagle* (left). William Grant Broughton (right) is consecrated Bishop of Australia.

**1837** The first Chinese agricultural-labourers arrive in Australia.

**1838** Henry Parkes and his family arrive in Sydney in February as assisted immigrants and in September Caroline Chisholm arrives and begins her philanthropic work with young women.

**1839** *Opuntia stricta* (prickly pear) is introduced into Australia from the Gulf of Mexico to the deep regret of later generations. It will be over 100 years before this pest is finally eradicated by the cactoblastis moth.

**1840** Horseracing begins at the Flemington racecourse in Melbourne.

reach into areas which would subsequently become parts of Queensland and South Australia. In 1824 Hamilton Hume and William Hovell explored from south of Sydney through to the Western Port district of Victoria. They had hoped to reach Port Phillip but they miscalculated.

Three years later, in 1827, Allan Cunningham headed north from the Upper Hunter Valley and reached the Liverpool Plains and the rich Darling Downs. All these explorers had been primarily concerned with finding and opening up good grazing land so that the inhabitants could be fed. They were people committed to practical exploration. In the 1830s such exploration gave way to journeys which were either to answer vexing questions like 'Why do so many of the rivers in New South Wales flow inland?' or to achieve status by being the first person to traverse the country from south to north.

In 1828–29 Charles Sturt, who wanted to know where the rivers flowed, explored the Macquarie, Darling, Castlereagh and Bogan. The following year he followed the Murrumbidgee downstream until he reached the Murray. He followed the Murray until it joined the Darling and continued until it emptied into Lake Alexandrina in South Australia.

In 1831 Major Thomas Mitchell explored the rivers in the north-west of New South Wales and in 1835 he made an epic journey through western New South Wales and north-western Victoria where, after crossing numerous rivers, he came across rich pastoral land which he named 'Australia Felix'.

The only other major exploration before 1840 occurred in 1839 when Angus McMillan and Paul

*Captain Charles Sturt.*

*Meeting of Eyre with French whalers.*

Strzelecki pushed down through the Snowy Mountains and opened up the rich pasturelands of western Victoria.

These early explorations concentrated on New South Wales and reached out to the limits of the state. In the following decades the true vastness of the country was explored. Ludwig Leichhardt travelled from Jimour in Queensland across to Port Essington (Darwin) in the Northern Territory. A. C. Gregory made epic journeys through outback South Australia and across the Northern Territory to the Victoria River, and the ill-fated Edward Kennedy struggled through dense tropical rainforest from Rockingham Bay up the coast of Cape York.

Throughout the 1850s, 1860s and 1870s major explorations occurred. Burke and Wills and John McDouall Stuart both crossed the continent from north to south. E. J. Eyre crossed the Great Australian Bight and John Forrest, Alexander Forrest, Edward Giles, A. C. and F. T. Gregory explored vast inland areas of Western Australia.

Slowly the continent was opened up. The dreams of vast pastures and of inland seas disappeared as explorer after explorer found that the inland reality was desert, heat, flies, disease and genuine hardship.

The period of exploration lasted for a century. By the end of the nineteenth century the inhabitants of Australia had a detailed, if not comprehensive, understanding of the continent. They realised that clinging to the coast was a necessity rather than a desirable option for the inland was such a vast emptiness.

## The creation of Australia's states and territories

In terms of its states and colonies Australia has changed its internal boundaries twelve times since the British government gave Captain Arthur Phillip his commission in 1786. In the original commission received by Phillip the continent, which at the time was still a blurry and inaccurate outline on a map, was divided down the 135th meridian of east longitude. This basically meant that all of Australia east of a line which ran from Arnhem Land down to the eastern edge of the Great Australian Bight (and which included both Van Diemen's Land and New Zealand) was known as New South Wales. The area to the west of the 135th meridian was not claimed.

Fear of possible French and Dutch settlement drove much of decision-making in early Australian history. By 1824, with the establishment of the brief and unsuccessful settlement of Fort Dundas on Melville Island the boundary of New South Wales was extended to the 129th parallel. Interestingly, this is the oldest permanent artificial state boundary in Australia. When the British claimed Western Australia in 1829 they defined it by the 129th parallel and that is still the state's eastern boundary.

In 1825 Van Diemen's Land was constituted as a separate colony. The territory of Van Diemen's Land included all the islands south of Wilsons Promontory including Macquarie Island which had been annexed by the British because of its popularity as a destination for whalers and sealers. The main island continued to be known as Van Diemen's Land until it was changed to Tasmania in 1855.

The next colony to be carved from greater New South Wales was South Australia which was created on 15 August 1834 by King William IV. Like New South Wales and Western Australia its boundaries were simply lines drawn on maps with no consideration to terrain (which was not known at the time) or natural features. Thus, the first South Australia was simply defined as all that territory bounded by the 132nd and 141st meridians of east longitude and by the 26th parallel south and the southern coastline. In 1861 the western boundary was extended to the 129th parallel so that it formed a border with Western Australia and from 1863, until it was taken over by the new Federal Government in 1911, the Northern Territory was included as part of the state.

Few Australians realise that New Zealand remained a kind of informal dependency of the

colony of New South Wales until 1840. In that year it became a formal dependency but the formal connection was shortlived because the following year it was proclaimed as a separate colony.

The goldrushes saw the most dramatic changes in the evolution of Australia's states. The rapidly expanding population along the continent's eastern seaboard meant that it became impossible for the rapidly growing goldrush towns to be administered from Sydney. Also the new goldrush ports of Melbourne, and later the towns along the north Queensland coast, could not be sensibly controlled from Sydney.

In 1851 the colony of Victoria was constituted. It had been known as the Port Phillip District. The definition of the colony reached beyond simple straight lines drawn on a map. Victoria was formally 'bounded on the north and north-east by a straight line drawn from Cape Howe to the nearest source of the River Murray, and thence by the course of that river to the eastern boundary of the colony of South Australia.' It was a colony with a natural boundary.

The last state to emerge was Queensland which was finally granted an independent administration on 6 June 1859. It effectively carved the northern two-thirds off New South Wales. In broad terms it was all the land from the coast to the 141st meridian of east longitude and all the land north of the 29th

*John McDouall Stuart.*

# The March of Time: 1840s and 1850s

| 1841–2 | 1843–4 | 1845–6 | 1847–8 | 1849–50 |
|---|---|---|---|---|

## EVENTS

**1841** John Eyre becomes the first European to cross from Adelaide to Albany over land. The trip was hampered by lack of water, and two Aboriginal members of the party killed Eyre's assistant and stole all the food.

**1842** Substantial deposits of copper are discovered in South Australia.

**1843** Benjamin Boyd establishes a large whaling station at Twofold Bay in southern NSW.

**1844** German naturalist, Ludwig Leichhardt, leads an expedition from the Darling Downs (Queensland) to Port Essington (Northern Territory). The journey takes fourteen months and covers 4800 kilometres.

**1845** Government House in Sydney is completed.

The near extinction of whales causes a decline in the whaling industry.

**1846** First proposals for a railway system are made at a public meeting led by James Macarthur, and the Sydney Tramroad and Railway Co. is established.

**1847** Melbourne is declared a city.

**1848** Ludwig Leichhardt's party disappears while trying to cross the continent from east to west.

**1849** Young Thomas Chapman discovers gold north-west of Melbourne.

A uniform two-penny postage rate is introduced by the government.

**1850** Western Australia's first convicts arrive at Swan River on board the *Scindian*.

## GOVERNMENT AND FOREIGN AFFAIRS

**1841** With very little help from the government, Caroline Chisholm establishes a Female Immigrants Home to shelter newly arrived females and to help them find work.

**1842** In July, Sydney is incorporated as a city and, in August, Melbourne is incorporated as a town.

**1843** A financial crisis in NSW is caused by drought, lack of wool sales, high bank interest rates and low wheat prices.

**1844** The Pastoral Association is formed by squatters to fight new squatting regulations introduced by the NSW government.

**1845** British troops are sent from Australia to New Zealand to fight in the Maori rebellion.

**1846** Transportation of convicts to Van Diemens Land is halted for two years. Sir Charles Fitzroy is appointed governor.

**1847** The forty-seven surviving Tasmanian Aborigines left on Flinders Island are returned to Van Diemens Land.

**1848** Western Australia conducts its first official census, counting 11 976 people. Aborigines are not included.

**1849** The wool industry grows rapidly, providing half of Britain's wool imports.

**1850** The Australian League is formed by the Reverend John Dunmore Lang to promote a national republic, universal male suffrage and an end to convict transportation.

## LEISURE AND LIFESTYLE

**1841** The first volume of *The Birds of Australia* by John Gould is published in London.

**1842** A North Shore ferry service begins in Sydney.

**1843** John Bede Polding (right) arrives back in Sydney with nineteen Roman Catholic priests, brothers and students. The enthusiastic welcome they receive causes consternation among Sydney Protestants.

**1844** *The Currency Lass*, a musical comedy by Edward Geoghegan, is first performed in Sydney.

**1845** A crowd of about 10 000 gathers outside Darlinghurst Goal when murderer John Knatchbull is executed.

**1846** The *Moreton Bay Courier* and the *Melbourne Argus* begin publication.

**1847** The Hon. James Graham lays out a golf course on the site later known as Flagstaff Gardens, in Melbourne.

**1848** John Gould completes his seven-volume work *The Birds of Australia*.

**1849** Caroline Chisholm establishes the Family Colonization Loan Society in London to help prospective emigrants to Australia.

**1850** Sir Thomas Mitchell and Stuart Donaldson exchange shots in a duel.

# The March of Time: **1840s and 1850s**

| 1851–2 | 1853–4 | 1855–6 | 1857–8 | 1859–60 |
|---|---|---|---|---|

## EVENTS

**1851** The goldrush begins, first in the area near Bathurst, then near Ballarat and Bendigo. Miners' licences are introduced.

**1852** The township of Gundagai is flooded by the Murrumbidgee River, and more than eighty people drown.

**1853** Paddlesteamers are first used on the Murray–Darling river system.

**1854** S. W. McGowan completes the telegraph line between Melbourne and Williamstown, the first in Australia.

**1855** A. C. Gregory leads an expedition south-east from the Victoria River and searches for traces of Leichhardt's party.

The first government-run steam railway in the British Empire is opened between Sydney and Parramatta

**1856** South Australia is granted responsible government.

**1857** Two major shipwrecks occur off Sydney: the clippers *Dunbar* (121 lives lost) and *Catherine Adamson* (21 lives lost).

**1858** John McDouall Stuart finds good sheep-grazing country in his exploration of South Australia.

**1859** The building of Leonard Terry's design for the Melbourne Club is completed.

**1860** Robert Burke (above left) and William Wills lead an expedition from Melbourne aiming to reach the Gulf of Carpentaria.

## GOVERNMENT AND FOREIGN AFFAIRS

**1851** The Port Phillip District becomes a separate colony named Victoria.

**1852** The British government agrees to stop sending convicts to the eastern colonies.

**1853** Gold becomes the country's chief export.

**1854** Troops attack the Eureka Stockade, built by Ballarat goldminers to protest high mining licence fees and other injustices. Peter Lalor leads the miners.

**1855** NSW, Victoria and Van Diemens Land are granted responsible government. Sir Charles Hotham becomes first Governor of Victoria.

**1856** The name Van Diemens Land is officially changed to Tasmania.

**1857** Anti-Chinese feelings intensify on the goldfields, and discriminatory laws are introduced.

Robert Torrens develops a system to stop confusion over land titles when deeds are lost and land changes hands.

**1858** Australia's white population reaches the one million mark.

**1859** The new separate colony of Queensland is established and granted responsible government.

**1860** The colonial warship, HMCS *Victoria*, is sent to New Zealand with British troops to help settlers fight Maoris.

## LEISURE AND LIFESTYLE

**1851** Two American Mormon missionaries arrive in Sydney.
  Scotch College is founded as the Melbourne Academy and the first Catholic and Presbyterian schools open in Melbourne.

**1852** In South Australia, the government stops aid to denominational schools.
  The opera *Norma* is performed in Melbourne.

**1853** The first Australian public library run on government funds is opened in Melbourne, and the Victorian Fine Arts Society is founded.

**1854** George Watson sets up the Melbourne Hunt Club.
  Opera singer Catherine Hayes visits Australia.

**1855** The NSW government imposes a tariff on sugar, coffee, tea, tobacco and alcohol.
  The first recorded Eisteddfod is held in Ballarat, Victoria.

**1856** Stonemasons in NSW and building trades workers in Victoria win an eight-hour working day.

**1857** The streets of Hobart and Melbourne are lit by gas.
  A pottery works is opened at Bendigo in Victoria.
  Fort Denison in Sydney Harbour is completed.

**1858** The country's first *Divorce Act* is passed.
  Australian Rules football begins in Melbourne and the Melbourne Australian Rules Football Club is founded.

**1859** Rabbits are introduced into Victoria as game animals.

**1860** The *Sydney Mail*, published by John Fairfax (above) & Sons, begins publication.

### The goldrushes change Australia forever

'Put it away Mr Clarke or we shall all have our throats cut!' the New South Wales Governor Sir George Gipps is supposed to have said when a geologist, the Reverend W. B. Clarke, first showed him some gold which he had found in a creek near Lithgow in New South Wales. The year was 1844 and the Governor of the Colony of New South Wales was worried that a public announcement of the discovery of gold, especially in a colony where the majority of the residents were convicts, would cause violence and chaos.

If the government didn't want a goldrush it was certain that the squatters and farmers didn't. The last thing they wanted was farm labourers leaving their lowly paid jobs to try their luck on the goldfields.

So pressure from the government and rural interests managed to keep the secret of Australia's gold away from the public for twenty-eight years. The first discovery of gold had occurred as early as 1823 when J. McBrien, a government surveyor, found gold in the Fish River near Bathurst. Then in 1839 Peter Strzelecki found gold near Hartley.

Transportation to the colony ended in 1840 and by the end of the decade the fears of the violence that a goldrush might produce had subsided. A mass exodus of the population to California searching for gold caused the New South Wales Government, under Governor Fitz Roy, to institute a policy of gold exploration in 1849.

The beginning of the Australian goldrushes occurred when Edward Hargreaves, after eighteen months working on the Californian goldfields, returned to Australia with a belief that the area around Bathurst and Orange might contain gold. On 12 February 1851, at the junction of Summer Hill Creek and Lewis Ponds Creek, Hargraves and a colleague, John Lister, successfully panned gold. In April, Lister and two brothers, James and William Tom, found gold at Ophir. In May 1851 Hargraves took 120 grams of gold to Sydney and showed it to the Colonial Secretary and on 14 May the gold discovery was announced. Within days men were pouring into the Ophir area. The goldrush had started.

The success of the New South Wales goldfields caused a rush of people from Victoria to New South Wales. To stop this a Gold Discovery Committee was formed and £200 was offered to anyone who could find gold in Victoria.

parallel with the easterly-most section of the border following the course of the Macpherson, Dumaresq and Macintyre rivers.

All that was left to complete the picture of modern Australia was for the Australian Capital Territory, a strange combination of 2360 square kilometres in New South Wales and 72 square kilometres at Jervis Bay (in case a port was required), to be handed over to the new Federal government in 1911 and for the Northern Territory to be moved from South Australia to the commonwealth in 1911, be carved up into North and Central Australia between 1926–31, and eventually be granted its own elected administration in 1976.

The evolution of Australia's states and territories was a mixture of cartographic whims and the changing nature of Australia's population in the nineteenth century. It is remarkable that with such flimsy reasons for division that, in less than one hundred years, the states began to assert their own identity.

The Gold Discovery Committee did not have to wait long. Only six weeks after the Ophir announcement James Esmond found substantial gold deposits near Clunes and within the next eight months the vast deposits at Ballarat and Bendigo had been discovered.

Inevitably the squatters' worst fears became a reality. Farm labourers, indeed anyone who was touched by gold fever, simply threw down their tools and using any available transport headed for the goldfields. Mostly the prospectors simply walked. Often they pushed their equipment in wheelbarrows. Only the affluent went to the diggings on horseback or in a coach. Usually the roads they travelled were little more than bush tracks which were dusty in summer and impossibly muddy in wet weather.

Prior to 1851 the Australian population was increasing in a slow and measured way. Australia had an average of 12 000 free immigrants a year from 1832 to 1842. After the discovery of gold the population of the country soared. From 1851 to 1861 the population trebled. In Victoria alone the population rose from 80 000 to 500 000. In September 1851, 19 000 people landed at Melbourne. In 1852, 95 000 people arrived in Australia.

It was common at this time for everybody who could make it to Australia to come and try their luck on the goldfields. The first to arrive were the experienced miners who were happy to leave the nearly exhausted Californian goldfields.

Interestingly, the majority of immigrants were English, Scottish and Irish. It is true that virtually every nationality on earth could be found on the goldfields but for the duration of the goldrushes the English, Scottish and Irish were by far the largest groups.

The Chinese, who were later to provoke considerable anger on the goldfields, did not start arriving in substantial numbers until as late as the mid-1850s. The first group, many of whom had come from the Californian goldfields, blended in with the rich racial mix on the diggings. Then in 1854–55, in a period of eighteen months, 18 000 Chinese arrived. The antagonism from European and Australian diggers was immediate. By the late 1850s the total number of Chinese on the goldfields had risen to 40 000 and they were establishing themselves as a separate community.

*A post office at the diggings.*

The attitude of European and Australian miners was that the Chinese wasted water, reworked other miners' shafts, smoked opium and gambled too much. The Chinese looked upon the Europeans with equal disdain.

These feelings of animosity finally burst into a series of riots at Bendigo and Buckland Valley in Victoria and Lambing Flat in New South Wales. The result was that the colonies began placing restrictions on the entry of Chinese into Australia. This was the beginning of what would eventually become known as the 'White Australia Policy'.

Although the goldrushes occurred in the 1850s prospectors continued to find new goldfields, particularly in Western Australia and Queensland, from the 1860s to the 1890s.

In Queensland there were a series of goldrushes in the 1870s to places which appeared and disappeared as the miners rushed to the diggings and then rushed on to the next goldfield. Towns like Maytown, Palmer and Croydon briefly enjoyed booms. The more important and long-lasting centres included Gympie, Charters Towers and Mount Morgan.

In Western Australia gold discovery occurred as late as the 1880s and 1890s with lodes being found in the Kimberley and Pilbara regions and major finds in the Kalgoorlie and Coolgardie fields.

The last region of Australia to be mined was the Northern Territory where successful gold discovery

# The March of Time: **1860s and 1870s**

| 1861–2 | 1863–4 | 1865–6 | 1867–8 | 1869–70 |
| --- | --- | --- | --- | --- |

## EVENTS

**1861** Alfred Howitt's search party finds the only survivor of the Burke and Wills expedition.

**1862** Cobb & Co.'s coach service, now owned by James Rutherford, extends its business into NSW.

**1863** Work begins on the Adelaide Town Hall, designed by Edmund William Wright.

**1864** Brisbane's city centre is ravaged by fires in April and December.

**1865** Bushrangers Dan Morgan, Ben Hall (left) and John Gilbert all killed by gunshot in separate arrests.

**1866** John McKinlay explores the country's north, looking for a coastal settlement site.

**1867** A telegraph line links Sydney and Melbourne.

**1868** An attempt is made on the life of visiting Prince Alfred, Duke of Edinburgh. The would-be assassin is hanged.

**1869** The Zig-Zag Railway is completed, an important stage in the crossing of the Blue Mountains by rail.

**1870** Construction begins of the 3000 kilometre long Overland Telegraph Line between Adelaide and Palmerston (later Darwin). It is completed in 1872.

## GOVERNMENT AND FOREIGN AFFAIRS

**1861** Violent anti-Chinese riots occur on the goldfields near Lambing Flat.

**1862** A minimum age of thirteen is set for NSW coal miners working underground.

**1863** Natives from the islands to the north-east of Australia are brought in to labour on Queensland cotton and sugar plantations.

**1864** Commercial grade sugar is made from Queensland sugar cane at Louis Hope's new sugar mill.

**1865** Coal is exported to Japan for the first time.

**1866** Victoria introduces a protectionist tariff, a first for Australian colonies.

**1867** NSW's anti-Chinese legislation is repealed.

**1868** The transportation of convicts to Australia ends with the arrival of the last convict ship, the *Hougomont*, in Western Australia.

**1869** George Goyder surveys the area around Port Darwin for a capital city for the Northern Territory. He names the site Palmerston.

**1870** The colonies become responsible for their own defence with the departure of the remaining British forces.

## LEISURE AND LIFESTYLE

**1861** The Victorian Turf Club runs a new event, the Melbourne Cup, with the prize money of 200 sovereigns won by Archer, ridden by J. Cutts.

**1862** Henry Kendall's *Poems and Songs*, his first work, is published.

**1863** Western Australia passes divorce legislation.

**1864** The *Australasian* (later the *Australasian Post*) begins publication.

**1865** Brothers William and David Arnott set up a bakery business in Newcastle.

**1866** Mother Mary McKillop establishes the sisters of St Joseph of the Sacred Heart as a teaching order of nuns.

← **1867** Adam Lindsay Gordon's first two poetry books are published.

**1868** A cricket team of thirteen Aborigines has a successful season touring England, with 'Twopenny' the bowler the star attraction.

**1869** The Agricultural Society of NSW has its first Exhibition (or 'Show'), at Belmore Park.
A nine-hole golf course is constructed in Adelaide.

**1870** Eugene von Guèrard is appointed as head of the new Victorian Academy of Arts.
One day after the publication of his *Bush Ballads and Galloping Rhymes* Adam Lindsay Gordon commits suicide.

# The March of Time: 1860s and 1870s

## EVENTS

**1871** Alexander Forrest leads an exploratory expedition in Western Australia, successfully locating good farming land.

**1873** Surveyor William Gosse discovers Ayers Rock, naming it after Sir Henry Ayers, Premier of South Australia. It is later renamed Uluru. ↓

**1875** Queensland, NSW, South Australia and Tasmania are all affected by floods.

**1877** Severe drought affects all the colonies with huge losses of crops and animals.

**1878** Telephones are established in Melbourne, the first one linking a hardware store with its head office.

**1879** Alexander Forrest's expedition discovers good farming land around the Ord River in Western Australia.

**1880** Two famous bushrangers are hanged: Captain Moonlight in NSW and Ned Kelly (below) in Victoria.

**1872** The discovery of gold at Charters Towers, Queensland, prompts a goldrush there.

**1874** The estimated NSW Aboriginal population is 9000.

**1876** Australia and New Zealand are linked by an undersea telegraph cable from Sydney to Wellington.

## GOVERNMENT AND FOREIGN AFFAIRS

**1873** Captain John Moresby claims New Guinea for Britain, but the British government repudiates his claim.

**1874** NSW exports wool to Japan for the first time.

**1877** The Port Arthur penal station is closed down. ←

**1878** The Victorian government is in chaos as Premier Berry tries to force the legislative council to pass a supply bill.

**1879** The NSW government dedicates about 8000 hectares of land for use as a 'national park'. The Sutherland National Park is the country's first.

**1871** The Queensland government attempts to supervise the recruitment of Pacific Islanders by plantation owners.

**1872** Henry Parkes begins his first term as Premier of NSW.

**1875** The Derwent ironworks in Tasmania and the Eskbank ironworks at Lithgow begin smelting operations.

**1876** Males aged 13–18 are limited to a 50½ hour working week by the *NSW Coal Mines Act*.

**1880** Peter Lalor (left) previously arrested for his part in the Eureka Stockade, becomes speaker of the Victorian Legislative Assembly.

## LEISURE AND LIFESTYLE

**1871** The Ballarat School of Mines is opened, giving Victoria its first technical college.
  Australia's first sheepdog trials are held at Forbes in NSW. The winner, a bitch named Kelpie, gives the breed its name.

**1872** Frederick Wolseley builds a working model of a sheep shearing machine.

**1873** Edward William Cole opens his Book Arcade in Bourke Street, Melbourne.

**1874** Smallpox vaccinations are made compulsory for Victorian infants.

**1875** T. S. Mort's refrigeration company brings chilled milk to Sydney from dairy farms in the country.

**1876** Edward Trickett wins the first world sculling championship, becoming Australia's first world sporting champion.

**1877** The *Sydney Morning Herald* begins publishing a weather map, with a weather forecast for the day.

**1878** The first artesian bore brings water to the surface near Bourke, NSW.

**1879** An American actor, J. C. Williamson, stages Gilbert and Sullivan's *H.M.S. Pinafore*, the first of his many productions.

**1880** Journalists John Haynes and John Archibald (left) begin publication of the *Bulletin* newspaper.

peaked in 1894 when over 1 million grams were discovered.

## Boom and bust in the 1880s and 1890s

It was inevitable that the incredible boom created by the goldrushes would not last. The goldrushes, particularly in Victoria and New South Wales, had stretched all the existing services and brought unprecedented wealth into the colonies. The population of Australia had grown dramatically in a very short period. In Victoria, for example, the population increased by 114 000 immigrants in the decade between 1881 and 1890. It was obvious that no colony could sustain such a demand on its services.

To compound the problem the wealth generated by the goldrushes had made some people very wealthy and they began to speculate on the development and growth of the cities of Sydney and Melbourne. Whole new suburbs were built, the age of the city high-rise (although it was rarely above four stories) had begun, and the governments, buoyed by their new-found wealth, began to borrow money from British investors to build railways and expand public works.

By the end of the 1880s two forces were at work. There was a great, and unjustified, belief that the rural sector in all the colonies could keep growing indefinitely and land companies and building societies were investing in the future real estate development of the big cities without any real consideration for the economic viability of their projects. It was a time of enthusiastic optimism where the signs of an imminent collapse were simply ignored.

Much of Australia's wealth at this time was determined by the annual wool clip. The country had become the world's largest producer of fine wool and this had produced a certain arrogance. When the wool price began to decline (due largely to competition from other markets) the local graziers and financiers did not heed the warning.

Thus, when wool prices and the housing market collapsed in 1890 the economy was totally unprepared. The result was the collapse of the banking industry and, although it is difficult to measure, it is likely that the 1890s saw the worst depression Australia has ever experienced.

In Victoria in January 1893 two-thirds of all the banks had closed their doors and suspended payments to depositors. The inevitable followed. Bankruptcies were commonplace. The queues of the unemployed grew alarmingly. Business became paralysed and fearful that anything it did may lead to further economic hardship.

The most frightening consequence of the collapse was the way it exacerbated class conflict. Graziers, trying to deal with falling wool prices and the collapse of the banks, decided that their workers would have to bear the full brunt of the depression. Disheartened rural workers started to leave the country and move either to the cities or to return to their countries of origin. The population of Victoria actually dropped during the depression.

To make matters worse Australia experienced an eight-year drought during the period. It was clear that the rural sector which had been so vibrant before the depression was likely to be the country's saviour but, with a drought, it had little ability to regenerate.

The country slowly pulled itself out of the crisis. The economy's dependence of wool was broken as farmers looked towards meat and dairy products. At the same time the discovery of silver and lead at Broken Hill and the rich gold finds on the Kalgoorlie–Coolgardie fields ensured that by the turn of the century the economies of the colonies were dragging themselves back to their pre-depression levels.

## The move towards federation

By the 1890s the inexorable and inevitable movement towards federation was occupying the minds of both politicians and the public. Ideas which had been debated for more than fifty years started to be important on the political agenda and the public meetings and conferences began to be held around the country.

In essence, federation reversed a process which had started in 1788 and continued until the 1850s. During this time the coherent, single island continent had been carved up (often at the whim of politicians and cartographers with a map and a ruler) into an ever-increasing number of states. Where once New South Wales had covered two-thirds of the continent, now it was broken up into a number of sparsely-populated colonies.

The foolishness of this fragmentation was recognised as early as 1846 when, in the New South Wales Legislative Council, the notion of some sort of legislation which linked the colonies was raised. The following year the British Secretary of State for the Colonies argued that some kind of central authority was probably necessary and, in 1851, Governor Fitz Roy's responsibilities were expanded from Governor of New South Wales to Governor-General of all Her Majesty's Australian possessions. It was a position which only lasted for a decade and fortunately was never seriously tested by Fitz Roy or his successor. A hint of the forthcoming battle occurred when both Tasmania and South Australia expressed grave reservations about the possibility of domination by New South Wales and Victoria.

Between 1850 and 1880 the idea of a federation was kept alive by isolated, quixotic politicians who believed in the merit of the idea. William Charles Wentworth was actively involved in the formation of the London-based General Association for the Australian Colonies in the mid-1850s. Select committees were formed by the New South Wales and Victorian parliaments to investigate the problems of establishing a federation. Unfortunately the suspicion and antagonisms which already existed between colonies conspired to scuttle any serious proposals. There is little doubt that a lack of any feeling of national identity combined with local political aspirations worked against any serious movement towards federation.

Inevitably during the 1860s and 1870s the colonies moved further and further apart. Some colonies prospered and others declined. Separate politicians on issues like immigration tariffs and defence began to emerge. Between 1863 and 1880 eight intercolonial conferences were held to resolve these basic issues. Federation had been so comprehensively dropped from the political agenda that it was rarely discussed at these conferences.

Eventually the problems became so great that during the course of the 1880 intercolonial conference Henry Parkes recommended the establishment of a permanent federal council. It was only supported by South Australia, Tasmania and

New South Wales. It seemed to fail although, when Germany and France began showing interest in colonising the Pacific, the states who had baulked at a federal council suddenly appreciated its value.

At the time there was a belief that Britain should take a more active role in colonising the Pacific. The major aim of the council was to exert pressure on Britain. In this it was successful and a Federal Council met for the first time in 1886. It continued to meet every two years until federation.

It is one of the ironies of the 'federation process' that Henry Parkes, who had recommended the establishment of the federal council, refused to have anything to do with it believing it to be flawed and ineffectual.

However, on 24 October 1889 at Tenterfield in northern New South Wales, Parkes addressed a meeting and argued persuasively that Australia had to develop a national defence force. Historians consider this speech to be the true starting point for the movement which culminated in federation eleven years later.

On 2 March 1891 forty-five delegates from all states gathered in Sydney for the first meeting of the National Australasian Convention. The convention established committees to draft a bill which would create the Commonwealth of Australia. If the political and economic forces had been different the Commonwealth of Australia may have become a reality within eighteen months but a severe depression and the emergence of the Labor Party ensured that it was once again pushed down the agenda.

Edmund Barton, who had effectively taken over

*An invitation to the Federation Inaugural Celebrations in Sydney, 1901.*

# *The March of Time:* **1880s and 1890s**

| 1881–2 | 1883–4 | 1885–6 | 1887–8 | 1889–90 |
|---|---|---|---|---|

## EVENTS

**1881** A smallpox epidemic begins in Sydney eventually claiming about forty lives.

**1882** Firemen are powerless as Sydney's 'Garden Palace' is destroyed by fire. The Palace was built for the International Exhibition of 1880.

**1883** The NSW and Victorian railway lines are linked, with passengers travelling from Sydney to Melbourne only needing to change trains at Albury.

**1884** The master and crew of the *Hopeful* are found guilty of the murder of Pacific Islanders they'd 'recruited' for work on Queensland sugar plantations.

**1885** Western Australia's first goldrush begins near Halls Creek after finds made by Charles Hall and Jack Slattery.

**1886** Californian irrigation experts George and William Chaffey sign an agreement with the Victorian government to pioneer irrigated farming on the Murray River at Mildura.

**1887** The practice of naming cyclones is introduced to arouse public interest in the weather bureau.

**1888** Tamworth in NSW becomes the first country town in Australia to introduce electric street lighting.

**1889** Lawrence Hargrave invents the rotary engine and develops a model of a flying machine powered by compressed air.

**1890** Dr Emma Constance Stone becomes the first registered woman doctor in Australia.

## GOVERNMENT AND FOREIGN AFFAIRS

**1881** Australia's first simultaneous census is taken. It reveals that the white population has reached two million.

**1882** The British government gives the screw corvette, *Wolverine*, to NSW, to be used as a training ship.

**1883** The Intercolonial Conference, attended by the colonies' leaders, agree to form a Federal Australasian Council to legislate on matters affecting the whole country.

**1884** The governments of NSW, South Australia, and Queensland introduce relief work to deal with high unemployment.

**1885** Troops from NSW leave to join the British troops in the Sudan after the death of General Gordon at Khartoum.

**1886** The Victorian Wharf Labourers' Union strikes for the eight-hour day, the first strike to be settled by arbitration.

**1887** Rallies protesting against Chinese immigration are held in Sydney.

**1888** British New Guinea (Papua) Protectorate becomes a Crown Colony administered by Queensland and Great Britain.

**1889** Lack of hygienic sewage disposal in Melbourne results in 558 deaths from typhoid. Victoria establishes a Department of Public Health.

**1890** The maritime strike over the right to unionism spreads to other industries in eastern and southern Australia causing industrial chaos. This strike is the first major clash between employers and the trade union movement in Australia.

## LEISURE AND LIFESTYLE

**1881** The Art Gallery of South Australia is opened.

**1882** The *Sydney Mail* begins publishing Rolf Boldrewood's *Robbery Under Arms* in serial form.

**1883** The Servants Training Institution is opened in Melbourne to train young women for domestic service.

**1884** Hugh McKay demonstrates his stripper harvester, an invention to make wheat harvesting easier.
  Bare knuckled boxing is declared illegal after the death of a boxer at Randwick, NSW.

**1885** A party of Seventh Day Adventist ministers and their families arrive in Melbourne.
  The National Gallery of NSW opens in Sydney.

**1886** The remodelled Princess Theatre opens in Melbourne with a performance of Gilbert and Sullivan's *The Mikado*.
  The first Angus & Robertson bookshop opens in Sydney.

**1887** Henry Lawson, aged twenty, has his first poem, 'Song of the Republic', published in the *Bulletin*.

**1888** J. T. Williams gives the first demonstration in Australia of a parachute when he jumps out of a balloon over Sydney.

**1889** The Heidelberg School of artists opens its first large exhibition of impressionist art in Melbourne. It is condemned by leading art critics.

**1890** 'Banjo' Paterson's bush ballad, 'The Man From Snowy River', is first published in the *Bulletin*.

# The March of Time: **1880s and 1890s**

| 1891–2 | 1893–4 | 1895–6 | 1897–8 | 1899–1900 |
|---|---|---|---|---|

**1891** H. Jones and Co. of Hobart (IXL label) pioneers fruit canning in Australia.

**1892** The complete skeleton of the prehistoric marsupial, *Diprotodon*, which grew to the size of a large rhinoceros, is found at Lake Callabonna, South Australia.

**1893** Patrick Hannan and friends discover gold nuggets at Kalgoorlie, Western Australia, an area which becomes known as the Golden Mile.

**1894** Frances Knorr is found guilty of murdering babies and hanged in Melbourne. Mrs Knorr ran a business where unmarried mothers paid her to act as a foster parent to their unwanted babies.

**1895** Very low rainfall this year begins a pattern which continues until 1902 causing a seven-year national drought. It hampers recovery from an economic depression which reduced sheep numbers by 50% and cattle by 40%.

**1896** Sir William Henry Bragg pioneers the use of the X-ray in Australia.

**1897** The NSW Post Office first officially uses bicycles to deliver the mail.

**1898** William Farrar produces two successful strains of drought resistant wheat.

**1899** John Norton, editor of the Sydney *Truth*, coins the word 'wowser' to describe puritanical fanatics.

**1900** Aborigines Jimmy and Joe Governor and Jackie Underwood kill nine people in NSW during the year. Joe Governor is shot and Jimmy and Underwood are hanged.

**1891** Three Labour candidates win seats in the South Australian elections, the first Labour Party members elected to an Australian parliament.

**1892** Queensland becomes the first government to introduce the 'preferential' voting system which was later adopted by the Federal Parliament in 1918.

**1893** Banks close due to a financial crisis. Thousands of small investors are very distressed.

**1894** The South Australian government gives women the right to vote and to stand for both houses of parliament—the first Australian colony to do so.

**1895** The *Closer Settlement Act* is passed in NSW making land available to farmers on easy terms on the condition it is lived on and improved.

**1896** Women vote for the first time in Australia at an election for the House of Assembly in South Australia.

**1897** Queensland adopts the *Aboriginal Protection Act* which transfers the control of Aboriginal reserves from missions to the government.

**1898** The NSW government creates a Bureau of Statistics and publishes the first statistics on childbirth and infant mortality.

**1899** The first contingent of Australian troops leaves for South Africa to support Britain in the Boer War.

**1900** Edmund Barton becomes Australia's first Prime Minister.

**1891** The famous French actress, Sarah Bernhardt, makes her first Australian appearance at Her Majesty's Theatre, Sydney.

**1892** The first Sheffield Shield cricket match played between NSW, Victoria and South Australia is won by Victoria.

**1893** The Tivoli Variety circuit begins and the first classical ballet choreographed in Australia is performed at the Princess Theatre, Melbourne.

**1894** Ethel Turner publishes her first novel, *Seven Little Australians*.

**1895** 'Banjo' Patterson composes the lyrics for the folk song, 'Waltzing Matilda', It is first sung in public at the North Gregory Hotel in Winton, central Queensland.

**1896** Edwin Flack, a Victorian and the only Australian competitor, wins the men's 800 metres and 1500 metres foot races at the first modern Olympic Games held in Athens.

**1897** Walter Withers is the first to win the Wynne Art Prize for his painting, *The Storm*.
    Artist Datillo Rubbo opens an art school in Sydney.

**1898** In Sydney, Greeks and Lebanese build a Christian Orthodox Church, the first in Australia.
    The Christian Science Church holds its first services in Australia, in Melbourne.

**1899** Major Joseph Perry of the Salvation Army begins work on *Soldiers of the Cross*, the first commercial film made in Australia.

**1900** Frederick Lane wins Australia's first gold medal for swimming at the Olympic Games in Paris.

33

*Ships at Sandridge Pier, Melbourne, c. 1878.*

from Henry Parkes as the federation champion in New South Wales, abandoned the slow parliamentary process and established a number of grassroots 'federal leagues' in towns and cities.

In 1893 a conference of these leagues was held at Corowa, New South Wales. The outcome of this conference was an agreement that each colony should elect representatives who would draw up a federal constitution which, in turn, would be put to a referendum. The breakthrough was that this was a practical way of carrying through the campaign for federation and seeing it resolved by a vote.

There was a mood of change in the air and it was now impossible for any of the state governments to resist. Thus, on 22 March 1897, after enabling legislation had been passed in every state apart from Queensland, the Federal Convention was convened in Adelaide. Two further sessions were held in Sydney and Melbourne in September 1897 and January–February 1898 respectively. By 13 March 1898 a draft constitution had been completed and in early June that same year the voters of New South Wales, Victoria, Tasmania and South Australia went to the polls. The result was 219 712 for federation and 108 363 against with Victoria recording an extraordinary 100 520 for and only 22 099 against.

Unfortunately, the referendum was only narrowly won in New South Wales (71 595 for and 66 228 against) and, given that the parliament had required a minimum of 80 000 votes for federation, the referendum did not pass. The premiers met in Melbourne in early 1899 to discuss possible amendments. Both Western Australia and Queensland were represented at this meeting. Minor changes were made to the draft legislation and during 1899 the states once again voted on the legislation. This time all requirements were satisfied with 377 988 voting for federation and only 141 386 voting against it.

The final process was for the bill to be taken to London where the British parliament had to enact it into legislation. A delegation comprising Edmund Barton, Alfred Deakin, C. C. Kingston, J. R. Dickson and Sir Philip Fysh travelled to London to ensure that the federation bill passed through the British parliament without amendment. At this time Western Australia was still resisting federation. It requested that the British parliament incorporate its amendments but the parliament refused. The bill remained relatively unchanged.

In July 1900 Western Australia voted to join the federation. On 17 September 1900 Queen Victoria signed a proclamation approving the establishment of the federation on the first day of the new century and thus, on 1 January 1901 the Commonwealth of Australian became a reality.

## Developing a concept of nationhood

World War I lasted from 1914 to 1918 and saw some 59 340 Australians die on foreign soils thousands of miles from their homeland. In spite of its distance from Australian shores, and the sense that Australian troops were fighting the wars of others, it is within the larger context of the war, and particularly the near-massacre Australian troops suffered at Gallipoli, that particular vital elements of the Australian character were wrought. Indeed it can be argued that those elements of our national identity which hover between myth and reality—the bronzed Anzac, independence, a natural sporting ability, an innate desire for fair play, a belief that we live in the lucky country, a healthy disrespect for authority, and a near-worship of individual enterprise—were actually forged on the battlefields of Europe and the Middle East.

It is easy to forget, however, that this emergent sense of nationhood had actually started before World War I. It seemed as though the moment people made the decision to become 'Australians' and create a federation that a sense of pride in country was immediately instilled. Australians seemed to see themselves as new and bursting with enthusiasm. It is hardly surprising then that when a contributor, obviously of British sympathies, wrote an article to *The Lone Hand* in 1910 declaring that Australians abroad were not liked because they were 'provincial, unreliable and have an irrepressible tendency to blow, brag and skite', he was greeted by a barrage of proud self-justification.

One writer summed up Australian pride when, replying to this perceived slur on Australian nationhood, he asked indignantly; 'Did Melba, or Ada Crossley, or Amy Castles prove "unreliable" when their voices were taken in hand? ... Is Brennan's torpedo and mono-rail any the worse for having been invented by an Australian? And what of Norman Brookes, who recently won the world's championship at lawn tennis? ... and in cricket and football have Australians proved their unreliability against England's best teams? ... did Lord Kitchener suppose them to be "unreliable" in the war, when he had every troop of them in the fighting line, whilst 90,000 British regulars, militia and South African volunteers defended the lines of communications? It almost seems that the Australian has a pretty fair right to an "irrepressible tendency" towards bragging.'

There was a wonderful buoyant sense of self-confidence, naïveté and optimism. The country sent men off to war because it thought of England as the 'Mother Country' and saw local obligations in terms of a kind of family commitment. Australians became inordinately excited at the aerial exploits of local aviators and of sportspeople.

This was a period of great achievements on a number of fronts. In 1912 John Flynn founded the Australian Inland Mission and, in that same year, Sir Douglas Mawson explored the icy wastes of Antarctica.

As a young geologist, Mawson had travelled to Antarctica in 1907 with Ernest Shackleton. By 1911 he had mustered sufficient funds and support to lead his own, and Australia's first, expedition to the southern polar region. With his two companions, one a German aristocrat, Xavier Mertz, and a member of the British fusiliers, Lieutenant Belgrave Ninnis, Mawson planned to explore 2400 kilometres of Antarctic coastline. Some 515 kilometres from the base camp Ninnis, along with the good supplies and vital equipment, disappeared into a crevasse. Mertz and Mawson decided return to base while trying to survive on dog meat, but the meat contained toxic levels of vitamin A which led to madness and death. When Mertz died, Mawson,

driven only by instinct, continued across the frozen wastes for 160 kilometres, only to arrive at his base camp the day his ship left. He had to wait a year before he could return to Australia where he became a national hero.

There seemed to be no end to the levels of confidence which existed at the time. In 1912 the then Prime Minister, Andrew Fisher, announced that the American Walter Burley Griffin was the winner of the worldwide competition to design a federal capital for the new nation of Australia. The flamboyant Minister of Home Affairs, King O'Malley, announced, 'This must be the finest capital in the world'.

The culture of the pre-war period was equally important in the way it defined the nation. The films of the period included *On Our Selection* which appeared in 1912 and *The Sentimental Bloke* in 1919. In fact C. J. Dennis' book, *The Sentimental Bloke*, had been published in October 1915 and had sold an incredible 66 148 copies by March 1917.

The pre-war period also saw the production of a range of important, defining works of literature. Henry Lawson wrote *Mateship* (1911) and *Backblock Ballads* (1913); C. J. Dennis followed his 1914 success (*The Sentimental Bloke*) with *The Moods of Ginger Mick* (1915) and the unofficial national anthem *The Australaise* (1915); Banjo Paterson published *Saltbush Bill* in 1917; and in that same year Henry Handel Richardson published *Australia Felix*, the first volume of her epic trilogy *The Fortunes of Richard Mahony*.

Musically, Nellie Melba (soon to be Dame Nellie Melba) strode through the pre-war years like the diva and prima donna that she undoubtedly was. In 1911 she toured Australia with the Irish tenor John McCormack; in 1915 she set up a singing school in Melbourne, and by 1918 she had been made a Dame Commander of the British Empire.

This was also a period of extraordinary Australian sporting prowess. In 1910 Frank Beaurepaire (who later made his fortune in motor-car tyres) toured Europe and competed in forty-eight races against the finest swimmers of the time. He raced over distances ranging from 100 yards to one mile and he won every race. In the same year an Australian professional runner, Jack Donaldson, ran the 100 yards in 9⅜ seconds. His achievement was so exceptional that his record was not beaten until 1948.

In 1912 T. J. Matthews took two hat tricks in one

# The March of Time: **1900s and 1910s**

| 1901–2 | 1903–4 | 1905–6 | 1907–8 | 1909–10 |
|---|---|---|---|---|

## EVENTS

**1901** The Australian flag is flown for the first time.

**1902** The Pacific Cable linking Southport, Queensland, with Vancouver, Canada, by submarine telegraph cable is opened, thus establishing trans-Pacific cable communications.

**1903** The following newspapers are first published this year: the *Brisbane Daily Mail*, the *Sunday Sun* (Sydney), the *Border Morning Mail* (Albury), and the *People's Daily* (Melbourne).

**1904** Electricity cables are laid across Sydney Harbour to provide household power and electric street lighting.

→

**1905** The Header Harvester is invented by Massey-Harris Co. It enables the harvesting of rain-damaged wheat crops.

**1906** The Marconi Co. officially establishes wireless telegraphy between Queenscliff, Victoria, and Devonport, Tasmania.

**1907** In Western Australia, the 'No. 1 Rabbit Proof Fence' is completed after five years work but is unsuccessful in stopping the spread of rabbits into that state.

**1908** The 'great white fleet' of the US Navy begins a month-long visit to Australia.

**1909** Severe flooding occurs in north-western NSW, south-eastern Queensland and the south-west of South Australia.

**1910** W. E. Raymond, the NSW Government Astronomer, photographs Halley's Comet on its transit of the sun.

## GOVERNMENT AND FOREIGN AFFAIRS

**1901** The Commonwealth of Australia comes into being at an inaugural ceremony in Centennial Park, Sydney, on the first day of the 20th century.

**1902** Women are granted the right to vote in federal elections.

**1903** The *Commonwealth Defence Act i*s passed making military service compulsory in time of war.

**1904** The recruitment of kanakas to work in the Queensland canefields ceases.

**1905** Western Australia, following Queensland's example, passes an *Aboriginal Protection Act* which establishes reserves and 'protectors', tightening control over many aspects of Aboriginal life.

**1906** The colony of British New Guinea is re-named Papua and comes under Australian administrative control.

**1907** The concept of a basic or minimum wage is legally established by Mr Justice Higgins when he hands down the Harvester Judgement. Initially it was seven shillings per day for a six-day working week.

**1908** The Commonwealth government passes a bill for old-age and invalid pensions of ten shillings per week.

**1909** The *Federal Defence Act* is introduced and provides for the establishment of a military college and compulsory military training for males aged 12–26.

**1910** The first Australian coins and banknotes are issued.

## LEISURE AND LIFESTYLE

**1901** *My Brilliant Career* by Miles Franklin is published.

**1902** The soprano, Nellie Melba, gives her first recital in Brisbane after returning from Europe.

**1903** *Such is Life* by Joseph Furphy is published.

**1904** W. A. Barton is selected as Australia's first Rhodes Scholar.

**1905** The first Melbourne–Sydney motor racing reliability trial is held. Mrs Ben Thompson is the first woman competitor.

**1906** *The Story of the Kelly Gang,* thought to be one of the first feature-length films in the world, is screened in Melbourne.

**1907** Australia wins the Davis Cup for the first time.

**1908** Australia's first surf carnival is held at Manly. The Bondi club demonstrates the march past drill.

**1909** Singers Peter Dawson and Amy Castles tour Australia and Dame Nellie Melba makes her third concert tour.

**1910** Cozens Spencer's narrative film, *The Life and Adventures of John Vane, the Notorious Australian Bushranger,* premieres in Melbourne.

# The March of Time: 1900s and 1910s

| 1911–12 | 1913–14 | 1915–16 | 1917–18 | 1919–20 |
|---------|---------|---------|---------|---------|

**1911** J. J. Hammond makes the first significant powered aircraft flight in Australia carrying passengers.

**1912** The Commonwealth Bank, owned and operated by the Federal government, opens as a savings bank.

**1913** The first penny postage stamp of the Commonwealth of Australia is issued. It is known as the kangaroo series, or 'roo' stamp.

**1914** Australia's first official airmail delivery is made from Melbourne to Sydney—1785 letters are delivered.

**1915** BHP opens its steelworks at Newcastle and begins large-scale steel production.

**1916** The Taronga Zoological Park opens in Sydney.

**1917** Due to anti-German feelings in South Australia, the names of over forty towns and districts with German origins are changed. German-speaking schools and newspapers are also closed down.

← **1918** Sydney receives the first direct overseas radio telephone transmission message sent in morse code from Britain.

**1919** A worldwide influenza epidemic kills 11 552 Australians.

**1920** Queensland and Northern Territory Aerial Services Ltd, now known as Qantas, is founded.

---

**1911** The newly formed Naval Board officiallly promulgates an order which establishes the Royal Australian Navy in October.

**1912** A maternity allowance of five pounds per child, known as the 'Baby Bonus', is paid to all white Australian mothers.

**1913** The new national capital is named Canberra and the first peg is driven in by Home Affairs Minister, King O'Malley.

**1914** Australia becomes involved in World War I when Britain declares war on Germany.

**1915** The Commonwealth introduces its own income tax as a temporary measure to pay for the war.
ANZAC forces land at Anzac Cove, Gallipoli.

**1916** ANZAC Day is first celebrated on April 25.

**1917** The Commonwealth Police Force is established.

**1918** Australia celebrates as the Armistice of 11 November ends World War I. Of the 329 000 Australians who served overseas, 166 819 were wounded and 59 342 lost their lives.

**1919** There are many strikes throughout the country. Working days lost because of strikes to now number 6 308 226.

**1920** The Communist Party of Australia and the Federal Country Party are both formed.

---

**1911** G. Hardwick wins gold medals for Australia in boxing and swimming at the Festival of Empire, the first of the sporting competitions now known as the Commonwealth Games.

**1912** Walter Burleigh Griffin (right) wins the international competition for the design of Canberra, Australia's capital city.

**1913** A documentary film entitled *Home of the Blizzard* is released by Frank Hurley, Douglas Mawson's official photographer for the Australasian Antarctic Expedition.

**1914** The tango dance from Argentina becomes popular in Melbourne and Sydney.

**1915** Visiting Hawaiian, Duke Kahanamoku, introduces surfboard riding to Australia.

**1916** Roy Rene, 'Mo', first appears at the Princess Theatre in Sydney.

**1917** The Australian boxer, Les Darcy, dies in Memphis, Tennessee, from pneumonia.

**1918** The children's classics, *Snugglepot and Cuddlepie* by May Gibbs, and *The Magic Pudding* by Norman Lindsay (left), are published.

**1919** The film, *The Sentimental Bloke*, produced by Raymond Longford, opens in Melbourne.

**1920** Raymond Longford releases the first film version of Steele Rudd's Dad and Dave stories, *On Our Selection.*

*William Morris Hughes.*

Test match in South Africa—a feat unequalled since. In 1912, 1913 and 1914 Bill Longworth won and held every New South Wales and Australian swimming title from 200 yards to one mile and in 1914 Norman Brookes won both the Wimbledon singles and doubles.

Among the sporting achievements there were also events which were to become part of the country's mythology. Les Darcy, the boxer from Maitland, may have become one of the world's great heavyweight boxers but the war deprived him of worthwhile opponents. Snowy Baker, the strongman archetype of the 'bronzed Aussie he-man', became a role model for Australian males. Fanny Durack won the 100 metres freestyle at the 1912 Stockholm Olympics thus becoming the first sportswoman to win an Olympic gold medal. At Freshwater Beach in Sydney Duke Kahanamoku introduced Australians to the mysteries of surfboard riding and Prince Wickyama (known in Australia as Alick Whickham) from the Solomon Islands, introduced the nation to the swimming stroke which became known as the Australian Crawl.

## World War I and the Anzacs

In the absence of any internal wars Australia has seen the experience of the two World Wars as hugely significant. In the case of World War I it did much to define the character of the nation.

If there is a theme which is common to all the wars involving Australians, it is the theme of departure. Wars have always been fought overseas and consequently the most potent images of war are images of wives and sweethearts waving farewell to troopships and ecstatic relatives greeting the returning warriors.

World War I, or the Great War, saw 329 000 soldiers leave the country. In the hearts and minds of Australians it was a confusing war. The posters and the politicians demanded unflinching patriotism and yet only one in twelve went to the war. Twice the Australian electorate rejected Billy Hughes' impassioned pleas for conscription powers.

For all this ambivalence, the war did create some remarkably potent myths. In the blood and destruction of Gallipoli, the image of the fearless Anzac, the jaunting slouch-hatted digger, the ever-optimistic patriot was forged. In the deserts of Egypt the legendary bushman's prowess with the horse was put to the test by the Australian Light Horse Brigade. At Gallipoli, a curly-headed larrikin named John Simpson found a donkey and transported hundreds of wounded soldiers from the front line back to the beach. After twenty-five days he was a legend—and he was dead. The nation's courage was measured in terms of sixty-six Victoria Crosses.

With war in Europe becoming inevitable, Andrew Fisher dissolved the federal parliament and declared a general election but, before the election could be held, Britain declared war on Germany (4 August 1914) and the war became the central election issue. Anticipating the outbreak of hostilities, Andrew Fisher proudly declared on 1 August:

> Turn your eyes to the European situation and give the kindest feelings towards the mother country at this time. I sincerely hope that international arbitration will avail before Europe is convulsed in the greatest war of any time ... But should the worst happen after everything has been done that honour will permit, Australia will stand by our own to help and defend her to our last man and our last shilling.

The government acted swiftly and the nature of Australia's military commitment to Britain was clearly established. The entire Australian navy was transferred to Britain and placed at Britain's disposal. On the voyage to England HMAS *Sydney* received two distress signals from the telegraph station on Cocos Island. Speeding towards the island, the *Sydney* caught the German battle cruiser *Emden* with half her crew ashore and pinned her between the island and the sea. In the battle which ensued the *Sydney* forced the *Emden* aground on a coral reef. It was one of the Allies' first sea victories. The *Sydney* and the rest of the naval convoy then continued on to Britain.

Apart from transferring its navy to Britain, Australia also established the Australian Flying Corps, seized the German south-west Pacific territories and, under Sir William Birdwood, formed the Australian and New Zealand Corps (ANZAC).

In 1915 the first Anzacs landed at Gallipoli and some 10 000 of them died in what was to be a pointless campaign. That same year no fewer than 250 000 Australians enlisted for service overseas—but this, according to the new Prime Minister, William Morris Hughes, was still not enough. Hughes introduced a 'Call to Arms' encouraging men to enlist in the military forces.

By 1916 Australia was deeply involved in the war in Europe. Thousands of men were fighting on the Somme, the Australian Light Horse had been committed to Syria and Palestine and the first Australian Flying Unit was being transported by ship to Egypt.

Hughes decided that conscription was essential. On 30 August 1916 he announced that a referendum on conscription would be held on 28 October. In the end the conscription referendum was lost due in part to an active anti-conscription campaign by the major unions and, so folklore has it, strong lobbying by soldiers at the front who didn't want their mates to suffer in the way they had. (In truth the soldiers at the front voted 'Yes' by a small majority.) The 'No' vote won by the slender margin of seventy-two thousand.

In May 1917 Hughes called a Federal election and won on a 'Win the War' platform. Once again Hughes went to the people to try and gain conscription powers and once again he was defeated—this time with twice the 'No' vote he had received the year before. Hughes resigned after his referendum defeat but in the absence of another leader he was re-elected.

The war finally came to an end in 1918. Some 59 340 Australians had been killed, 166 819 wounded and 329 000 had served overseas. Hughes and the war had decimated the Labor Party and it was in such an environment that Earl Page founded the Country Party.

At home, the war had a strange effect. Cut off from European imports, Australia was forced to manufacture its own goods. In 1915 BHP opened a blast furnace at Newcastle and by 1916 Wunderlich were manufacturing three million terracotta roof tiles (replacing the tiles previously imported from France) and, as the advertisements said, 'painting the town red'.

For most Australians, the war was something far away. It is interesting that on the night of 11 November 1918, the night peace was declared, the singer Gladys Moncrieff was performing in Sydney. The performance was interrupted to announce the cessation of hostilities and, at the finale of the first act, white pigeons were released from the stage.

*Dee Why Beach, Sydney, in about 1939.*

## World War II and postwar prosperity

On 3 September 1939 the then Prime minister Robert Menzies went on radio to announce : 'Fellow Australians, it is my melancholy duty to inform you officially that, in consequence of the persistence by Germany in her invasion of Poland, Great Britain has declared war upon her, and that as a result, Australia is also at war.'

The nation's passion for war and the belief that it was nation-building and character-building was clear. People queued to join the forces and the newspapers wrote eulogies about the brave men who were going off to fight for their country.

The *Sydney Morning Herald* described the departure of six thousand soldiers from Sydney on 5 January 1940.

Six thousand young soldiers of the Second A.I.F., proud bearers of the standard bequeathed to them by the original Anzacs, marched through the streets of the city yesterday. A tumultuous reception was given them by dense crowds, estimated to number nearly 500,000.

The long khaki columns thrilled the heart of Sydney as it has not been thrilled for a quarter of a century, since that still spring day in 1914 when the First A.I.F. marched through the same streets on its way to Anzac and imperishable glory.

These men of Australia's brave new army, young, bronzed, clear-eyed, and so obviously conscious in their demeanour of their high responsibility and the confidence which a nation reposes in them, were the answer to Berlin's wishful propaganda. They were worth, in terms of patriotic showmanship, ten times all the supply ships and the food ships which Australia

# *The March of Time:* **1920s and 1930s**

| 1921–2 | 1923–4 | 1925–6 | 1927–8 | 1929–30 |
|---|---|---|---|---|

## EVENTS

**1921** The Ford Motor Co. begins assembling cars in Australia.

**1922** The Smith Family Welfare Organisation and the Country Women's Association are both established.

**1923** Fred Walker and Co. begins producing Vegemite.

**1924** The longest recorded heatwave in Australia ends. The temperature at Marble Bar, Western Australia, had exceeded 100° F (37° C) for more than 170 consecutive days.

**1925** Radio 2UE begins operating. It was to become Australia's oldest commercial radio station.

**1926** The prickly pear infestation is successfully eradicated by the release of eggs from a South American moth.

**1927** The Flying Doctor Service is established by the Reverend John Flynn.

**1928** Bert Hinkler makes the first solo flight from England to Australia and Charles Kingsford Smith (left) and Charles Ulm make the first trans-Pacific flight from California to Brisbane.

**1929** Noel Hunt introduces airconditioning into Australia.

**1930** The first commercial radio telephone service is established between Australia and England.

## GOVERNMENT AND FOREIGN AFFAIRS

**1921** Prominent social worker and Nationalist, Edith Cowan, becomes the first female member of any Australian Parliament when she is elected to the Western Australian Legislative Assembly.

**1922** Payment for six days sick leave per year is introduced by the Commonwealth Arbitration Court.

**1923** Queensland's Labor government introduces Australia's first unemployment benefits scheme.

**1924** About two million koala skins are exported this year resulting in near extinction of koalas in the eastern states.

**1925** Working hours are reduced to forty-four hours per week in NSW and Queensland.

**1926** The Council for Scientific and Industrial Research (later CSIRO) is established.

**1927** Parliament House, Canberra, is officially opened by the Duke of York. ←

**1928** A Court of Enquiry justifies the killing of thirty-two Aborigines by whites in retaliation for an Aboriginal attack on a station holder and the killing of a white dingo shooter.

**1929** The Scullin Labor government abolishes compulsory military training and voluntary enlistment is introduced.

**1930** Unemployment of workers reaches 20% as Australia experiences the effects of the worldwide Depression.

## LEISURE AND LIFESTYLE

**1921** W. B. McInnes wins the first Archibald Prize for his portrait of Mr H. Desbrowe-Annear.

**1922** 'Along the Road to Gundagai', written by Melbourne songwriter Jack O'Hagan, is published in sheet music.

**1923** The English novelist, D. H. Lawrence, writes his novel, *Kangaroo,* while living at Thirroul, NSW.

**1924** Three Australians win gold medals at the Paris Olympics: A. W. Winter for the hop, step and jump, R. C. Eve for diving and Andrew 'Boy' Charlton (left) for the 1500 metres freestyle (sets record).

**1925** The first professional jazz record is made featuring the trombone and trumpet playing of Frank Coughlan.

**1926** The Russian ballerina, Anna Pavlova, tours Australia promoting public interest in ballet. Robert Helpmann studies with her company during the tou

**1927** Australia's first greyhound races are held at Harold Park, Sydney.

**1928** The first 'talkies' films are screened for the Australian public in Sydney: *The Jazz Singer* at the Lyceum and *The Red Dance* at the Regent Theatre.

**1929** Doris Fitton establishes the Independent Theatre in Sydney.

**1930** Phar Lap wins his second Melbourne Cup.

# The March of Time: 1920s and 1930s

## EVENTS

**1931** Western Australia's largest nugget, the Golden Eagle, weighing 35 303 grams, is found at Coolgardie.

**1932** The Sydney Harbour Bridge is officially opened by Premier Jack Lang.

**1933** The *Australian Women's Weekly* begins publication.

**1934** 'Cook's Cottage' arrives from England and is reassembled in Fitzroy Gardens, Melbourne.

**1935** The Shark Arm murder mystery is the main news in Sydney.

Kingsford Smith and Tom Pethybridge are lost over the Bay of Bengal in the *Lady Southern Cross*.

**1936** The Hume Dam on the Murray River is completed. It is Australia's largest public works to this time.

**1937** A serious epidemic of infantile paralysis (poliomyelitis) breaks out in all states.

The *Spirit of Progress* begins its first run from Melbourne to Albury

**1938** Australia's first Empire Games (now the Commonwealth Games) are held in Sydney as part of Australia's 150th Anniversary.

**1939** Devastating bushfires in Victoria, NSW and Tasmania destroy millions of hectares of forest and claim seventy-one lives.

**1940** Dr Howard Florey and Dr E. Chain successfully prove the antibiotic qualities of penicillin. They are awarded the Nobel Prize in 1945. Florey is the first Australian to receive this award.

## GOVERNMENT AND FOREIGN AFFAIRS

**1931** The Commonwealth Arbitration Court reduces the basic wage by 10% to try to combat the worsening depression.

**1932** Dole queues lengthen and unemployment peaks at 30% as Australia becomes seriously affected by the Depression.

**1933** Australia takes control of six million square kilometres of the Antarctic continent when the Australian Antarctic Territory is created.

**1934** A dictation test is used to bar a Czech Communist, Egon Kisch, from entering Australia to address an anti-war congress.

**1935** Mild trade sanctions are imposed against Italy after it invaded Ethiopia, and HMAS *Sydney* is sent to join the international force at Gibraltar.

**1936** The Federal Arbitration Court grants a week's paid annual leave to commercial printers.

**1937** A Federal government conference adopts a policy of assimilation for part-Aborigines and reserves for the segregation of full-blood Aborigines.

**1938** Australia agrees to accept Jewish refugees from Nazi Germany.

**1939** Prime Minister, Robert Menzies, announces Australia is at war with Germany.

**1940** The government bans the Communist and Fascist political parties in Australia believing them to be subversive to the war effort.

## LEISURE AND LIFESTYLE

**1931** The first fully Australian newsreel, *Cinesound Review*, has its first showing.

**1932** West Australian Walter Lindrum becomes the world billiard champion.

**1933** The 'bodyline' bowling controversy begins with the Australia v England Test cricket series. ←

**1934** Science House in Gloucester Street, Sydney, is the first winner of the John Sulman Award for Architecture.

**1935** The ABC begins school radio broadcasts.

**1936** 'Dad and Dave' radio serial begins. It will be broadcast for fifteen years. ↓

**1937** The Police Citizens Boys' Club movement is opened in Sydney to help in the fight against juvenile delinquency.

**1938** Albert Namatjira, an Aboriginal artist, holds his first exhibition in Melbourne, selling all forty-one paintings.

**1939** Edouard Borovansky opens a ballet school in Melbourne which eventually becomes the Australian Ballet.

**1940** George Russell Drysdale begins his landscape paintings of the Australian outback.

*R. G. (later Sir Robert) Menzies.*

has sent to the European war zone since the war began...

By the beginning of 1940 Australia's overseas 'obligations' were clear. That year was notable for its preparations to defend Australia against possible invasion: a Volunteer Defence Corps was established; Bass Strait was closed to shipping after a British ship hit a mine; and the first of many rationing measures—petrol rationing—was introduced.

Perhaps the most significant moment of World War II (as far as Australia was concerned) occurred in 1942 when Japan entered the war and started its push south which, by the end of the year, would see the first attacks on Australian soil since European settlement.

The year before (1941) had seen the Australian Government suffer a crisis of confidence, the ruling coalition collapse, and Robert Menzies resign as Prime Minister. In his wake came John Curtin, and it was Curtin's hapless duty to announce the nation's greatest naval disaster as 645 servicemen died when HMAS *Sydney* was destroyed by the Germans off the coast of Western Australia.

In 1942, for the first time in history, foreign invaders killed civilian Australians on Australian soil (243 died in Darwin as a result of Japanese air raids). It was the year when the Australian towns of Broome and Wyndham were bombed, and when three midget Japanese suicide submarines broke through the safety net and attacked shipping in Sydney Harbour.

Rationing was intensified as the demands of the war ate deeper into the healthiness of the Australian economy. By 1943 there were restrictions on the sale of cooking appliances and rationing of household drapery.

By 1943 the Japanese were on the retreat. In that year too, Darwin saw the last bombing raid after some fifty-nine attacks. Signs that the war was drawing to a close were apparent as work was completed on Hobart's famous floating bridge across the Derwent and in Western Australia the Australian National Airways was established.

Although the war did not finish until 1945, the major events of 1944—with the obvious exceptions of the introduction of meat rationing and the Japanese prisoner-of-war breakout of Cowra (which resulted in the deaths of 232 prisoners)—were domestic issues. The country was racked by natural disasters with bush-fires in Victoria claiming fifty-one lives and the worst dust storms on record sweeping across south-eastern Australia.

In 1945, just a month before the end of the war, John Curtin died in office. He was succeeded for just five days by Francis Forde before Ben Chifley, 'a true product of the Australian Labor movement' (as *The Times* in London described him), became Prime Minister.

The postwar years were characterised by demobilisation, immigration and reconstruction. As Minister for Immigration, Arthur Calwell instituted a huge drive for European migrants which, by the late 1950s, had brought more than a million Greeks and Italians, and substantial numbers of Dutch, Yugoslavs, English and Spaniards to Australia. The program was rationalised as humanitarian aid to a war-torn Europe but it was also driven by a fear of imminent invasion from the north—a fear which had proved to be a reality during 1942 and 1943.

Reconstruction and recovery saw the establishment of Trans Australian Airlines, the development of Woomera as an experimental site and the opening of the Australian National University (ANU); Qantas was nationalised and an Antarctic survey station was built on Heard Island.

In 1946 cars finally outnumbered horses and thus became the country's main mode of transport. This fact was neatly reinforced two years later when, on 29 November 1948, Prime Minister Ben Chifley stood at the end of a production line at Fisherman's Bend and watched the first Holden 48/215 (the first 'Australian' car) come off the assembly line. For Chifley it fulfilled his dream of a low cost, hardy, people's car. It cost £733 10s and by 1951 General Motors-Holden's (GMH) were producing over a hundred vehicles a day.

The recovery from the Great Depression and World War II was complete and people settled back into a comfortable society where thoughts of war and strife were pushed to the back of their minds.

### Towards an Australian identity—A decade of change

Major cultural changes are usually the product of complex and subtle factors which occur slowly and are often hard to identify. In recent times Australians have started to discuss the possibility of becoming a republic, have seen the need for a recociliation treaty with Aborigines, and the importance of focussing the country's industrial activity more towards the buoyant economies of Asia.

It is hard to account for the winds which swept through Australian political life in the decade between 1965 and 1975. Why should we change? The postwar years had been good to Australia. Robert (later Sir Robert) Menzies had ruled over the country like some benign medieval prince. There had been little or no unemployment. Large projects like the Snowy Mountains Hydro-Electricity Scheme and the Murrumbidgee Irrigation Scheme had started. England was 'home' and Queen Elizabeth II was loved and admired. Australia may not have been very exciting but it was very comfortable.

As much as any generalisation has validity it would seem that the defining force of change in the mid-1960s was the sudden explosion of young adults known as 'the baby boomers'. A new word, 'teenager', entered the language. The conservative

*Building of the Sydney Opera House continues during 1966.*

forces—education, the law, parents, social morality—were being challenged by a phalanx of youth whose catch-cry was 'The times they are a'changin'. Movies like *Blackboard Jungle* and *The Wild Ones*, actors like James Dean and Marlon Brand, musicians and singers like Elvis Presley and Jerry Lee Lewis, had given notice in the 1950s

*Sydney's Warringah Expressway under construction in 1966.*

# The March of Time: **1940s and 1950s**

| 1941–2 | 1943–4 | 1945–6 | 1947–8 | 1949–50 |

## EVENTS

**1941** Dr Norman Gregg establishes the connection between rubella (German measles) and congenital defects in babies.

**1942** Darwin is bombed by Japanese aircraft and three midget submarines enter Sydney Harbour and sink HMAS *Kuttabul*.

**1943** Japanese torpedo the hospital ship *Centaur* off the south Queensland coast with the loss of 268 lives.

**1944** Japanese prisoners-of-war attempt to escape from their POW camp at Cowra, NSW. Four Australian guards die and 234 Japanese are killed or commit suicide.

**1945** War with Germany concludes on 8 May and Japan surrenders 15 August.

**1946** The government-owned Trans-Australian Airlines is established.

**1947** The Australian National Antarctic Research Expedition sets up a permanent scientific research station on Heard Island, Antarctica.

**1948** The Holden, an entirely Australian-made car, is produced at General Motors-Holden.

**1949** Prime Minister Chifley officially opens the Snowy Mountains Hydro-Electric Scheme for irrigation and power generation.

**1950** The CSIRO successfully introduces the myxomatosis virus to the Murray Valley to control the rabbit population.

## GOVERNMENT AND FOREIGN AFFAIRS

**1941** Australians of the 6th Division capture Tobruk—including 40 000 Italian soldiers— a great morale booster for the people at home.

**1942** To conserve fuel and electricity daylight saving begins. Petrol, tea, butter, sugar and clothing are rationed and a uniform Federal income tax replaces state taxes.

**1943** The first two women elected to Federal Parliament are Dame Enid Lyons (above left) and Dorothy Tangney.

**1944** The Commonwealth government extends social welfare and introduces unemployment and sickness benefits.

**1945** 500 000 people are out of work due to strikes over wage claims, the forty-hour week and company policies.

**1946** The Immigration Advisory Committee suggests mass immigration from Britain and Europe to increase Australia's population. A. Calwell (above) is first Immigration Minister.

**1947** The Northern Territory moves towards self-government when it is granted a partly elected and partly nominated Legislative Assembly.

**1948** The forty-hour week becomes effective on 1 January throughout Australia.

**1949** The Australian Security Intelligence Organisation (ASIO) is established.

**1950** The Minister for External Affairs, Sir Percy Spender, proposes the establishment of the Colombo Plan, an aid program for less developed nations.

Australian volunteer troops are committed to United Nations forces in Korea. ←

## LEISURE AND LIFESTYLE

**1941** *The Timeless Land* by Eleanor Dark (above) and Ernestine Hill's novel *My Love Must Wait* are published.

**1942** *The Pea Pickers*, a novel by Eve Langley, is published.

**1943** There is much controversy when the Archibald Prize is won by William Dobell for his portrait of Joshua Smith.

**1944** Charles Chauvel's film *Rats of Tobruk* is released and Kenneth Slessor publishes *One Hundred Poems, 1919–39*.

**1945** The first Sydney–Hobart yacht race begins on Boxing Day with nine competitors.

**1946** Two poets publish their first books of poetry: Judith Wright with *The Moving Image* and James McAuley with *Under Aldebaran*.

At the movies, Chips Rafferty stars in the Australian film *The Overlanders*.

**1947** Sydney Nolan exhibits his first Ned Kelly series of paintings.

**1948** After twenty years of Test cricket, Donald Bradman retires with a record of 117 centuries.

**1949** 'Blue Hills', the popular ABC radio serial, commences. It runs for the next twenty-seven years.

**1950** Frank Hardy (below) publishes *Power Without Glory* and Nevil Shute publishes *A Town Like Alice*.

| 1951–2 | 1953–4 | 1955–6 | 1957–8 | 1959–60 |
|---|---|---|---|---|

## EVENTS

**1951** Extensive bushfires throughout all states in Australia claim sixteen lives.

**1952** There are heavy rural losses as one of the worst recorded floods in Australian history strikes southern NSW.

Jubilee celebrations are held throughout to Australia to mark the fifty years since Federation.

**1953** The Atomic Energy Commission is created to co-ordinate the research and development of atomic energy and uranium which has been discovered in Australia.

**1954** Queen Elizabeth II and Prince Philip tour Australia, the first visit by a reigning monarch.

**1955** The first hydro-electric power for the Snowy Mountains Authority is generated by the Guthega Power Station.

**1956** The CSIRO manufactures the Salk vaccine for polio and governments begin a free mass vaccination program.

**1957** Danish architect Joern Utzon wins the inter-national competi-tion to design the opera house for Sydney and the Sydney Opera House Lottery begins.

**1958** Qantas begins its first commercial around-the-world air service travelling between Sydney and London, with one route via the US, the other via India and the Middle East.

**1959** Qantas takes delivery of its first jet aeroplane, an American-made Boeing 707.

**1960** Eight-year-old Graeme Thorne is kid-napped and murdered, the first case in Australia of child kidnap for ransom. His parents had won the Opera House Lottery.

## GOVERNMENT AND FOREIGN AFFAIRS

**1951** ANZUS, Australia's first defence treaty with a foreign country, is signed by Australia, New Zealand and the United States.

**1952** Assisted immigration is reduced because of rising unemployment among Australian workers.

**1953** The Commonwealth Medical Benefits Scheme is introduced paying pharmaceutical, medical and hospital benefits to members of registered health funds.

**1954** Australia becomes a member of the South-East Asia Treaty Organisation (SEATO), the main aim being to prevent communist expansion in South-East Asia.

**1955** Australia receives its one millionth post-World War II migrant, Mrs Barbara Porritt from Yorkshire, England.

**1956** Britain begins its first testing of atomic weapons on the Australian mainland at Maralinga, South Australia.

**1957** The Australia–Japan Trade Agreement provides better access to each country's products.

With no need for a large peacetime army the numbers of National Service trainees are reduced with the introduction of a ballot system based on birth date.

**1958** NSW is the first state to introduce equal pay for women doing equal work. Female state school teachers are the first to benefit.

**1959** Australia restores diplomatic relations with Egypt (broken off during the Suez crisis) and the USSR (broken off over the Petrov affair).

**1960** Social security benefits such as pensions and child endowment are now being paid to Aborigines.

## LEISURE AND LIFESTYLE

**1951** 'The School of the Air' begins broadcasting to children in remote areas from the Flying Doctor Service in Alice Springs.

**1952** Australia's first world boxing title is won by bantamweight Jimmy Curruthers.

**1953** The exhibition, 'French Painting Today', begins a nine-month tour of Australia, encouraging abstract impressionism.

**1954** The Elizabethan Theatre Trust is formed to encourage the development of drama, opera and ballet.

**1955** Barry Humphries' Edna Everage impersonation first appears during a Christmas review in Melbourne.

**1956** Television commences transmission in Australia in time to broadcast the Melbourne Olympics, the first time the Olympics have been broadcast on TV.

← ↓

**1957** Slim Dusty records 'A Pub With No Beer' and it becomes Australia's first gold record.

**1958** Sydney's Radio 2UE presents Australia's first Top 40 chart and Brian Henderson's program 'Bandstand' begins on TV.

**1959** The musical *My Fair Lady* opens in Melbourne and runs for five years. The ABC's '6 O'Clock Rock' begins on TV, compered by Johnny O'Keefe, Australia's 'King of Rock'.

**1960** The largest exhibition of Australian Aboriginal art yet seen tours Australia.

During the fifties women's fashions had been chic, with a well groomed look.

*Melbourne's Westgate Bridge, almost completed in 1976.*

that change was in the air.

In the 1960s, there was an even more potent force at work. The pre-eminent cultural force was popular music. Singers and groups like Bob Dylan, The Beatles and the Rolling Stones not only provided the soundtrack they also provided the hairstyles, clothes, recreational activities, and the political focus.

In Australia an era symbolically ended when Sir Robert Menzies retired on 20 January 1966. It was as though, at that moment, the easy postwar security and conservatism was over. Already Australia was embroiled in Vietnam and the first baby boomers were old enough to vote.

The unfortunate Harold Holt tried to maintain the status quo but events were beyond his control. He could proudly declare that he was 'All the way with LBJ' but Lyndon Baines Johnson would retreat from office under a welter of anti-Vietnam rallies and protests.

The tide of world events had been running against the Liberal Party. The moral and economic conservatism and the blind allegiance to Britain and the United States which had been the cornerstone of the Menzies years were coming under attack. Australian jingoism was being replaced by an informed nationalism. The commitment in Vietnam was under attack in both the United States and Australia. The 'swinging sixties' with their new liberalism and sexual freedom were challenging the morality of the early postwar years.

It was an accident of history which jettisoned John Gorton into this period of flux. When Harold Holt drowned at Cheviot Beach near Portsea on 17 December 1967 the Liberal Party was thrown into chaos.

The contenders for the prime ministership included Senator John Gorton, Leslie Bury, Billy Snedden and Deputy Leader William McMahon. McMahon was eliminated when John McEwan, Leader of the Country Party, threatened to break the coalition if he won the leadership ballot. All the other candidates seemed lacklustre.

To the surprise of many, John Gorton won. Thus, on 10 January 1968, he became the first senator to be elected Prime Minister, although shortly afterwards he moved to the House of Representatives, having won Harold Holt's seat in a by-election.

Gorton caught the mood of the times. He challenged the stuffy formality of the Liberal Party and his brief prime ministership (he voted himself out the office on 10 March 1971) was characterised by a liberalism and commitment to change which anticipated the Whitlam era.

Gorton is a near-perfect example of John Kenneth Galbraith's argument that history is driven by the necessity of events not the ideology of individuals. Although he was a conservative he was driven by the mood of the times. During his brief period in office he saw changes in Australian society which included the creation of the Australian Council for the Arts, the completion and opening of the National Library of Australia, the establishment of the liberal–conservative Australia Party, the introduction of the concept of equal pay for women, an agreement to establish Australia's first legal gambling casino at Wrest Point near Hobart, the creation of the Metric Conversion Board, the liberalising of abortion laws in South Australia, the first Aborigine to enter Federal Parliament and Aborigines included in the national census.

In many ways, 1971 was a watershed year for Aborigines. It was a year when the changing attitudes in Australian society began to have an impact on the rights of Aborigines. Still, in a very real sense, victories were tempered by setbacks.

The fight for land rights, which was to dominate Aboriginal thinking throughout the 1970s and 1980s, saw both victories and defeats. In January the Victorian Government of Sir Henry Bolte announced that the Aboriginal reserves at Lake Tyers in the Gippsland region and around Framlington would be handed over to the local Aboriginal communities. However, in April the people of Yirrkala lost their land rights battle in the Northern Territory Supreme Court.

In May 1971, when a casual Senate vacancy occurred in Queensland, Neville Bonner became the first Aborigine to take a seat in the Federal Parliament. Although he was hardly a radical, Bonner did attempt to champion the Aboriginal cause.

Then, on 30 June, for the first time since 1901, full-blooded Aborigines were included in a Federal Census. Against this background C. D. Rowley's *The Destruction of Aboriginal Society* was published.

*The Brisbane city skyline in 1979.*

It was the first major acknowledgment by white society that white settlement in Australia had been the cause of the decimation of the Aboriginal people.

In hindsight it has been common to attribute these changes to Gough Whitlam and the ALP. The fact was that the mood of the late 1960s could not be denied by any politician. Perhaps the only difference between Gorton and Whitlam was that Gorton was caught up and swept along by events and Whitlam, sniffing the changes, embraced them with enthusiasm.

In 1971, after a party room vote of confidence which resulted in a tie, John Gorton, who had the casting vote, voted himself out of office and William McMahon came to power. But, by now, the ALP juggernaut was unstoppable.

On 13 November 1972 Gough Whitlam, Leader of the Federal ALP, opened the party's election campaign at Blacktown Civic Centre with the famous lines:

Men and women of Australia, the decision we will make for our country on 2 December is a choice between the past and the future, between the habits and fears of the past and the demands and opportunities of the future. There are moments in history when the whole fate and future of nations can be decided by a single decision. For Australia, this is such a time.

After twenty-three years of Liberal government the Australian electorate was being asked to choose between a party which had been ruled by four leaders—Menzies, Holt, Gorton and McMahon— in six years and a party which had been dominated by Gough Whitlam since 1966.

The Labor campaign, with the slogan 'It's Time' and a catchy pop song accompanying its television commercials, caught the popular imagination. When the election was held on 2 December Whitlam achieved 49.6 per cent of the vote, giving him a nine-seat majority.

Whitlam was a man in a hurry. He could not wait for the formal establishment of a new ministry. For three weeks he ran the country with his Deputy Prime Minister, Lance Barnard. This two-man ministry controlled twenty-seven portfolios. In three weeks they set out to wipe away the detritus of twenty-three years of Liberal government. They repealed the Conscription Act, released National Service protesters from gaol, looked into the issue of

# The March of Time: **1960s and 1970s**

| 1961–2 | 1963–4 | 1965–6 | 1967–8 | 1969–70 |
|---|---|---|---|---|

## EVENTS

**1961** Large-scale iron-ore deposits are found in Western Australia and the first commercially viable oilfield is discovered in Queensland.

**1962** The *Southern Aurora* begins through-services by train between Sydney and Melbourne.

**1963** The Bogle–Chandler inquest begins. Their bodies had been found in Sydney bushland, the cause of death remaining a mystery.

**1964** HMAS *Voyager* sinks with the loss of eighty-two lives after colliding with HMAS *Melbourne* (above) during naval exercises off the coast of NSW.

**1965** English model, Jean Shrimpton, wears an above-the-knee dress, no hat and no stockings to Flemington. She is asked to dress more conventionally for the Melbourne Cup.

**1966** Decimal currency is introduced.

**1967** Australia's first satellite is launched from Woomera, and a national four-digit postcode system is introduced to assist in the sorting of mail.

**1968** Australia's first heart transplant operation takes place in Sydney. The patient survives for forty-five days.

**1969** Television pictures of man's first landing on the moon are relayed to the world from the CSIRO's radio astronomy telescope near Parkes, NSW. Great UK train robber Ronald Biggs (below) is reported living in Melbourne.

**1970** The Royal Family and Pope Paul VI (the first pope to visit Australia) help celebrate the 200th anniversary of Captain Cook's landing.

## GOVERNMENT AND FOREIGN AFFAIRS

**1961** Un-employment reaches 3.5% during the Menzies government 'credit squeeze' which particularly affects the motor vehicle, building, timber and steel industries.

**1962** Aborigines in Western Australia, Queensland and the Northern Territory gain the right to vote in Federal elections; the same right that Aborigines in other states have had since 1949.

**1963** Australia signs the Nuclear Test Ban Agreement.

**1964** Financial assistance is given to government and non-government secondary schools for science education, thus re-introducing state aid to private schools after a lapse of over 100 years.

**1965** Australia sends troops to Vietnam, a decision which is bitterly opposed by the Labor Party, and the first National Service call-up ballot is held.

**1966** As a result of a strike on Wave Hill Station (Northern Territory) the Northern Territory Aboriginal stockmen are granted white rates of pay and working conditions and the Council for Aboriginal Rights is established.

**1967** A record 'yes' vote in the referendum grants Aborigines full citizenship rights giving the Federal government power to legislate for Aboriginal policy and include them in the census.

Prime Minister Harold Holt drowns in the surf at Cheviot Beach, Victoria.

**1968** The 12-mile fishing limit around Australia is introduced to protect the Australian fishing industry. John Gorton (left) succeeds Harold Holt as Prime Minister

**1969** The Conciliation and Arbitration Commission grants equal pay to women for equal work.

**1970** Tempers flare when thousands march in Vietnam War Moratoriums in all states to protest against Australia's participation in the Vietnam War.

## LEISURE AND LIFESTYLE

**1961** Government-run Totalizator Agency Boards (TABs) have been introduced to take over control of off-course betting in Victoria and Western Australia.

**1962** Firsts in tennis—Rod Laver wins the Grand Slam (Australian, French, Wimbledon and US singles titles) while Margaret Smith wins the US, Australian and French singles titles.

**1963** The Reverend Alan Walker of the Central Methodist Mission in Sydney establishes Lifeline, Australia's first telephone counselling service.

**1964** The Beatles tour Australia and 'Beatlemania' spreads.

**1965** The Seekers' song 'I'll Never Find Another You' becomes the first Australian record to sell a million copies; Joan Sutherland returns home for an Australian opera tour; the Australian Ballet makes its first overseas appearance at Covent Garden.

**1966** The film *They're A Weird Mob* premieres and Geoffrey Blainey publishes *The Tyranny of Distance*. The Mavis Bramston Show begins on the Seven Network.

**1967** The ABC's current affairs program, 'This Day Tonight', is launched with Bill Peach as compere.

**1968** The Australian Council for the Arts and the National Literature Board of Review are established.

**1969** Harry M. Miller presents the live rock-musical *Hair* at the Sydney Metro.

**1970** Rosie Sturgess and Graham Kennedy continue to delight viewers in IMT on the Nine Network.

The Women's Liberation Movement is greatly influenced by the publication of Germaine Greer's *The Female Eunuch*.

| 1971–2 | 1973–4 | 1975–6 | 1977–8 | 1979–80 |
|---|---|---|---|---|

## EVENTS

**1971** The South African Springbok Rugby Tour sparks anti-apartheid demonstrations wherever the team plays. A State of Emergency is declared in Queensland.

**1972** The Ord River Dam, part of the Ord River Scheme in the Kimberleys, Western Australia, is officially opened.

**1973** The Sydney Opera House is officially opened by Queen Elizabeth II and the Wrest Point Casino, the first legal casino in Australia, is opened in Hobart.

**1974** There is severe flooding in Brisbane caused by Cyclone Wanda and on Christmas Day Darwin is devastated by Cyclone Tracy.

**1975** The bulk carrier, *Lake Illawarra*, sinks, losing twelve lives, when it rams and destroys a span on the Tasman Bridge, Hobart, and a fire claims fifteen lives when it destroys the Savoy Hotel in Sydney.

**1976** The ACTU calls the nation's first general strike to protest against proposed changes by the Fraser government to Medibank.

**1977** Eighty-three lives are lost in Australia's worst rail disaster, at Granville in Sydney.

**1978** Refugee 'boat people' arrive in Darwin from Vietnam, Laos and Cambodia.

**1979** The British government takes responsibility for the disposal of plutonium waste excavated from the Maralinga bomb test site in South Australia.

**1980** An anti-venene for the funnel-web spider bite is discovered by CSIRO scientists.

## GOVERNMENT AND FOREIGN AFFAIRS

**1971** Queensland's Neville Bonner becomes the first Aboriginal parliamentarian.

**1972** Gough Whitlam becomes the first Labor Prime Minister since 1949. His government ends conscription and recalls the remaining Australian troops from Vietnam

**1973** The Federal government grants Papua New Guinea self-government (comes into effect in 1975), gives eighteen-year-olds the right to vote in Federal elections, abolishes tertiary education fees and appoints Elizabeth Reid adviser to the government on women's affairs (first in the world).

**1974** The Bankcard credit system is introduced by government and private banks.

**1975** Medibank is introduced, the *Commonwealth Racial Discrimination Act* becomes effective and the Whitlam government is controversially dismissed by the Governor-General, Sir John Kerr (above).

**1976** The Family Court of Australia introduces 'no-fault' divorce based on twelve months' separation as proof of irretrievable breakdown.

**1977** The NSW government appoints a Royal Commission into Drug Trafficking as a result of the disappearance of anti-drug campaigner, Donald Mackay.

**1978** Three die as a terrorist bomb explodes outside the Sydney Hilton Hotel where the Commonwealth Heads of Government Meeting is being held. A State of Emergency is declared.

**1979** Up to twelve months unpaid maternity leave is granted to working women by the Commonwealth Arbitration Commission.

**1980** After much controversy, the Tasmanian government decides to dam the Gordon River as part of a hydro-electricity scheme, at a place least damaging to the environment, and the

## LEISURE AND LIFESTYLE

**1971** The NSW Builders Labourers Federation imposes 'green bans' on the Rocks area in Sydney.

**1972** Shane Gould, aged fifteen, is Australia's outstanding performer at the Olympic Games when she becomes the first to hold all women's freestyle swimming records at once.

**1973** Patrick White becomes the first Australian to win the Nobel Prize for Literature and the National Australian Gallery purchases Jackson Pollock's *Blue Poles*.

**1974** 'Advance Australia Fair' becomes the new national anthem.
Women's fashions favour wide flairs and high platform soles.

**1975** Peter Weir's film *Picnic At Hanging Rock* premieres and colour TV is officially introduced.

**1976** The Australian films *Caddie, The Devil's Playground* and *Don's Party* are released.

**1977** Methodist, Congregational and some Presbyterian churches join to form the Uniting Church of Australia.

**1978** A female, Pat O'Shane, becomes the first Aboriginal law graduate and barrister.

**1979** Karen Pini and Mike Walsh launch the first Lotto draw in New South Wales. The Federal government introduces the 'Life Be In It' campaign.

**1980** Candice Reed, Australia's first 'test tube' baby, is born in Melbourne.
Alan Bond makes a challenge for the America's Cup with his yacht *Australia*.

*In October 1986 the Royal Australian Navy hold their 75th Anniversary Celebrations on Sydney Harbour. HRH the Duke of Edinburgh is on board the white ship, HMAS* Cook, *taking the Royal salute.*

equal pay for women, banned sporting teams from Rhodesia and South Africa, set up an inquiry into Aboriginal land rights, withdrew troops from Vietnam, and investigated grants to public and private schools.

On 18 December a full ministry was chosen. Again the pace of legislation was rapid and by the end of 1972 the Whitlam government's popularity had soared. The public perception was that here was a government which was going to improve both Australian society and the well-being of individuals within that society.

The end result was the Whitlam government changed Australian society irrevocably. Although, on balance, he was an unsuccessful Prime Minister, his vision of a new, liberal, adventurous society was to persist. It still dominates Australian thinking today.

## The emergence of modern Australia

Edward Gough Whitlam may have been a man in a hurry but he was also a Prime Minister with a vision of a new, more independent and self-confident Australia.

There are thousands of vantage points for looking at the way societies change. Each has its own merits. One image that seems to sum up the changes of the 1970s, and which impacts on a book such as this, is the way the publishing industry began to view the 'Australiana' market.

In 1971 if you wanted a large, glossy book with lots of good photographs of Australia you bought *The Australians* (text by George Johnson, photographs by Robert B. Goodman). It had been first published in 1966 and in the following five years it seemed as though every home had a copy.

By 1981 whole sections of bookshops had been given over to 'Australiana'. Huge books, commonly with a photograph of what was then called 'Ayers Rock' on the cover, were piled on shelves which sagged under their weight. From a point of indifference we had become a nation eager to devour everything about the country.

Somewhere in the 1970s Australia became very proud of its uniqueness and identity. This process probably reached its apotheosis in 1988 when the bicentennial was celebrated with an orgy of self-congratulation and pride.

There are moments throughout the 1970s and 1980s which still loom large in the nation's consciousness. These are moments when pride in country felt good and when we seemed to be capable of matching the achievements of any other society. There are also moments when Australians asserted their independence from the historic control of Britain and the United States.

If, for example, the anti-Vietnam rallies of 1970 challenged the relationship Australia had with the United States then so too did the Proclamation of Australia Act which was signed by Queen Elizabeth in Canberra in 1986 and which finally broke the legal ties between Australia and Britain. In themselves these two acts seem small but in the way that they defined a new feeling of independence they were significant. On 8 May 1970 an estimated

*Australia's Aussat I communications satellite is launched from the space shuttle* Discovery *on 31 August 1985.*

200 000 people marched in the streets of Australia's capital cities to protest about Australian involvement in Vietnam. This wasn't just student radicalism it was a spontaneous outpouring of a belief that Australia could make decision without being cajoled into them by larger powers.

Similarly the final cutting of the legal umbilical cord between Britain and Australia which started in 1982 when the High Court became the final court of appeal and appeals to the British Privy Council were stopped was also a change in mood. Again it was Australia saying that it could sort out its own problems. There was no need to be dependent on Britain for legal decisions.

On a more superficial, but no less powerful, level the assertion of Australianness manifested itself in enormous public gatherings and celebrations. The official opening of the Sydney Opera House in 1973 saw a huge fireworks display and the lighting up of the harbour. Again this kind of celebration would be repeated over and over again in the coming years. In 1988 it was estimated that two million people lined the shores of the harbour on 26 January to celebrate the Bicentennial and once again to watch fireworks and extravagant displays on the harbour. Similarly the outpouring of joy when Sydney won the right to host the 2000 Olympics again saw the harbour lit

# *The March of Time:* **1980s and 1990s**

| 1981–3 | 1984–6 | 1987–9 | 1990-92 | 1993-4 |
|---|---|---|---|---|

## EVENTS

**1981** Kakadu National Park, the Willandra Lakes and the Great Barrier Reef are given world heritage listing.

**1982** The first shipment of uranium ore leaves for processing in America.

**1983** The 'Ash Wednesday' bushfires destroy large areas of rich grazing country in Victoria and South Australia; seventy-one people die and seven townships are destroyed.

**1984** The Federal government appoints a National Advisory Committee on problems associated with AIDS.

**1985** Australia's first communications satellite, Aussat I, is successfully deployed from the space shuttle *Discovery*.

 **1986** Halley's Comet reappears in Australian skies but is barely visible to the naked eye.

**1987** Dick Smith becomes the first person to reach the North Pole by solo helicopter.

 **1988** On Australia Day, about two million people watch the First Fleet Re-enactment as Australia begins celebrating 200 years of white settlement.

**1989** The most severe earthquake in Australia's history devastates Newcastle, NSW.

**1990** Catastrophic floods destroy townships in Queensland, NSW and Western Australia.

**1991** Sydney is shocked and saddened when heart transplant specialist, Dr Victor Chang, is shot dead in a Mosman street.

**1992** Inventors and engineers, headed by Doug Tarca, develop a portable oil containment system so that ships can contain their own oil spills immediately.

**1993** Compass Airlines goes into liquidation.

**1994** The worst bush fires in NSW's documented history destroy bushland and property and claim four lives.

## GOVERNMENT AND FOREIGN AFFAIRS

**1981** Australia's immigration policy emphasises family reunion and filling gaps in the labour market.

**1982** Australian troops join United Nations Peacekeeping Forces in the Sinai during Israel's withdrawal from Egyptian territory.

 **1983** The Labor Party, led by Bob Hawke, wins the federal election as unemployment reaches 10.7%, the highest level since the Depression years.

**1984** Medibank is replaced by Medicare which is financed by a 1% levy on taxpayer's wages.

**1985** The Mutitjulu people are now the official owners of an area of national park which encompasses Uluru (Ayers Rock) and Mount Olga.

**1986** The *Proclamation Act*, which breaks the legal ties between Australia and Britain, is signed by Queen Elizabeth II in Canberra.

**1987** The Fitzgerald Inquiry into police and political corruption and organised crime in Queensland opens.

**1988** Australia's new Parliament House is opened in Canberra by Queen Elizabeth II.

**1989** The Muirhead Royal Commission Report into Aboriginal Deaths in Custody is released and recommends law reform for minor offences.

**1990** Four hundred Australian sailors and five ships leave for the Persian Gulf to join the United Nations Gulf blockade after Iraq invades Kuwait.

 **1991** Paul Keating replaces Bob Hawke as Prime Minister.

**1992** The High Court hands down the 'Mabo Judgement' which rejects the doctrine that Australia was *terra nullius* at the time of British settlement in 1788.

**1993** The Prime Minister, Paul Keating, continues to campaign for an Australian republic and a new flag. He is supported by public opinion polls.

**1994** NSW MP John Newman is killed, an unprecedented political assassination.

## A LEISURE AND LIFESTYLE

**A1981** The government-funded Australian Institute of Sport opens in Canberra.

**1982** The Commonwealth Games are held in Brisbane, Thomas Keneally (below) wins the Booker Prize for  *Schindler's Ark*, The Australian National Gallery opens in Canberra and the Australian film *Mad Max II* is an unprecedented success.

**1983** Alan Bond's winged-keeled yacht, *Australia II,* wins the America's Cup.

**1984** Many movie theatres and drive-ins close as the video movie industry gains popularity.

 **1985** The first Australian Formula One Grand Prix is held in Adelaide, South Australia, and the last NSW Opera House Lottery is drawn.

**1986** Pope John Paul II visits Australia. Catholicism has become the nation's most popular religion.

**1987** Kylie Minogue and Jason Donovan are popular stars in the TV show 'Neighbours'.

**1988** Brisbane hosts World Expo '88.

**1989** The Adelaide Plaza is completed with the opening of Exhibition Hall.

**1990** Joan Sutherland gives her farewell performance in the Sydney Opera House before retiring.

**1991** Yothu Yindi becomes Australia's first Aboriginal musical group to be internationally recognised.

**1992** The film *Strictly Ballroom* premieres to the best box office attendance of all movies released in Australia this year.

 **1993** Australians celebrate as Sydney is awarded the Olympic Games for the year 2000.

**1994** The films *The Adventures of Priscilla, Queen of the Desert* and *Muriel's Wedding* are huge box office successes, with *Priscilla* winning best costume design at the 1995 Academy Awards.

up and huge celebrations on the shore. These were all acts of pride. People were gathering to declare a love of country and a commitment to the nation.

Behind these public displays were the more subtle changes. The arts, which had never enjoyed a huge profile, came to prominence during the Whitlam era when in 1973 Patrick White became the first Australian to win the Nobel Prize for Literature. That same year the Australian National Gallery purchased Jackson Pollock's *Blue Poles* for $1.3 million amid considerable public debate. But the quiet artistic achiever was the Australian film industry.

Starting tentatively with a series of superbly filmed historic dramas—*Picnic At Hanging Rock* (Russell Boyd won a British Academy Award for the Best Photography), *The Getting of Wisdom, Sunday Too Far Away, Newsfront* and *My Brilliant Career*—the 1970s ended with the industry making commercial movies which were enjoying huge success in international markets.

The change occurred at the end of the decade when *Mad Max* became Australia's most successful international film ever. Through the 1980s it was followed by such acclaimed and successful moves as *'Breaker' Morant, Gallipoli, Mad Max 2, The Year of Living Dangerously, Bliss, Mad Max: Beyond Thunderdome, Crocodile Dundee, Crocodile Dundee II, Evil Angels, Young Einstein, Dead Calm* and, in the 1990s, movies like *Strictly Ballroom, The Piano, Ferngully: The Last Rainforest, Priscilla, Queen of the Desert* and *Muriel's Wedding.*

The arts may have gloried in their successes but the sense of sporting achievement was equally significant and defining. In the 1950s Australians had been naturally good sportspeople. The nation's swimmers, tennis players, footballers and cricketers were the best in the world but they were all enthusiastic amateurs. As sport took on a more rigorous, more professional complexion Australian athletes found that they could not match the expertise of highly paid, full-time sportspeople.

This change in the nature of Australian sport occurred with the establishment of the government-funded Australian Institute of Sport. The AIS's most obvious early success was Robert de Castella who, in 1981, joined the organisation as a sports biophysicist and went on to become one of the finest marathon runners of his generation.

In the world of commercial sport the highlights of the era included Pat Cash's win at Wimbledon in 1983, the holding of the first Australian Grand Prix motor race in Adelaide in 1985 and, looming large over the 1980s, the victory of Alan Bond's winged-keeled yacht *Australia II*, which had been designed by Ben Lexcen and skippered by John Bertrand. After twenty-one years of trying to win the elusive cup it was a victory that seemed to capture the mood of optimism which existed in the country in 1983.

Almost forgotten in this hub-bub of success were the smaller events which were symbolic of a more confident, more relaxed nation. In 1976 the liberal-minded and progressive Premier of South Australia, Don Dunstan, achieved a significant breakthrough when he appointed Pastor Sir Douglas Nicholls Governor of South Australia. It was a symbolic gesture. Nicholls became Australia's first Aboriginal State Governor.

Equally, the decision to grant leasehold title to the Gurundji people in 1975 was the beginning of a process which would culminate in the admission that land had been taken from Aborigines. The historic Mabo decision would attempt to redress this perception of unfairness.

This was also a time when Australia finally embraced the concept of a universal health insurance system, changed its national anthem, and looked toward the future with a sense of optimism and genuine enthusiasm. It seemed as though the country had achieved a sense of independence and nationhood which had been accepted broadly by the majority of citizens.

## Looking towards the future

In the 1990s, under the leadership of Paul Keating, a Prime Minister who prides himself on his ability to see 'the big picture', Australian society has been nudged towards a need to redefine itself.

The old image of a predominantly Anglo-Saxon outpost of the British Empire is redundant. The country has genuinely become multicultural and multinational. Inevitably there has been racial friction but it has, by the standards of other countries with large immigration programs, been low level and rarely seriously violent.

The Australia of the 1950s was a society where tea and beer were the most popular adult drinks, where restaurants offered lamb or beef 'with two veg', where men wore grey suits and ties and women wore furs, pearls and 'sensible' clothes and where cheddar cheese, brawn and devon were the high points of the local delicatessan and where brown bread was considered a bit daring. It was a deeply conservative society emotionally tied to Britain which, in the minds of many, was referred to as 'home' and 'the mother country'. The Union Jack was flown higher than the Australian flag at important occasions, 'God Save the Queen' was Australia's national anthem and images of a youthful Queen Elizabeth II were neatly framed on a wall in every public building.

In forty years the country has changed dramatically. Wine, boutique beers and endless Mediterranean variations of coffee have over-whelmed beer and tea. Urban centres offer a bewildering variety of cuisines ranging from American fast food through Vietnamese, Thai, Indian, Spanish and Mexican to African and South American. Suits and furs have given way to casual attire, multicoloured elegance and, for young people, the persuasiveness of designer labels.

Delicatessans are bewildering storehouses of international meats and cheeses and exotic delicacies. The conservatism of the 1950s has given way to a society eager to embrace change—Australians have purchased electronic toys with extraordinary enthusiasm—and eager to be seen as part of the international community, not a colonial outpost.

It is easy to see these changes as cosmetic. In fact they are symbolic of deeper changes in the nature of Australian society. These changes can be summarised as a belief that Australia needs to define itself according to its future rather than its past. Thus, a society which once actively discouraged migration from Asia now recognises that its future is inextricably linked with the rapidly developing economies of south-east Asia and the Pacific rim.

A society where once Latin and French were the most popular languages taught in schools now focusses its language education programs on Japanese and Indonesian.

A society which traditionally relied on its primary production—particularly wool, wheat, meat and mining products—for its economic prosperity now declares that its future lies in becoming a 'clever country'.

The vision for the future is rich and complex. It can be summed up as a combination of a need for national identity, a need to find a realistic place in an increasingly complex modern world, and a need to take our place alongside the great, independent nations of the world.

Australians have been talking about a sense of national identity for most of the twentieth century. In the years immediately prior to federation the *Bulletin*, and writers like Henry Lawson, had championed the notion that a fiercely independent, hard-working and resilient rural worker was the true Australian. It was an image which mixed the courage of the Eureka Stockade, the tenacity of The Drover's Wife, the anti-authority feelings of the early convicts, with liberal doses of drought, dust, flies and hardship and added pain and suffering for good measure.

This image seemed to become a reality during World War I. When the image of Australian soldiers on the battlefield connected with the image of the resilient rural worker. This image, subsequently made more potent by actors like 'Snowy' Baker and Chips Rafferty, persisted until the 1980s. It may well be the case that Bryan Brown and Bob Hawke, particularly the latter in his 'larrikin' mode, were the last hurrahs of this image.

What Keating has done is to change Australia's perception of itself. The Australian of the future will be a person who is part of Asia. They will be able to speak Asian languages, they will contribute to the high tech. productivity of Asia, and they will see themselves as an integral part of the world's most dynamic economic zone.

The Australian of the future will be distanced from any notion of England as 'home'. They will acknowledge that the Europeanisation of Australia was a result of British colonial expansionism in the late eighteenth century and will admit that there was once a society which looked to Britain for its political and legal institutions. This new Australian will see the country as a republic, will be happy with a flag which does not have the British flag in one corner, will acknowledge that Australian Aborigines were forcibly dispossessed of their land, and will rejoice in the sense that modern Australia is a melting pot of cultures where people enjoy the benefits of older cultures while not being tied to the superiority of those cultures.

In many ways such an image of Australia is a dream. However, the changes which have occurred in Australia in the past twenty years do suggest that the old order will never return and that Australia in the twenty-first century will hold its head high in the world community of nations. It will rejoice in its independence and its dynamism.

# New South Wales: THE HERITAGE

In the beginning, New South Wales was the term applied to more than half of the Australian continent. Captain James Cook, having sailed up the eastern coastline of Australia stood on Possession Island at the tip of Cape York on 22 August 1770 and claimed the entire eastern coastline of Australia in the name of King George III, the reigning British monarch. It was, as history has shown, an extraordinary act. All the way up the coast Cook had seen the fires from Aboriginal camps and at numerous places he had sighted Aborigines on beaches and headlands and yet, in spite of British regulations regarding inhabited lands, he claimed the east coast as though it had not human habitation. By doing so he set in motion the forces which, fifteen years later, would result in England establishing a penal colony at Port Jackson.

When Cook claimed the east coast he did not name it. Evidence shows that the term 'New South Wales' came to him on the homeward journey and he recorded it in his journal.

The decision to create a penal colony in this far-flung land was the result of forces which created a serious shortage of facilities for convicts in Britain in the late eighteenth century and after the American War of Independence North America could no longer be used for this purpose. Equally the Industrial Revolution saw people pouring into the larger cities and consequently the crime rate in London had risen to a point where it could not be handled by the prisons in Britain.

In 1786 the British parliament decided that Botany Bay would be a suitable penal colony and so, on 13 May 1787, a fleet of eleven ships carrying convicts and marines set sail from Portsmouth bound for New South Wales. They reached their destination on 18 January 1788 but it became immediately obvious that the lack of fresh water would ensure the failure of the colony. Governor Arthur Phillip, who was in charge of the settlement, sent an exploration party north where, only a few kilometres up the coast, they entered Port Jackson. In Phillip's assessment it was 'the finest harbour in the world'. It also had reliable fresh water.

Thus, on 26 January 1788 Phillip raised the Union Jack in Sydney Cove and the colony of New South Wales was formally established. The early life was hard. The settlement started with nothing. Houses had to be built, streets and lanes carved out of the slopes on either side of the Tank Stream, quarters constructed for the soldiers and convicts, fields planted, animals grazed and the countryside explored. This was the true origin of New South Wales. A dirty and desolate penal colony at the end of the world.

The first years in the colony were very difficult. The supplies which had been brought on the First Fleet were inadequate. The tools were unsuitable and the expertise of both the convicts and the soldiers was limited. The colony waited for every new ship from England, Batavia and the Cape of Good Hope. When a ship did not arrive the colony was on the edge of starvation.

The rapid development of the colony was driven by necessity rather than some adventurous

*The Gap, near South Head, Sydney.*

*Sydney Harbour from Shark Point in the 1880s.*

Foveaux (1808–09), and Colonel William Paterson (1809). Some achieved fame and notoriety. King, for example, was responsible for extensive coastal exploration and was the governor who granted John Macarthur land (which led to the establishment of the very lucrative market in fine wool); and Bligh, already the victim of a mutiny, was publicly humiliated and forced to leave the colony after he attempted to control the power of the military.

At this time all of the east coast and hinterland was part of New South Wales so the exploration of the coast which ranged from the discovery of the Hunter and Hawkesbury rivers in the north to the circumnavigation of Van Diemen's Land was all considered part of the larger exploration of New South Wales.

The great challenge, however, lay inland from Sydney. The Blue Mountains seemed impassible to the explorers who made their way across the Sydney basin. When, after numerous attempts, they were finally crossed in 1813 by the explorers Blaxland, Wentworth and Lawson, it was merely a question of the time before the whole of New South Wales was settled.

It is appropriate that this major exploration milestone was reached during the governorship of Lachlan Macquarie. Macquarie, who was Governor from 1810 to 1823, transformed the struggling colony into a thriving and successful region.

During his administration numerous public buildings were constructed with the help of the gifted ex-convict Francis Greenaway, education and the treatment of women and children was addressed, the first bank (the Bank of New South Wales) was granted a charter, and exploration and settlement proceeded at a dramatic pace. By the time Macquarie returned to England the colony had been explored from Port Macquarie in the north to the Lachlan and Macquarie rivers in the west and Jervis Bay in the south.

In 1823 Macquarie established the basis for the state's Legislative Council. It was the first move towards some kind of self government. That same year the Supreme Court was given full independence and the old military rule (which had existed since 1788) began to be phased out.

The history of New South Wales from 1825 until the 1860s is that of a colony which kept shrinking due to the establishment of independent new colonies. In 1825 Van Diemen's Land was separated. This was followed in 1851 by Victoria and 1859 by

management program. By 1791 land had been granted to over 150 people in the hope that the agricultural base of the infant settlement could be broadened. The problem was still one of expertise and Phillip eventually pleaded with the British government to send out free settlers with farming experience so that New South Wales could become self-sufficient. This call was answered and by the mid-1790s farms, with convicts as the workers, were providing Sydney with supplies.

Given that he had started with a beach and no water and had, in the space of four years, found water, settled the land and made it productive, it is important that Arthur Phillip is recognised as the true father of New South Wales. It was his tenacity and determination which converted Sydney into a viable colony and set the base upon which New South Wales, the most populous of the Australian states, was created.

In the years that followed a series of Governors, most of them with military or naval backgrounds, battled to solve the problems of the new colony. In order, the governors were: Major Francis Grose (1792–94), Captain William Paterson (1794–95), Captain John Hunter, RN (1794–1800), Captain Philip Gidley King, RN (1800–06), Captain William Bligh, RN (1806–08), Lieutenant-Colonel George Johnston (1808), Lieutenant-Colonel Joseph

Queensland. In each case the development of a community with interests which were different from those emanating from Sydney resulted in new colonies being given some measure of autonomy.

During this period the penal nature of the colony was replaced by a society where free settlers and emancipated convicts worked together.

As the population increased the needs of New South Wales changed. During Major-General Ralph Darling's governorship (1825–31) the colony's Legislative Council was enlarged and government customs offices, postal services and a land office were all created.

The colony's focus on agriculture during this period resulted in a population of 2.75 million sheep in 1838. By the 1840s explorers like Sir Thomas Mitchell and others reached the Darling Downs (now in southern Queensland), Portland Bay (Victoria) and the Murray River (South Australia). They were quickly followed by squatters and settlers who claimed the land as soon as it was explored.

The great turning point in the state's history occurred in the area around Bathurst and Orange on 12 February 1851 when Edward Hargraves and a colleague, John Lister, successfully panned gold. In May 1851 Hargraves took 120 grams of gold to Sydney and showed it to the Colonial Secretary and on 14 May the gold discovery was announced.

The impact of this event sent shock waves through all the Australian colonies and changed the nature of Australian society. Over night, workers in Sydney downed tools and headed for the goldfields. Miners and prospectors from all over the world arrived in Sydney eager to get to the goldfields and try their luck.

It was now clear that the old administrative mechanisms which had kept New South Wales tied to the British parliament were irrelevant. The British handed over control of land policy to the NSW Legislative Council in 1852 and a form of responsible government was granted when, in 1855, an elected lower house, the Legislative Assembly, was created.

In the decade from 1851 to 1861 the population of the state nearly doubled—from 197 000 to 350 000. The rural squattocracy which had traditionally controlled the state were now in a minority but, because of the unfairness of the electoral system, they still controlled both houses of parliament.

The state continued to expand throughout the

*The Argyle Cut, Sydney, in the 1880s.*

1870s and 1880s. Railways were built across the Blue Mountains and the combination of Cobb & Co. coaches and bullock wagons (which had to travel on appalling bush tracks) and railway lines, opened up the state. The prosperity of the agricultural sector of the state's economy in the last years of the nineteenth century ensured an enduring and strong economic base.

The period leading up to the outbreak of World War I was a boom time for New South Wales. The area of the state under wheat, greatly helped by the Federation strain of the grain developed by William Farrer, grew to a massive 1.4 million hectares. Rural credit was readily available to farmers wishing to expand. The advent of refrigeration opened up overseas and interstate markets. Mining of silver-lead at Broken Hill and coal in the Hunter Valley expanded rapidly.

*Fort Macquarie (where the Sydney Opera House now stands) in the 1880s.*

The outbreak of World War I fuelled this already buoyant economy and by 1918 New South Wales had the strongest economic base in Australia. This continued until the Great Depression forced the government to protect the economy. The political leader at the time, J. T. Lang, fought running battles with bankers and the Federal government and attempted to repudiate interest payments on state loans which had been generated overseas.

The state Governor, Sir Phillip Game, sacked Lang and in the election that followed the anti-Labor parties won an overwhelming victory. They retained office until the outbreak of World War II when Labor under William McKell regained government. The Labor Party then held power in the state until 1965 when Robert Askin's Liberal-Country Party coalition won a victory which kept them in power for the next nine years. In recent times the Labour party have held power from 1976 to 1988 when the Liberal-National coalition under Nicholas Greiner won government.

These relatively long periods of stable government have ensured that progress within the state has been coherent and sustained.

The post-World War II development of the state has seen the construction of the Opera House, the creation of sophisticated urban transport in the Sydney metropolitan area, the development of the vast Snowy Mountains Hydro-Electricity project, the enormous growth of suburban Sydney so that it is now a city similar in size to Los Angeles, and the modernisation of the city centre. The success of New South Wales has been based on the strength and diversity of its economic base and the unchallenged position of Sydney as the financial and industrial capital of Australia.

The diversity of the state's resources ranges from the silver–lead deposits of Broken Hill to the vast coal reserves of the Illawarra and Hunter Valley regions. The cotton growing in the state's north is matched by the huge sheep properties in the west, the rich dairy country along the coast, the cattle country of the Great Dividing Range and the crops of the Riverina.

Modern changes in technology have resulted in Sydney becoming the home of the major television networks and the headquarters for most national media organisations.

Sydney airport is the primary destination for the majority of overseas flights arriving in Australia and Sydney Harbour is still regarded as the premier urban tourist attraction in the country.

New South Wales is the dominant state in Australia. It is rich and prosperous and with nearly six million residents it accounts for more than a third of the nation's population.

# WHERE TO GO AND WHAT TO SEE

## New South Wales and the Australian Capital Territory

### Sydney and Environs

Agar Steps, The Rocks
Anzac War Memorial, Hyde Park
Aquarium, Darling Harbour
Archibald Fountain, Hyde Park
Argyle Centre, The Rocks
Argyle Place, The Rocks
Art Gallery of New South Wales,
  Art Gallery Road,
  Domain
Australian Museum,
  6 College Street,
  Sydney

Barrenjoey Lighthouse, Palm Beach
Bondi Beach
Botanic Gardens,
  Macquarie Street,
  Sydney
Brett Whiteley Studio,
  2 Raper Street,
  Surry Hills

Cadman's Cottage,
  110 George Street,
  Sydney

Captain Cook's Landing Place,
  Kurnell
Cenotaph, Martin Plaza
Centrepoint Tower
Chinese Gardens, Darling Harbour
Conservatorium of Music,
  Maquarie Street,
  Sydney
Customs House, Circular Quay

Darling Harbour

Earth Exchange, Geological and
  Mining Museum, The Rocks
El Alamein Fountain, Kings Cross
Elizabeth Bay House—colonial
  restoration,
  7 Onslow Avenue,
  Elizabeth Bay
Elizabeth Farm,
  70 Alice Street,
  Parramatta
Ervin Museum and Art Gallery,
  Observatory Hill
Experiment Farm Cottage,
  9 Ruse Street,
  Parramatta

Flemington Market (Friday and
  Saturday)
Fort Denison ('Pinchgut'), Sydney
  Harbour

Garden Island
Garrison Church (Holy Trinity),
  Lower Fort Street,
  Millers Point
General Post Office, Martin Plaza
Great Synagogue,
  160 Castlereagh Street,
  Sydney

Harbour Bridge
Hero of Waterloo Hotel,
  81 Lower Fort Street,
  Millers Point
Hyde Park
Hyde Park Barracks Museum,
  Queens Square,
  Sydney

Jewish Museum,
  148 Darlinghurst Road,
  Darlinghurst

Justice and Police Museum, Circular
    Quay

Kings Cross
Ku-ring-gai Chase National Park

Lancer Barracks,
    Smith Street,
    Parramatta
Law Courts,
    Queens Square,
    Sydney
Library of New South Wales, State,
    Macquarie Street,
    Sydney
Lindesay—colonial restoration,
    Carthona Avenue,
    Darling Point

Macquarie Place, Sydney
Manly
Martin Plaza, Sydney
Mary MacKillop Place,
    7 Mount Street,
    North Sydney
Mint Museum, Queens Square,
    Macquarie Street
Mitchell Library,
    Macquarie Street,
    Sydney
Monorail
Motor Museum, Harris Street
Mrs Macquarie's Chair,
    Royal Botanic Gardens,
    Sydney
Museum of Contemporary Art,
    Circular Quay
Museum of Sydney, Cnr Bridge and
    Phillip Streets

National Maritime Museum, Darling
    Harbour
National Trust, Observatory Hill
Northern Beaches

Observatory, Observatory Park,
    Watson Road,
    Millers Point

Oceanworld, Manly
Old Customs House, Circular Quay
Old Government House,
    Parramatta Park,
    Parramatta
Opera House, Bennelong Point

Paddington Bazaar,
    395 Oxford Street,
    Paddington (Saturdays only)
Paddy's Markets, Haymarket
    (Saturday and Sunday)
Palm Beach

Parliament House, Macquarie Street
Powerhouse Museum,
    Harris Street,
    Ultimo
Pylon Lookout, Sydney Harbour
    Bridge

Quarantine Station,
    North Head,
    Manly
Queen Victoria Building, George
    Street

Randwick Racecourse, Randwick
Royal National Park

St Andrew's Cathedral,
    Sydney Square,
    Sydney
St James' Church,
    King Street,
    Sydney
St John's Church, Parramatta
St Mary's Cathedral,
    College Street,
    Sydney
St Philip's Church,
    York Street,
    Sydney
St Stephen's Church,
    197 Macquarie Street,
    Sydney
Southern Beaches
Sydney Hospital, Macquarie Street

Taronga Zoo Park
The Rocks, Sydney
Town Hall, Sydney Square

University of New South Wales,
    Anzac Parade,
    Kensington
University of Sydney,
    Parramatta Road,
    Newtown

Vaucluse House,
    Wentworth Road,
    Vaucluse
Victoria Barracks,
    Moore Park Road,
    Paddington

Waratah Park,
    Namba Road,
    Duffys Forest
West Head

**Beyond Sydney**
Abercrombie Caves
Australian Village, Wilberforce

Barrington Tops National Park
Ben Boyd National Park
Berrima Village and Gaol, Southern
    Highlands
Blue Mountains
Bouddi National Park
Brisbane Water National Park
Burrendong Dam

Camden Park Homestead—historic
    house, Camden

Dharug National Park
Dorrigo State Park

Gibraltar Range National Park

Hartley—historic township
Hill End—historic township
Hunter Valley—vineyards and
    wineries

Jenolan Caves

Karingal Village, near Bathurst
Kinchega National Park
Kosciusko National Park

Lachlan Vintage Village, Forbes
Lake Burragorang
Lake Eucumbene
Lake Macquarie
Lightning Ridge Opal Fields
Lord Howe Island

Menindee Lakes
Mootwingee Historic Site
Morton National Park
Mount Canobolas, Orange
Mount Kaputar
Murrumbidgee Irrigation Area
Myall Lakes National Park

New England National Park
New England University, Armidale
Old Sydney Town—historic
   re-creation, near Gosford
Overseas Telecommunications
   Station, Moree

Perisher Valley (skifields)

Radio Telescope, Parkes
Richmond RAAF Base

St Matthew's Church, Windsor
Snowy River Hydro-electric Scheme
Southern Highlands
Sturt National Park
Surveyor-General Inn—historic
   house, Berrima

Thredbo (skifields)

Warrumbungle National Park
Wellington Caves
Western Plains Zoo, Dubbo
Wineries and vineyards—Griffith,
   Hunter Valley, Mudgee, Wellington
Wombeyan Caves

Yarrangobilly Caves


**Australian Capital Territory**

All Saints' Anglican Church, Ainslie
Academy of Science,
   Gordon Street,
   City
Australian-American Memorial,
   Russell Drive,
   Canberra
Australian National Gallery,
   14 Molonglo Mall,
   Fyshwick
Australian National University
Australian War Memorial,
   Anzac Parade,
   Canberra

Blundell's Farmhouse

Captain Cook Memorial, Lake Burley
   Griffin
Carillon, Aspen Island, Lake Burley
   Griffin
Cockington Green,
   Gold Creek Road,
   Gungahlin
Cotter Dam

Duntroon Military College,
   Duntroon

Government House,
   Dunrossil Drive,
   Yarralumla

High Court of Australia,
   King Edward Terrace,
   Parkes

Lake Burley Griffin
Lanyon—historic house

Mount Ainslee
Mount Stromlo Observatory

National Library,
   Parkes Place,
   Canberra

Old Parliament House,
   King George Terrace,
   Canberra

Parliament House

Red Hill Lookout
Royal Australian Mint, Deakin

St John's Church,
   Constitution Avenue,
   Reid
Space Tracking Stations—
   Honeysuckle Creek,
   Tidbinbilla

Telecommunications Tower, Black
   Mountain
Tidbinbilla Nature Reserve

Above: *The Australian flag flies proudly atop the modern Parliament House on Capital Hill in Canberra.*

Right: *Shoppers relax under autumn foliage in Petrie Plaza near the huge Monaro Mall shopping complex in Canberra.*

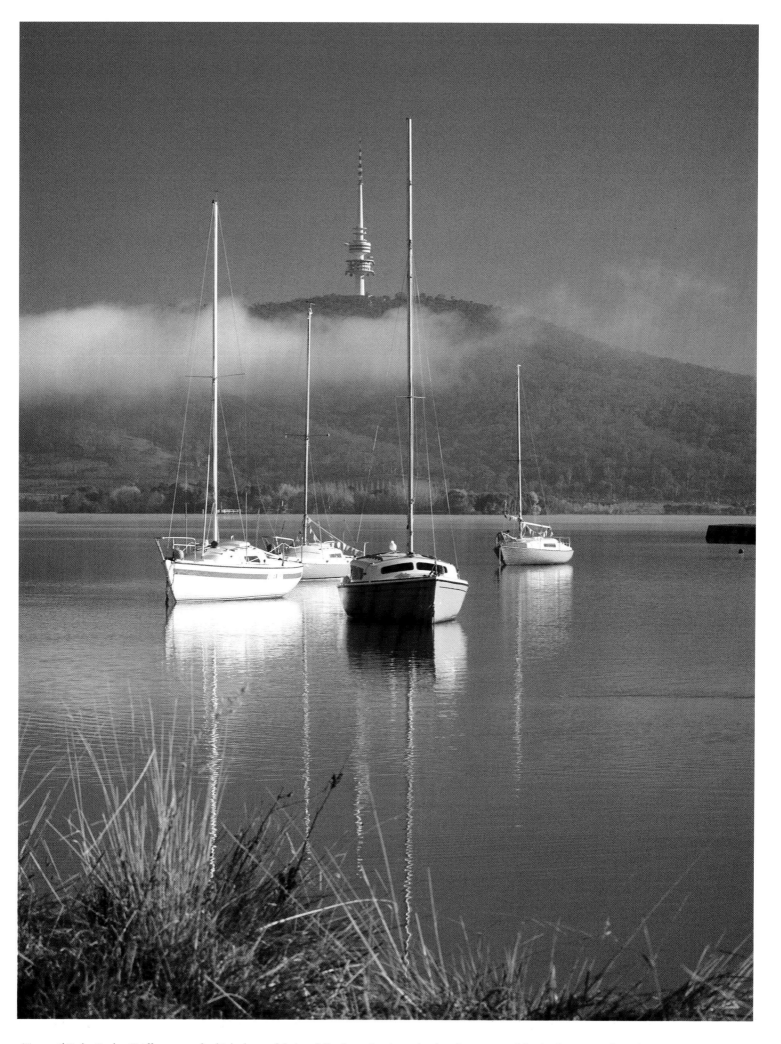

*Tranquil Lake Burley Griffin, around which the model city of Canberra has been developed, was created by the damming of a tributary of the Murrumbidgee River. In the background, the Telecommunications Tower rises 195.2 metres above ground level on the summit of Black Mountain.*

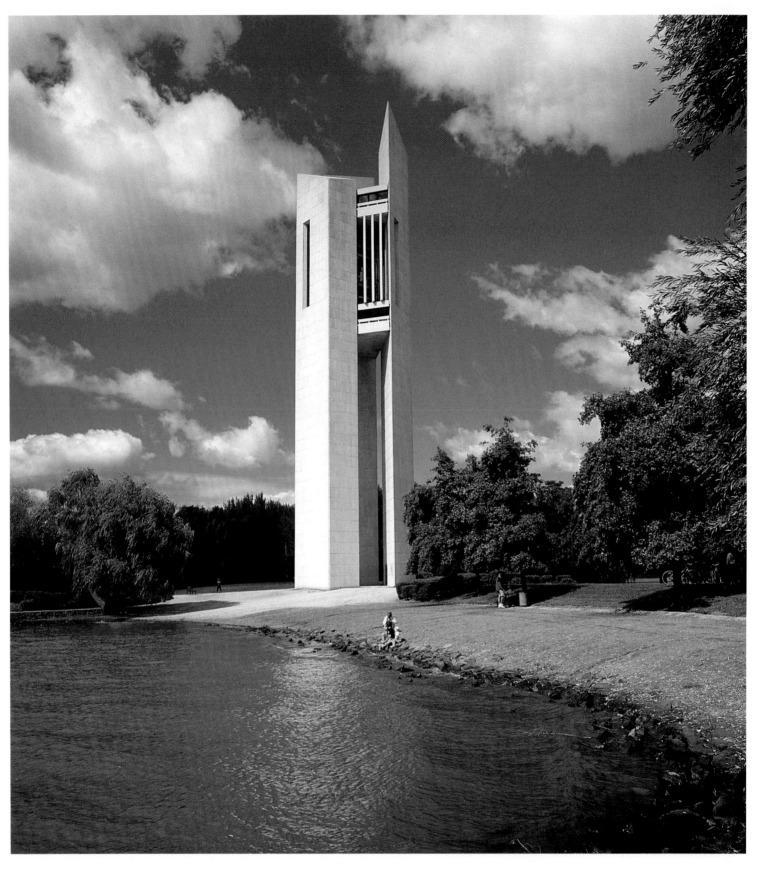

Above: *The fifty-three bells of the Canberra Carillon regularly resound over the shores of Lake Burley Griffin. The Carillon was given to Australia by the British Government to mark the Jubilee of the founding of Canberra and stands on Aspen Island in Lake Burley Griffin. It provides regular Sunday afternoon recitals.*

Opposite, top: *Blundell's Farmhouse in Canberra was built in 1858 by the Campbells of Duntroon for a ploughman employed on the property. It was later occupied by the Blundells who worked the small surrounding farm for fifty years.*

Opposite, right: *The dome-shaped Academy of Science building in Canberra is surrounded by a water-filled moat.*

Opposite, far right: *The foundation stone of the historic Anglican Church of St John the Baptist in Canberra was laid in 1841. The church is built entirely from local materials and contains many memorials to those of Canberra's pioneer past.*

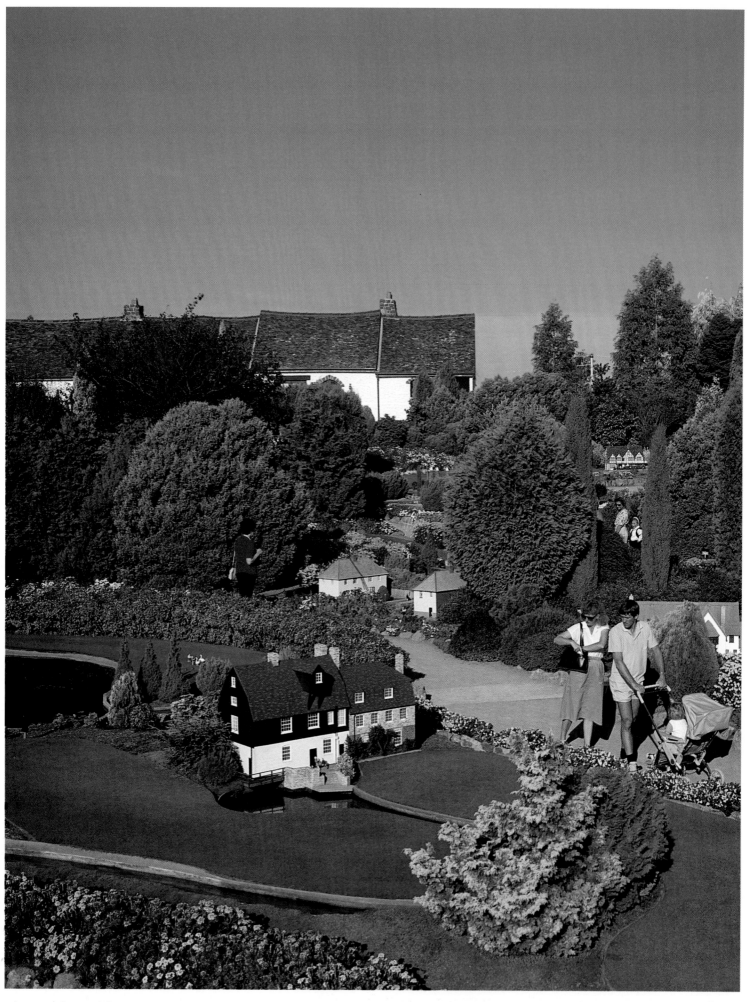

Above: *A drawcard for young and old, the fascinating model English village of Cockington Green is one of Canberra's most famous attractions.*

Opposite: *Bondi Beach in Sydney is Australia's most famous stretch of surf, sand and sunshine. It is one of the thirty-four ocean beaches that the city has to offer.*

68 *Two of Sydney's most famous landmarks, the Opera House and the Harbour Bridge, at dusk.*

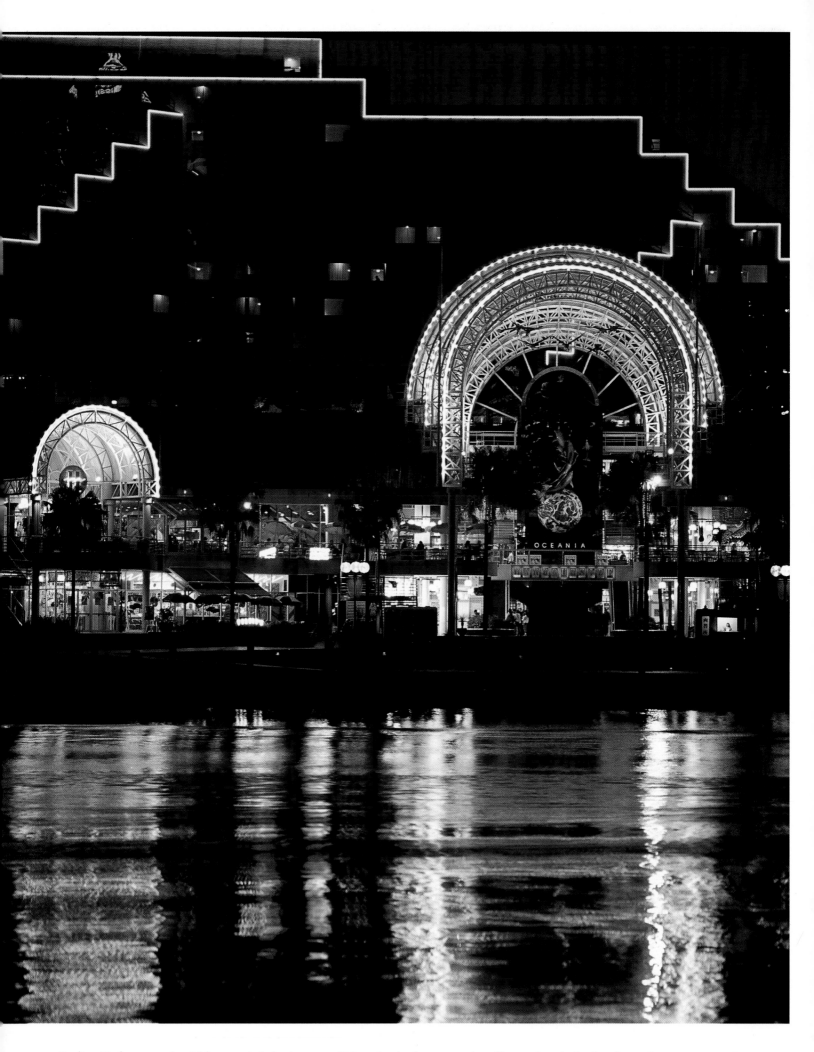

*Darling Harbour, covering 54 hectares, is Sydney's most ambitious city development to date. Shown above is the shopping and restaurant complex at*
70  *night. The bustling recreation and commercial area is a waterfront redevelopment of the former shipping and storage area for the Port of Sydney.*

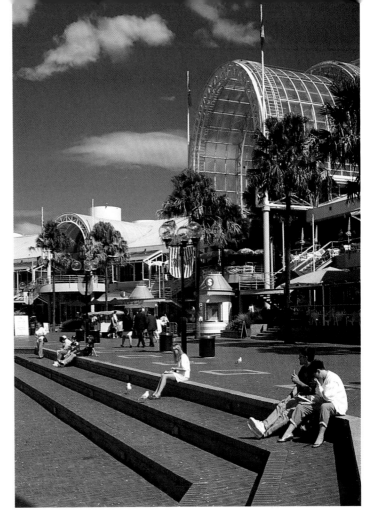

Above: *Centrepoint Tower forms a backdrop to the Chinese Gardens on the eastern side of Darling Harbour. The gardens were a gift to the people of Sydney from the people of Guangzhou, Sydney's sister city.*

Above: *Looking towards the Convention Centre at Darling Harbour.*

Below: *Spanish dancers perform for the crowds during a daytime multicultural performance at Darling Harbour.*

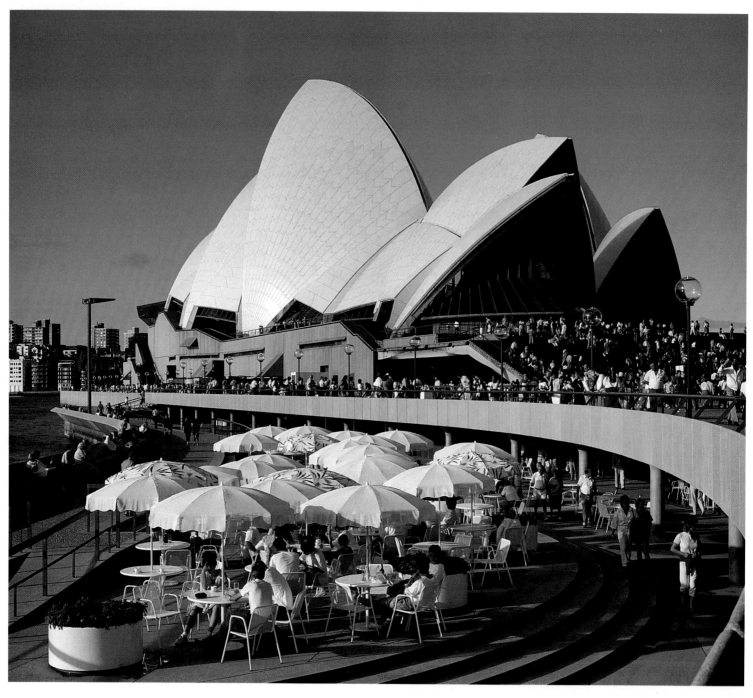

Above: *The spectacular Sydney Opera House on Bennelong Point was officially opened by Queen Elizabeth II in October 1973—it cost a staggering $102 million to construct.*

Right: *Rows of colourful and quaint terrace houses at Glebe contrast with modern high rises, creating the juxtaposition that characterises Sydney.*

Above: *Looking towards the Sydney Harbour Bridge from Lavender Bay, on the northern shore of the harbour. The refurbished Luna Park with the space age big dipper can be seen on the left.*

Below: *The monorail heads towards Darling Harbour Station from the city.*

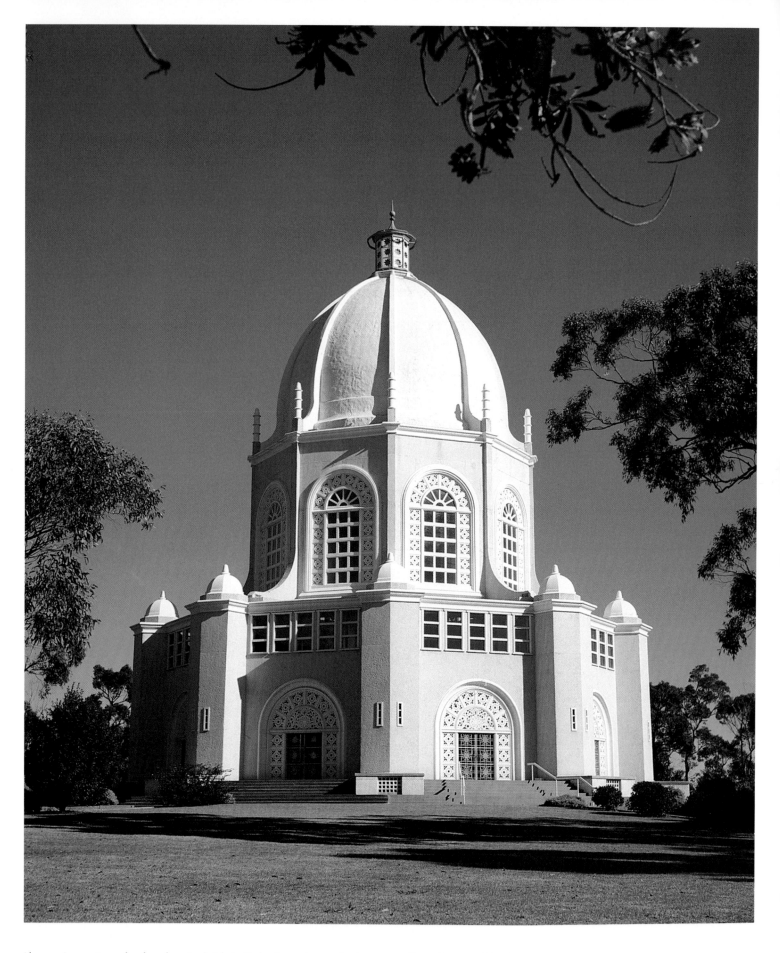

Above: *A prominent landmark at Ingleside in Sydney's northern suburbs, the Bahá'i House of Worship is a unique nine-sided building rising to a height of 40 metres.*

Opposite, top: *Vaucluse House in Sydney was once home to William Wentworth, one of Australia's most colourful pioneers. Set in beautiful gardens and housing many fine antiques, the mansion is open for public inspection.*

Opposite, bottom: *Designed by convict architect Sir Francis Greenway in 1821, the Sydney Conservatorium of Music was originally used as horse stables for Government House.*

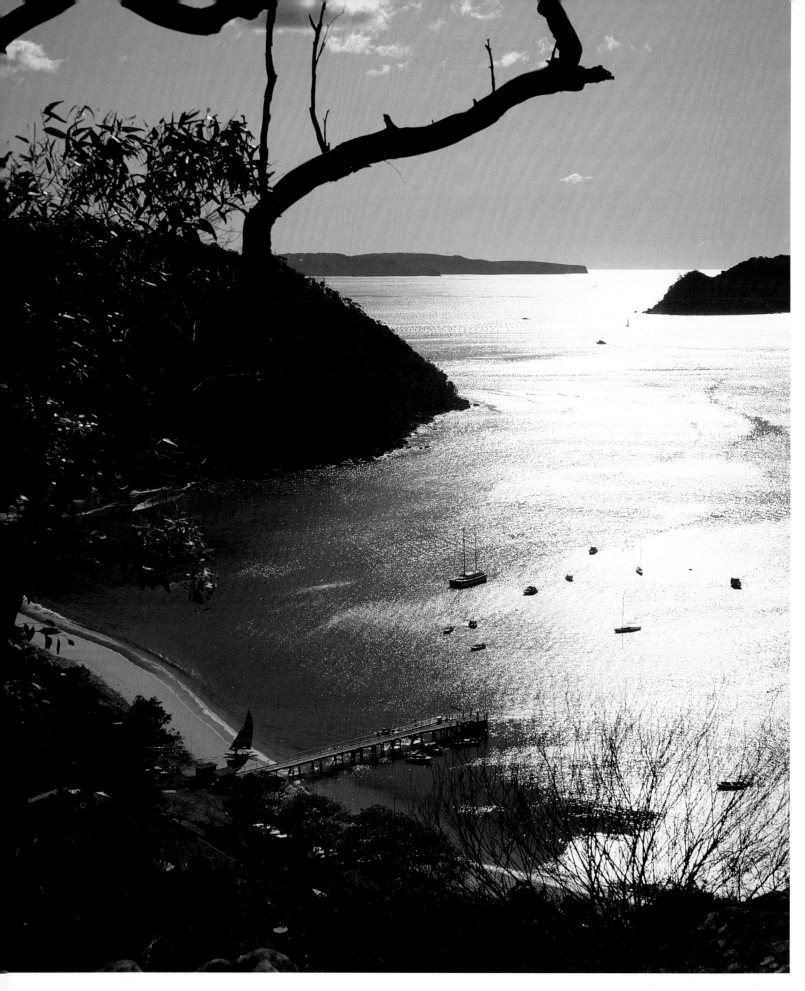

Above: *The vast waterways of Sydney's Pittwater and the adjacent Broken Bay are famous for their scenery and gentle boating conditions.*

Opposite, top: *Relaxing on the paddlewheeler showboat* Turrumburra *which operates on the bush-lined Lane Cove River in Sydney.*

Opposite, bottom: *A huge steel section of the Spit Bridge at Sydney's picturesque Middle Harbour swings up to enable pleasure craft to pass through.*

Above: *Boating on Lake Macquarie, the largest seaboard lake in Australia.*

Left: *The General Grocer and Produce store at the historic goldfield site of Hill End.*

Opposite: *Grand and rugged, with tall stands of timber and natural rock amphitheatres, the Blue Mountains are one of the most impressive scenic attractions within easy reach of Sydney.*

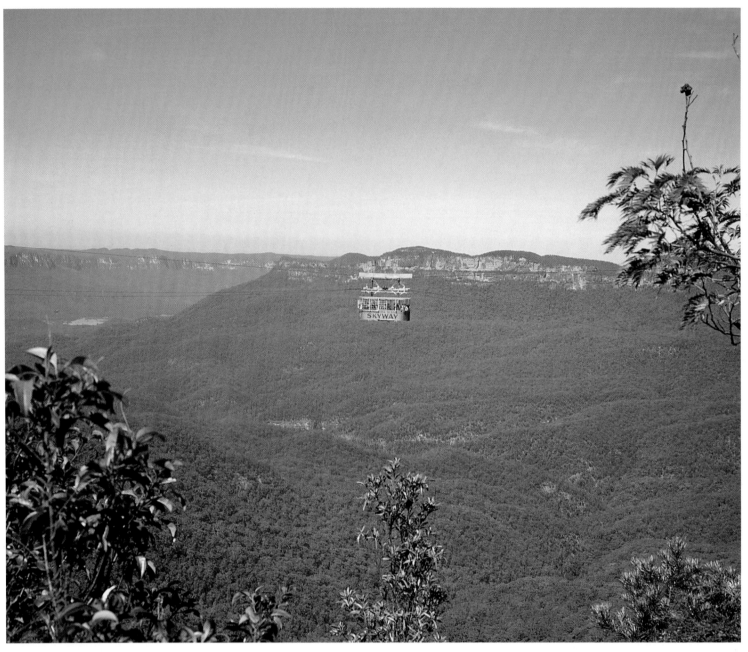

Above: *The Scenic Skyway soars above a gorge at Katoomba in the Blue Mountains, New South Wales. Built in 1958, it was the first passenger-carrying horizontal ropeway in the Southern Hemisphere.*

Below, left: *Caves House, a delightful and popular hotel at Jenolan Caves, the most spectacular limestone caves in New South Wales.*

Below: *Cooma Cottage at Yass, built about 1830, was home to explorer Hamilton Hume who was responsible for opening much of southern New South Wales.*

Above: *Vibrant gardens at Narrandera, a pastoral and wheat town south-west of Sydney at the gateway of the Murrumbidgee Irrigation area.*

Below: *Celebrating Australia's heritage—a mural at Broken Hill in far western New South Wales.*

Below: *The old slab huts of New South Wales' early pioneers were honest and simple in design, blending in with the surrounding countryside.*

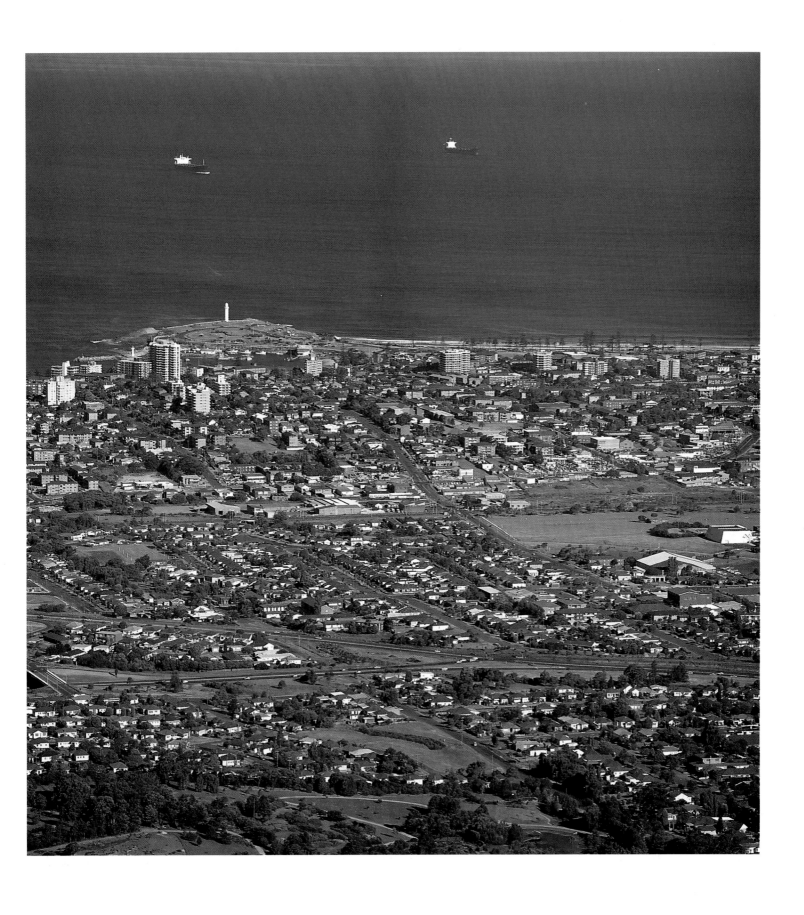

Above: *Looking over Wollongong from Mt Keira Lookout. This heavily industrialised area is the third largest city in New South Wales.*

Opposite: *An unusual view of one of the Three Sisters, probably the best known of the sandstone rock formations to be found in the Blue Mountains*

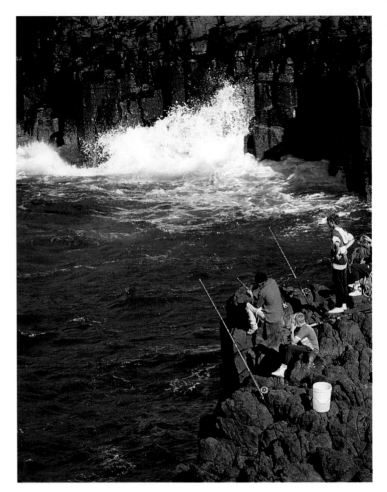

Above: *St Matthew's Church, Windsor, is the oldest Church of England church in Australia. Built in 1817, it was designed by convict architect Francis Greenway who was transported to the colony for forgery in 1814.*

Below: *Birds of a feather flock together at The Entrance on the Central Coast of New South Wales.*

Above: *Rock fishing at the south coast township of Kiama, New South Wales, where the fishing is reputed to be among the best in the country.*

Below: *Magnificent deeply indented coastline and tumbling wooded slopes are features of Bouddi National Park.*

Above: *The surf rolls in at Flynns Beach, Port Macquarie, one of the oldest towns in the state and now a major holiday resort.*

Below: *Enjoying the ambience of The Entrance, one of the most popular holiday resorts on the Central Coast.*

85

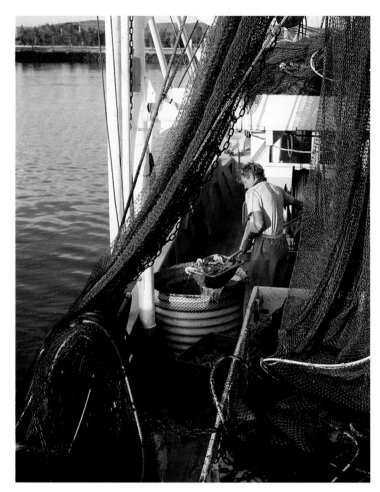

Above: *Mt Warning looms behind the picturesque Tweed River near Murwillumbah, in the centre of the banana and sugarcane growing district near the Queensland border.*

Above: *At work at Evans Head fishing port, centre of the New South Wales' prawning industry.*

Below: *Rows of oyster beds decorate the water at Brunswick Heads, a fine fishing town at the mouth of the Brunswick River.*

Below: *Fog shrouds the impressive forest scenery near the timber town of Dorrigo.*

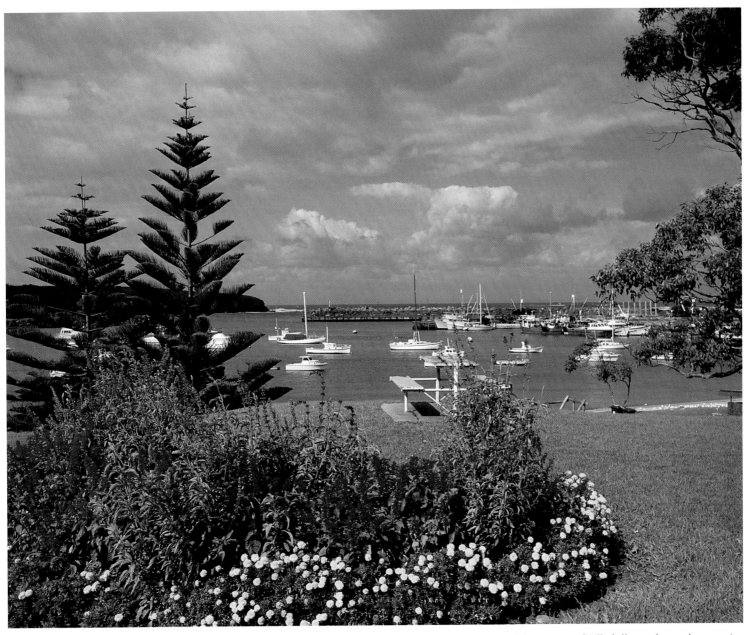

Below: *The convict-built Sea Horse Inn, which still functions as a licensed inn, is one of the few buildings in Boydtown. The town was formerly a rival settlement to Eden and now has little standing, apart from ruins that include a church and lighthouse.*

Above: *The picturesque fishing town of Ulladulla on the south coast. A colourful ceremony is held here each Easter to bless the fishing fleet.*

Below: *Sunset over the Clyde River at the charming resort town of Batemans Bay on the south coast.*

Left: *Siding Spring Observatory, near the Warrumbungle National Park where the extreme clarity of the air greatly facilitates astronomical observation.*

Below: *Early morning sun highlights the Post Office building in the former goldmining town of Forbes. Bushranger Ben Hall's final resting place is in the town's cemetery.*

Opposite: *Water lillies enhance the beauty of the Macquarie Marshes.*

Above: *St Bernard's Church and Presbytery (1842), one of the many fine historic buildings at Hartley, an important stop-over for travellers crossing the Blue Mountains in colonial days.*

Right: *The awesome beauty of Hanging Rock in the Blue Mountains*
*National Park.*

Above: *Snow sculpted trees at Kosciusko National Park in the heart of the Snowy Mountains.*

Left: *Early morning fog clothes the town of Tumut on the Snowy Mountains Highway.*

Right: *The Chalet at Charlotte Pass, a popular ski resort in Kosciusko National Park. Some of Australia's highest peaks and most spectacular ski runs are accessible from here.*

Above: *Historic ruins at the ghost town of Silverton where silver chlorides were discovered in 1883.*

Right: *Opals are mined at the small town of White Cliffs where there is also a walk-in opal mine museum.*

Opposite, top: *Early snowfall at Three Mile Dam in the Snowy Mountains.*

Opposite, far left: *Cattle country at Khancoban near the Snowy Mountains.*

Opposite, left: *Sunrise throws reflections on one of the huge dams of the Snowy Mountains Hydro-electric Scheme.*

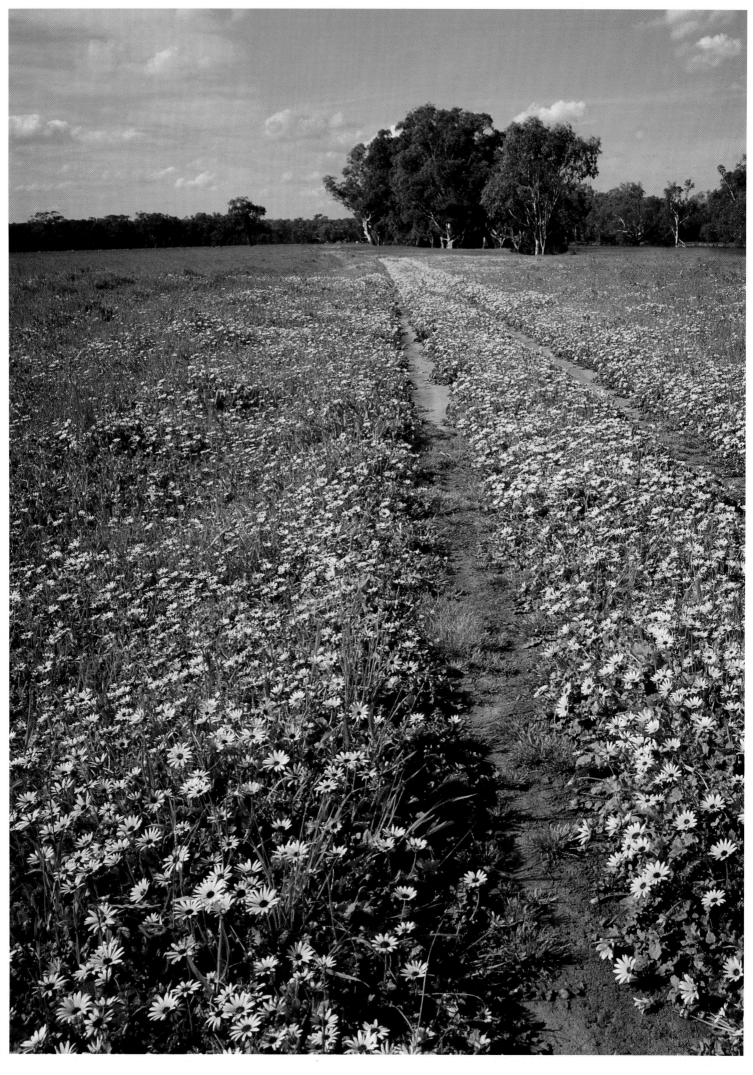

Opposite: *Spring is bursting out all over this farm track near the pastoral town of Narrandera, south-west of Sydney.*

Right: *Grape picking in the Hunter Valley, one of Australia's most important wine districts. The country's oldest commercial wine-producing area, wine was first made here in the 1830s.*

Below: *Reminiscent of an English village, historic Carcoar was the scene of New South Wales' first bank hold-up in 1863.*

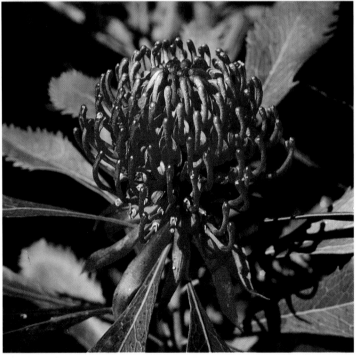

Above: *Heavy rainfall plays havoc with road networks in the usually arid wastelands of far western New South Wales.*

Left: *Most magnificent of all Australian wildflowers—the waratah* (Telopea speciosissima), *floral emblem of the State of New South Wales.*

Opposite: *Lit by the early morning sun, this ancient rock formation near Tibooburra is a reminder of the extreme age of the Australian continent.*

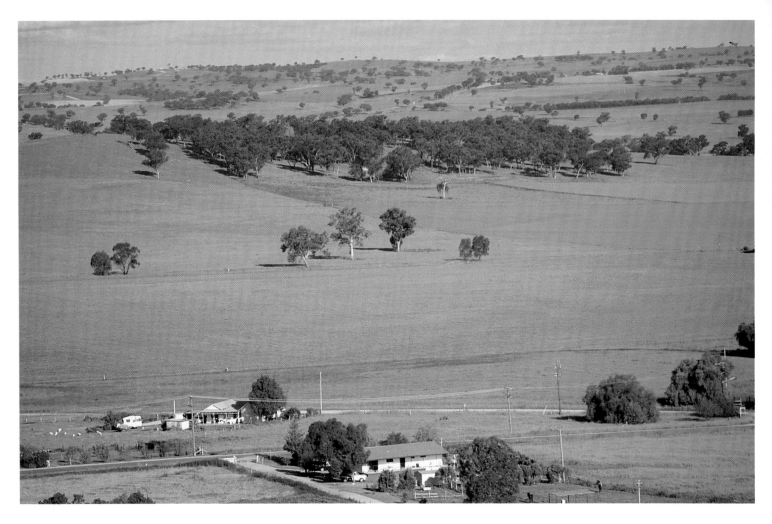

Above: *Rolling farmland at Canowindra, a township once commandeered by Ben Hall and his gang of bushrangers.*

Below: *The Civic Theatre at Wagga Wagga, a thriving city on the Murrumbidgee River.*

Opposite: *Waterfalls cascade through the densely timbered Barrington Tops National Park which straddles the Great Dividing Range.*

Above: *Many of Canowindra's graceful old buildings have been classified by the National Trust.*

Above: *A great place for a drink—Ettamogah Pub, near Albury.*

Below: *Camerons Corner—the meeting of the New South Wales, South Australian and Queensland borders.*

Below: *The Wall of China—crumbling sedimentary deposits in Mungo National Park in south-western New South Wales.*

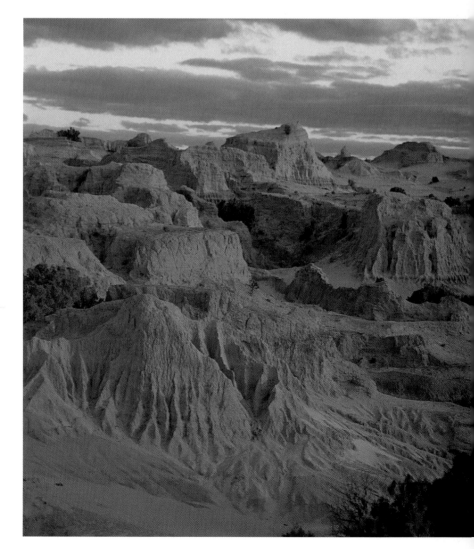

Right: *The War Memorial and a section of the gardens in the Civic Centre at Bathurst in western New South Wales.*

Below: *Nestled between Wollongong and Shell Harbour, Lake Illawarra near Windang is a peaceful retreat.*

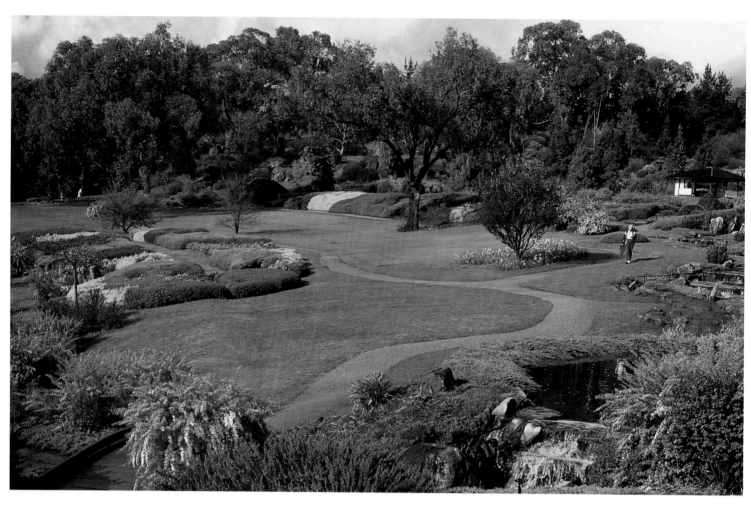

Above: *The beautifully laid out Japanese Gardens and Cultural Centre at Cowra. During World War II Japanese prisoners attempted to escape from a nearby POW camp, 234 of them dying in the struggle. Many committed suicide.*

Opposite: *Ghostly gums reach out from the water at Gumswamp Reserve, Forbes.*

Below: *Beautiful gardens in Albury, the principal city of the Murray district.*

Opposite: *Mellow autumn tones soften a country lane near Tumut, a town with distinctive seasons and ever-changing European treescapes.*

Above: *Golden daffodils form part of colourful spring flower displays in Canberra.*

Below: *Berowra Waters, a popular weekend retreat for fishermen and boating enthusiasts, is situated on an arm of the Hawkesbury River.*

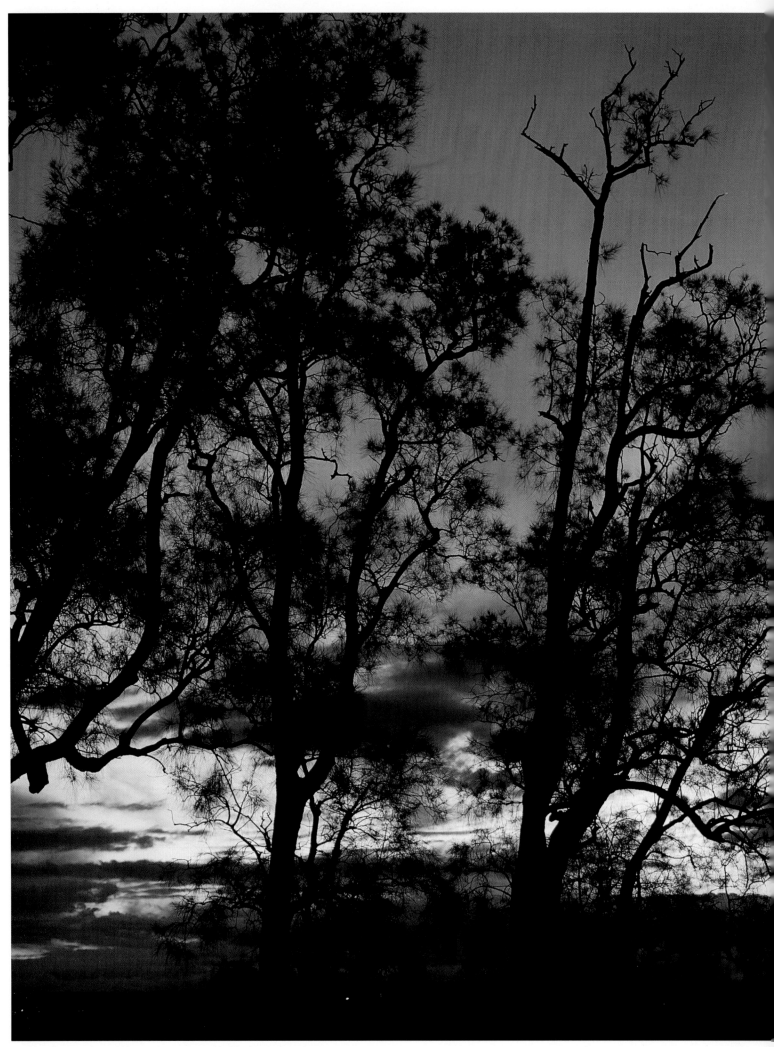

108   *A typical Australian skyline—native trees backlit by an impressive sunset.*

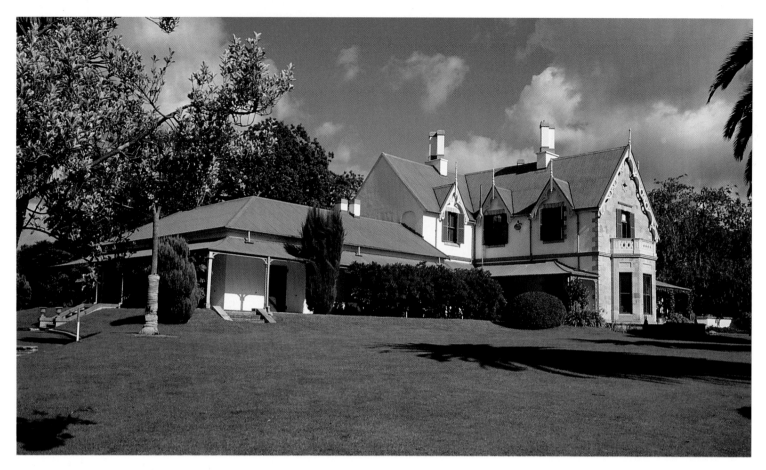

Above: *Duntroon House, the Royal Military College, Canberra, stands on the former Duntroon station, established in 1825 by banker and pastoralist, Robert Campbell.*

Below: *Goulburn courthouse is one of the many fine historic buildings in this provincial city, centre of a wealthy farming district.*

*The spectacular Ebor Falls, at Ebor near the New England National Park.*

Right: *Sydney's ever-changing harbour scenery, seen here from Elizabeth Bay in the eastern suburbs.*

Below: *The sun sets over Wallis Lake, a popular holiday area of the Great Lakes District, north of Sydney.*

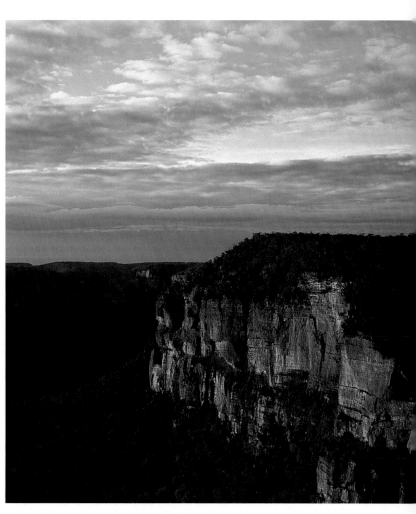

Above: *Heavily laden golden boughs of the spring flowering Cootamundra wattle* (Acacia baileyana).

Right: *Sunrise over Govetts Leap in the Blue Mountains.*

Left: *Wheat growing is one of the major agricultural activities in New South Wales.*

Below, left: *Rural tranquillity in the rich dairylands of the Bellinger Valley.*

Below: *The Zig Zag Steam Railway near Lithgow was regarded as an engineering masterpiece when first built in 1868.*

Bottom: *Tebbutt's Observatory, Windsor, was built in 1863 for the distinguished astronomer John Tebbutt who discovered the comet that bears his name.*

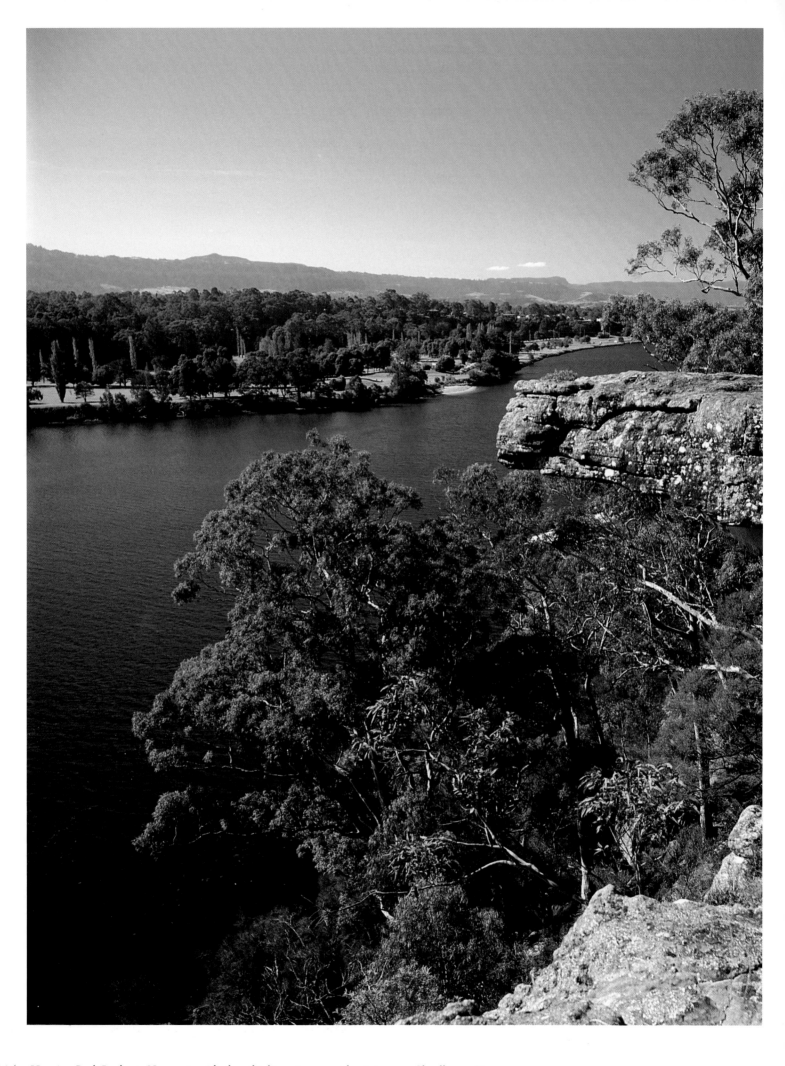

114   *Hanging Rock Lookout, Nowra, provides breathtaking views over the picturesque Shoalhaven River.*

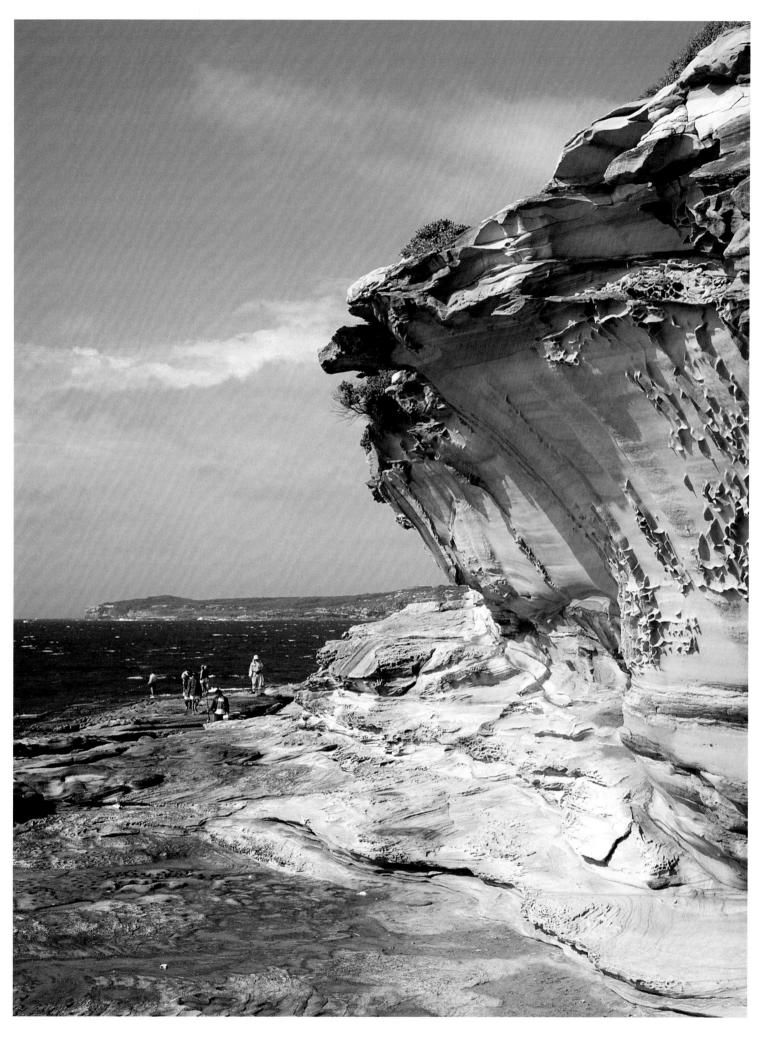

*Sandstone cliffs at La Perouse on Botany Bay. This area was named after the French navigator, Comte de la Perouse, who arrived six days after Governor Phillip and the First Fleet.*

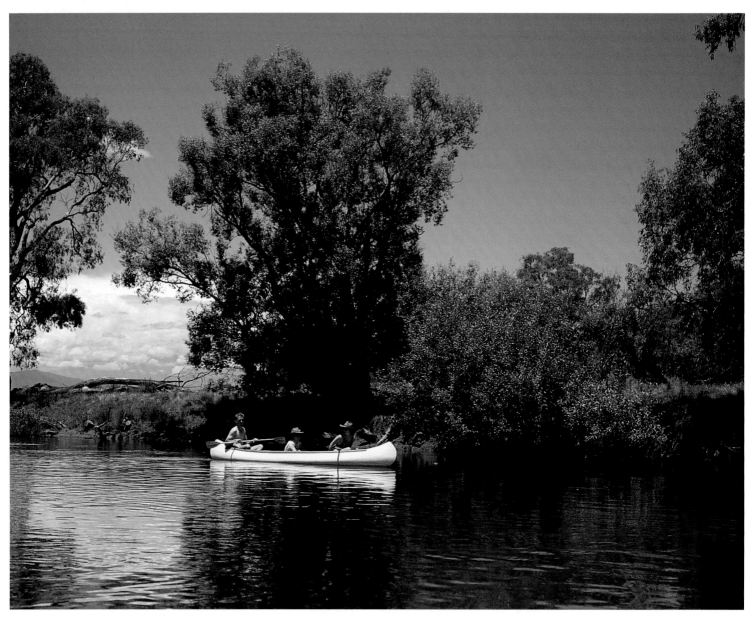

Above: *Canoeing on the Murray River, which has its source in the heart of the Snowy Mountains.*

Below: *Terrace houses in the inner-Sydney suburb of Paddington.*

Opposite: *A mineshaft is silhouetted at Broken Hill in the heart of the rich silver, lead and zinc mining country of the Barrier Range in far western New South Wales.*

Below: *Dinkum outback dunny—seen here at Lachlan Vintage Village, a re-creation of the goldrush town.*

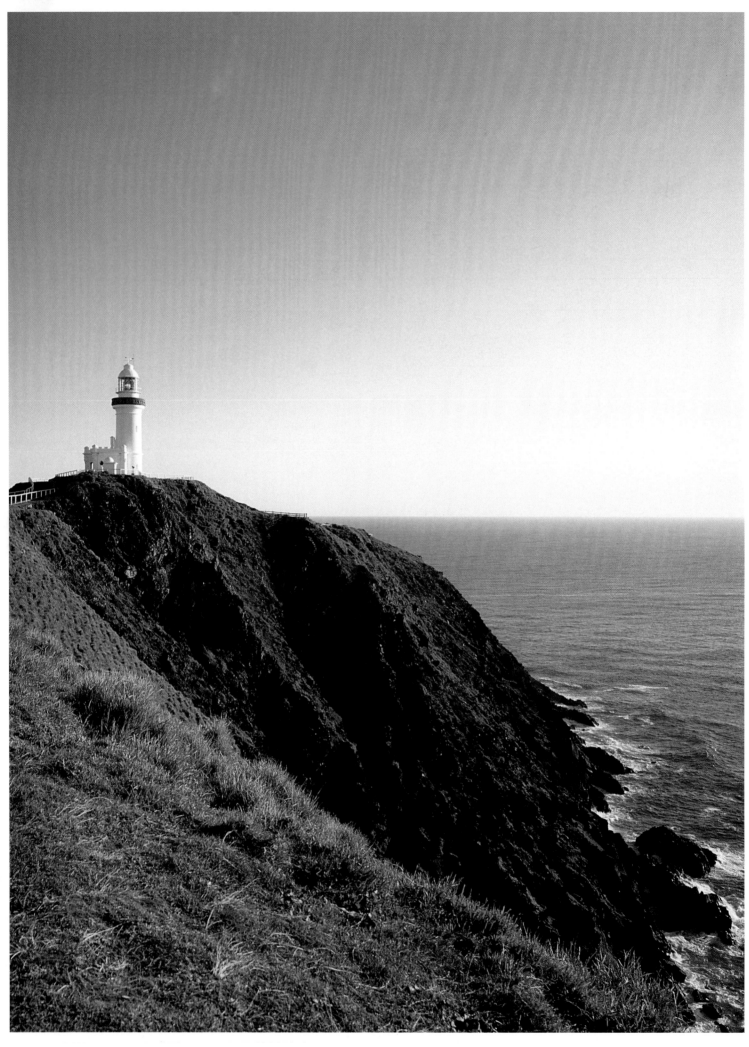

*Australia's most powerful lighthouse is situated on the continent's most easterly point at Cape Byron.*

# ANNUAL EVENTS—NEW SOUTH WALES AND AUSTRALIAN CAPITAL TERRITORY

The following list is a general guide only. Precise information may be obtained from Tourism NSW.

JANUARY–MARCH
**Albury** Tractor Pull and Mud Bash; Woolcraft and Sheep Show
**Armidale** Autumn Festival
**Batemans Bay** Festival of Yachting; Open Game Fishing Tournament
**Bourke** National Wool Bale Rolling Championships; National Yarn Spinning Championships
**Bowral** Horse Show
**Broken Hill** Big Australia Day BBQ
**Brunswick Heads** Festival of Fish and Chips
**Carcoar** Australia Day Handicraft Fair
**Forster** Surf Carnival
**Goulburn** Day
**Jindabyne** Mountain Muster; Strzlecki Festival
**Kiama** Jazz Festival
**Mittagong** Autumn Country Fair; Easter Festival
**Nelson Bay** Game Fishing Championships
**Newcastle** Harbour Regatta
**Orange** Banjo Paterson Festival
**Parramatta** Heritage Week
**Sydney** Australia Day at the Opera House; Carnivale; Dragon Boat Races; Eastern Creek Motor Cycle Grand Prix; Festival of Sydney (whole of January); Great Ferry Race; Greek Festival; Opera in the Park
**Tamworth** Rodeo and Country Music Festival
**Thirlmere** Festival of Steam
**Thredbo** Alpine Flower Week
**Ulladulla** International Fishing Competition
**Wagga Wagga** Antique Fair
**Wauchope** Lasiandra Festival
**Wollongong** Blessing of the Fleet

APRIL–JUNE
**Batemans Bay** Sailing Regatta
**Bathurst** James Hardie 12-hour
**Bermagui** Big Game Fishing Competion
**Berry** Spinners and Weavers Exhibition
**Bowral** Southern Highlands Arts Festival
**Bundanoon** Art Show; Highland Gathering
**Burrawang** Bunyip Fun Run and Folk Music Festival; Village Market
**Central Tilba** Festival
**Coonabarabran** Fair; Warrumbungle Show
**Crookwell** Autumn Festival; Polo Cross Carnival
**Deniliquin** Jazz Festival
**Dubbo** Orana Easter Country Music Festival
**Forster** Jumping Jazz Festival
**Gooloogong** Ben Hall Easter Harvest Drive
**Grenfell** Henry Lawson Festival of the Arts and Pinnacle Guinea Pig Races
**Griffith** Food and Wine Festival
**Kendall** Henry Kendall Festival
**Lemon Tree Passage** Market Day and Fireworks Spectacular
**Lightning Ridge** Great Goat Race
**Maitland** Equestrian Centre 3-Day Event; Hunter Valley Steamfest

**Merimbula** Jazz Festival
**Port Macquarie** Easter Regatta
**Sydney** Darling Harbour Jazz Festival; Film Festival; Manly Food and Wine Festival; Royal Easter Show
**Ulladulla** Blessing of the Fleet
**Wagga Wagga** Veterans Vintage Car Rally
**Wollongong** Antique Fair; Easter Jazz Festival

JULY–SEPTEMBER
**Ballina** Boat & Leisure Expo; Kingsford Smith Festival
**Batemans Bay** Carnival and Field Day
**Bellingen** Jazz Festival
**Bowral** Tulip Time Festival
**Broken Hill** Outback Tent Pegging Competition; Silver City Show
**Camden** Camden Park Open Weekend
**Coffs Harbour** Australian German Beer Festival
**Gunnedah** Dorothea Mackellar Day; Gallop
**Lightning Ridge** Opal Festival
**Maclean** Cane Harvest Festival
**Mildura** Country Music Week; Mallee Balloon Rally
**Moree** Arts Festival
**Newcastle** Jazz Festival
**Perisher Valley** Festival Ski Week
**Port Maquarie** Festival of Theatre
**Singleton** Hunter Valley Wine Show
**Stroud** International Brick and Rolling Pin Throwing Competition
**Sydney** Aboriginal Week; City of Sydney Eisteddfod; City to Surf Fun Run; Festival of the Winds, Bondi Beach; Rugby League Grand Final; Spring Racing Carnival, Randwick
**Thredbo** Carnival Week; Top to Bottom Downhill
**Warners Bay** Oktoberfest, Lake Macquarie

OCTOBER–DECEMBER
**Adaminaby** Snowy Mountains Trout Festival
**Bathurst** Eisteddfod; Tooheys 1000
**Berry** Gardens Festival
**Bingara** Rodeo
**Bowraville** Back to Bowra
**Branxton** Wine Expo
**Bulahdelah** King of the Mountain Endurance Run
**Camden** Rose Festival
**Coffs Harbour** City Festival
**Coonabarabran** Siding Spring Observatory Open Day
**Cowra** Sakura Matsuri Cherry Blossom Celebration
**Forster** Oyster Festival Long Weekend
**Glenbrook** Village Festival
**Gosford** Festival of the Arts
**Goulburn** Spring Show
**Grafton** Jacaranda Festival
**Griffith** Festival of Gardens; Orchid Show
**Inverell** Sapphire City Festival
**Jindabyne** Rodeo
**Kempsey** Country Truck Show
**Kiama** Seaside Festival
**Lake Conjola** Great Lake Conjola Raft Race
**Leura** Footsteps Festival; Gardens Spring Festival; Village Fair
**Lismore** North Coast National Show

**Maitland** Garden Ramble; Show and Rodeo
**Manilla** Festival of Spring Flowers
**Merimbula** Country Music by the Sea; Spring Festival
**Mittagong** Jazz in the Highlands
**Moree** Carnival of the Golden Grain
**Narrandera** Country Music Festival
**Newcastle** King Street Fair; Mattara Festival
**Nowra** Shoalhaven Rodeo; Spring Festival
**Orange** Bloom 'n' Blossom
**Parkes** Country Music Spectacular
**Penrith** Jazz Festival
**Pokolbin** Festival of Jazz
**Richmond** Macquarie Towns Festival
**Singleton** Northern Agricultural show
**Speers Point** Children's Festival Day
**Sydney** Carolfest; Glebe Street Fair; International Food and Wine Festival; Iron Man Competition, Bondi; Iron Man Competition, Freshwater; Kings Cross Carnival; Manly to Darling Harbour Surfboat Marathon; Music for Spring; Sydney-Hobart Yacht Race
**Tenterfield** Federation Festival; Granite Belt Spring Wine Festival
**The Entrance** Mardi Gras Festival
**Tooraweenah** Agricultural Show
**Tumut** Spring Fair; Rodeo
**Windsor** Bridge to Bridge Water Ski Classic
**Wollongong** Highland Games, Berkley; Iron Man Competition
**Yass** Berinba Art Festival; Fishing Carnival; Rodeo

## AUSTRALIAN CAPITAL TERRITORY

JANUARY–MARCH
Black Opal Stakes
Canberra Day Celebrations
Canberra Festival
Lisensed Clubs Association World Buskers Festival
Royal Canberra Show
Sri Chinmoy Triathlon
St Valentine's Day Jazz Festival
World Cup Showjumping

APRIL–JUNE
Australian Science Festival
Autumnfest
Embassy Open Day
International Balloon Festival
National Folk Festival

JULY–SEPTEMBER
Floriade Spring Festival

OCTOBER–DECEMBER
Canberra Cup
Floriade Spring Festival
International Car Rally
Oktoberfest
Scottish Week
Street Machine 'Summernats'
National Wine Week

# Victoria:
## THE HERITAGE

Victoria enjoys a unique position in Australian history. Until 1851 it was part of New South Wales then, in a period of forty years, it rapidly became the premier state due to the vast wealth which was being generated by its goldfields. This wealth turned Melbourne into the financial and administrative centre of Australia, a position which the city enjoyed at the time of federation and which it managed to retain until the 1960s and 1970s when the head offices of many federal government departments and most of the country's largest companies were still based in the city.

Like most Australian colonies the original reason for the British occupation of Victoria was the fear of possible French settlement. By the end of the eighteenth century the coast had been explored extensively by both British and French adventurers. Reacting to a perceived French threat Lieutenant David Collins, accompanied by a party comprising both convicts and free settlers, landed on the shores of Port Phillip (near the modern-day site of Sorrento) in October 1803 and a short-lived colony was established. By May 1804 Collins had gained permission to move the colony to Van Diemen's Land and his brief attempt at settlement had been abandoned.

Through the 1810s and 1820s Port Phillip was regularly visited by whalers and sealers who worked the coast from Van Diemen's Land to South Australia.

The real impetus for permanent settlement came as a result of the land-based explorers who, having explored south from Sydney, had crossed the Murrumbidgee River and pushed on towards the southern coast. Hume and Hovell reached Port Phillip in 1824. They mistook it for Western Port and two years later, acting on their incorrect advice, a military and convict outpost was established on Western Port. It lasted thirteen months.

Around this time the entrepreneurial John Batman, who was living in Van Diemen's Land, tried to gain approval from the Governor of New South Wales to settle the area around Western Port. He had been encouraged by reports that the land was fertile and the pastures rich. The Governor, fearing problems if a second colony was created, denied Batman permission. This proved to be a hollow gesture. Eight years later, in November 1834, Edward Henty ignored the rulings of the New South Wales Governor and settled at Portland Bay. In early 1835, spurred on by Henty's example, Batman crossed Bass Strait and in June 1835 infamously 'purchased' the land on the western shore of Port Phillip from the local Aborigines.

At this time Batman explored the shores of Port Phillip and chose a site for a village. Within a year the township of Melbourne began to grow on the banks of the Yarra River.

The subsequent exploration of Victoria occurred rapidly. The New South Wales Surveyor-General, Major T. L. Mitchell, traversed Victoria in 1836 establishing routes to the Upper Murray and pushing through to Portland Bay. The settlement which followed was rapid. By 1845 squatters, following the lead of Edward Henty, had occupied nearly all of the Western District, settled along the Murray River and, led by Angus McMillan, moved down into the Gippsland area. Effectively the state, although it was still part of New South Wales, had been settled in 1850.

In 1837 the township of Melbourne was surveyed and named and a magistrate, Captain William Lonsdale, was sent from Sydney to maintain law and order. The attempts to stop settlement had clearly failed and the administration of New South Wales was forced to deal with Victoria as a successful, and semi-autonomous, colony. This was converted into a reality in September 1839 when Charles La Trobe, the newly appointed Superintendant of the Port Phillip District, arrived from England. In his wake the colony established a separate police force, a customs office and, perhaps most importantly, a separate Lands Office.

By 1 July 1851, when the colony of Victoria was officially proclaimed, there were already more than 80 000 people living south of the Murray–Murrumbidgee and over six million sheep were being grazed on well-established properties.

In theory, Victoria would have remained a rural economy (although in 1851 it was true that more than 20 000 of the state's 80 000 people were living in Melbourne) but the discovery of gold changed everything.

The gold discoveries in New South Wales had attracted labourers north to the goldfields around Bathurst. This trend was short lived. By November 1851 alluvial gold had been discovered at Clunes, Anderson's Creek, Buninyong, Ballarat, Mount Alexander and Bendigo, which at the time was known as Sandhurst. Gold fever had struck the state. The streets of Melbourne were virtually deserted and, by early 1852, ships from all over the world were disgorging eager miners on the wharves of Melbourne.

By 1854 the colony's population had grown from 80 000 to 300 000, the value of imported goods had reached an extraordinary £18 million, and everything needed for mining, from food to houses and equipment, was being shipped into the colony. In 1856 more than 86 million grams of gold were mined. This would form the basis for unprecedented development which would establish Melbourne as Australia's major financial centre and Victoria as an extremely wealthy colony.

A total of more than £100 million worth of gold was won from the earth in the 1850s. This was not

*The Exhibition Buildings, Melbourne.*

without its problems. The early supplies of alluvial gold disappeared and companies were quickly formed to extract the ore. The government, eager to cash in on the goldfields, established an expensive licence fee which had to be paid by every miner regardless of their success. The licence fee became a major source of discontent with local administrations seeming to use it to harass miners. The situation boiled over into the closest thing Australia has ever had to civil war. On 3 December 1854 a group of miners, led by Peter Lalor, fought a brief and bloody battle with government forces at the Eureka Stockade on the Ballarat goldfields. Thirty men were killed and a large number of agitators were subsequently arrested. When they were brought before the courts in Melbourne juries refused to convict them. This was symbolic of the complex, radical forces which were working in the colony at the time.

Victoria's development was dramatically different from other colonies in the sense that its independence coincided with huge wealth, huge influxes of migrants and rapid changes in the nature of the society.

In 1855 a Legislative Council and Legislative Assembly were created to administer the colony. The problem was that membership and voting rights were tied to ownership of substantial tracts of land. Thus, the first parliament was made up almost entirely of lawyers, successful businessmen, affluent squatters and merchants. They may have represented the 80 000 people who lived in the state in 1851 but they hardly represented the 300 000 in 1855.

The Legislative Assembly politicians were sufficiently aware of the changing face of Victorian society that, with admirable pragmatism, they introduced a series of reforms. In 1856 Victoria saw the introduction of the secret ballot (possibly the first in the world), the following year universal male suffrage was introduced and in 1870 the parliament agreed that parliamentary members should be paid.

Unfortunately the members of the colony's Legislative Council were less flexible. In spite of the changes in the lower house this upper house remained a bastion of conservatism and exclusivity with membership restricted to males with more than £5000 in property. They were elected to ten-year terms. They remained an anachronism unable to meet the changing circumstances of the colony.

Similar tensions began to emerge on the goldfields as different cultures confronted each other. The Chinese were the brunt of racist attacks. By 1855 there were 17 000 Chinese in Victoria and most of them were working on the goldfields. The diggers, looking for someone to blame as the easy wealth of the fields dried up, turned their anger on the Chinese. The Victorian parliament introduced a series of particularly offensive pieces of racist legislation which would eventually form the basis for the White Australia Policy.

As the diggings declined the government had to deal with the problem of unemployed miners. The government offered a range of incentives to try to encourage miners to turn to farming. While it was fraught with problems the arrangement was basically successful. By the 1890s large areas of Victoria had been cleared and wool and wheat dominated the rural economy.

Inevitably, the wealth generated by gold could not be sustained. The state experienced a major economic downturn in the last two decades of the nineteenth century. It recovered in the early years of the twentieth century when the combination of successful exporting of dairy products, expanding open-cut coal mining in Gippsland, and significant

growth in the state's manufacturing sector ensured economic stability.

This economic recovery established a stable base. After World War I, when imports were in short supply, the Victorian economy expanded rapidly to meet the demands of the local economy. Unfortunately, the success of the manufacturing sector had an unforseen effect. The Great Depression decimated the sector and by October 1931 more than 25 per cent of the state's workforce were unemployed and over 170 000 people were dependent on welfare assistance. The situation was not helped by the success of the newly emergent Country Party which was committed to the problems of rural workers and less interested in the problems the Depression had created for urban workers.

It seemed as though the tensions which had emerged after the goldrushes—the tensions between radicalism and conservatism, the tensions between established rural landowners and 'get-rich-quick' entrepreneurs, the tensions between primary producers and manufacturers—were to be enduring characteristics of Victoria's personality and character.

The vitality and dynamism of the state continued after World War II with rapid rural growth being accompanied by successful and sustained industrial and manufacturing success. By 1992 the state's population was 4 458 895. Victoria had attracted large numbers of non-English speaking settlers (particularly from Italy and Greece) and they had impacted significantly on the character of the state. Lygon Street in Melbourne, famed for its international cuisine, is a symbol of the cultural diversity of the city.

In recent times Victoria has experienced severe economic problems. The recession of the late 1980s, combined with a series of spectacular collapses of industries and financial institutions, ensured that the state's Labor government which had come to power in 1982 after twenty-seven years of Liberal rule, was swept from office.

The new Liberal Party, under Jeff Kennett, instituted a strict economic regime to rein in state expenditure. After initial resistance the state accepted the 'harsh medicine' with the result that, while still experiencing considerable economic problems, the future promised a return to confidence and stability.

# WHERE TO GO AND WHAT TO SEE

## Melbourne and Environs

Albert Park Lake,
   Albert Road,
   Melbourne

Block Arcade,
   Elizabeth–Collins Street,
   Melbourne
Botanic Gardens
   Birdwood Avenue,
   South Yarra
Bourke Street Mall,
   Melbourne

Captain Cook's Cottage,
   Fitzroy Gardens,
   Wellington Parade,
   Melbourne
Carlton—Lygon Street Italian
   restaurants, bistros and cafés

Chinatown,
   Bourke Street,
   Melbourne
City Circle Tram
City Square,
   Collins Street,
   Melbourne
Como Gaslight Gardens, cnr Toorak
   Road and Chapel Street—food
   court, restaurants, fashion and
   lifestyle shops
Como—historic house,
   Como Avenue,
   South Yarra

Exhibition Building and Gardens,
   Nicholson Street,
   Carlton

Fitzroy Gardens,
   Wellington Parade,
   Melbourne
Fitzroy—Brunswick Street ethnic
   restaurants and shops

Flemington Racecourse
Fort Gellibrand,
   Williamstown

Government House,
   St Kilda Road,
   Melbourne

Jam Factory shopping and
   entertainment centre, South Yarra

La Trobe Library,
   La Trobe Street,
   Melbourne
La Trobe's Cottage,
   Birdwood Avenue,
   Melbourne
Luna Park, St Kilda

Maritime Museum,
   Williamstown
Melbourne Concert Hall,
   Southgate
Melbourne Cricket Ground

Melbourne University,
  Grattan Street,
  Parkville

Melbourne Zoo,
  Elliott Avenue,
  Parkville
Model Tudor Village,
  Fitzroy Gardens,
  Wellington Parade,
  Melbourne
Mornington Peninsula
Myer Music Bowl,
  Kings Domain,
  Melbourne

National Gallery of Victoria,
  St Kilda Road,
  Melbourne
National Museum,
  285 Russell Street,
  Melbourne City

Old Melbourne Gaol,
  Lygon Street,
  Melbourne
Olympic Park,
  Melbourne

Parliament House,
  Spring Street,
  Melbourne
Performing Arts Museum,
  Southgate
*Polly Woodside* Maritime Museum
Prahran Market,
  Prahran

Queen Victoria Market,
  Victoria and Elizabeth Streets,
  Melbourne

Railway Museum,
  Spotswood
Rialto Towers Observation Deck,
  476 Flinders Lane,
  Melbourne City

Richmond—Greek and Vietnamese
  restaurants, shopping
Rippon Lea—historic house,
  192 Hotham Street,
  Elsternwick
Scienceworks, Museum,
  Williamstown
Shrine of Remembrance,
  Domain,
  St Kilda Road,
  Melbourne
South Yarra—elegant restaurants and
  shopping
Southgate,
  St Kilda Road,
  Melbourne
St James' Old Cathedral,
  King and Batman Streets,
  West Melbourne
St Kilda
St Kilda Botanic Gardens,
  Blessington Street,
  St Kilda
St Kilda Esplanade (Sunday market)
St Patrick's Cathedral,
  Albert Street,
  East Melbourne
St Paul's Cathedral,
  Flinders Lane,
  Melbourne
State Library,
  328 Swanston Street,
  Melbourne

Toorak Village, Toorak
Treasury Gardens

University of Melbourne,
  Grattan Street,
  Parkville

Victorian Arts Centre,
  100 St Kilda Road
  Melbourne

World Trade Centre,
  Flinders Street,
  Melbourne

# Beyond Melbourne

Air World—aircraft museum,
  Wangaratta
Apollo Bay—fishing village,
  Great Ocean Road
Arthurs Seat

Balconies
  Grampians National Park
Ballarat Art Gallery, Ballarat
Baw Baw National Park
Bells Beach, near Torquay, Surf
  Coast—surfing
Bellarine Peninsula
Bonnie Doon,
  Lake Eildon

Cape Shanck Coastal Park
Castlemaine
Coal Creek Historical Park
Croajingalong National Park

Dandenong Ranges
Daylesford Botanic Gardens

Eureka Stockade Memorial and
  Exhibition,
  Ballarat

Falls Creek Ski Village
Fern Tree Gully National Park
Flagstaff Hill Maritime Village,
  Warrnambool
Fraser National Park

Geelong Art Gallery,
  Little Mallop Street,
  Geelong
Geelong Botanic Gardens
Gippsland Lakes National Park
Goldfields—Ballarat, Bendigo and
  Stawell
Gold Museum,
  Ballarat
Goulburn Valley
Grampians National Park

Great Ocean Road—picturesque
   coastal drive

Hanging Rock, Mount Macedon
Hattah Lakes National Park
Healesville Wildlife Sanctuary
Hepburn Springs, spa resort town

Island Arch,
   Great Ocean Road

Jaws of Death,
   Grampians National Park

Kingslake National Park

Lake Eildon
Lakes Entrance
Lake Wendouree
Lind National Park
Little Desert National Park
Loch Ard Gorge, Great Ocean Road
Lorne—holiday resort,
   Great Ocean Road

Maldon—authentically preserved
   nineteenth-century buildings
Mount Buffalo National Park

Mount Buller
Mount Eccles National Park
Mount Hotham
Mount Macedon
Mount Richmond National Park
Murray River Cruises
Murray River towns—Mildura, Swan
   Hill, Echuca, Yarrawonga and
   Albury-Wodonga

National Wool Museum, Geelong
Ninety Mile Beach

Oasis Country—Swan Hill, Mildura
   and Horsham

Phillip Island—fairy penguins
Port Campbell National Park
Puffing Billy,
   Dandenongs

Queenscliff–Sorrento Ferry,
   Port Phillip Bay

Seal Rocks—seal colony,
   Phillip Island
Sovereign Hill, Ballarat—re-creation
   of early gold-mining town

Surfworld, national surfing museum,
   Surf Coast Plaza,
   Torquay
Swan Hill Pioneer Settlement, Swan
   Hill

Talking Tram Tour
   Bendigo
Timber Tramway,
   Fraser National Park
Twelve Apostles, Great Ocean Road

Werribee Park, K Road, Werribee
Wilsons Promontary National Park
Wineries and vineyards—Geelong-
   Yarra Valley, Goulburn Valley,
   Great Western, Mildura-Robinvale,
   Rutherglen
Wonderland Range,
   The Grampians
Wyperfeld National Park

Yallourn Power Station, Yallourn

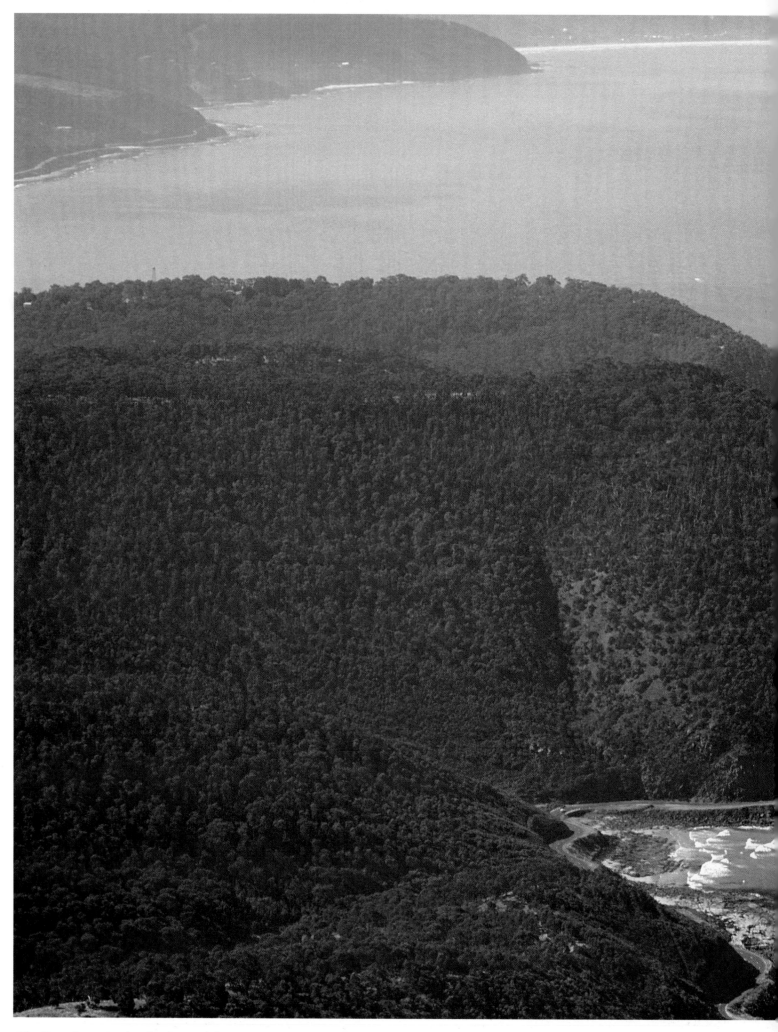

*The Great Ocean Road snakes for 300 kilometres along the scenic south-west coast of Victoria. Carved into the cliffside to honour the servicemen of World War I, it is one of the world's greatest coastal roads.*

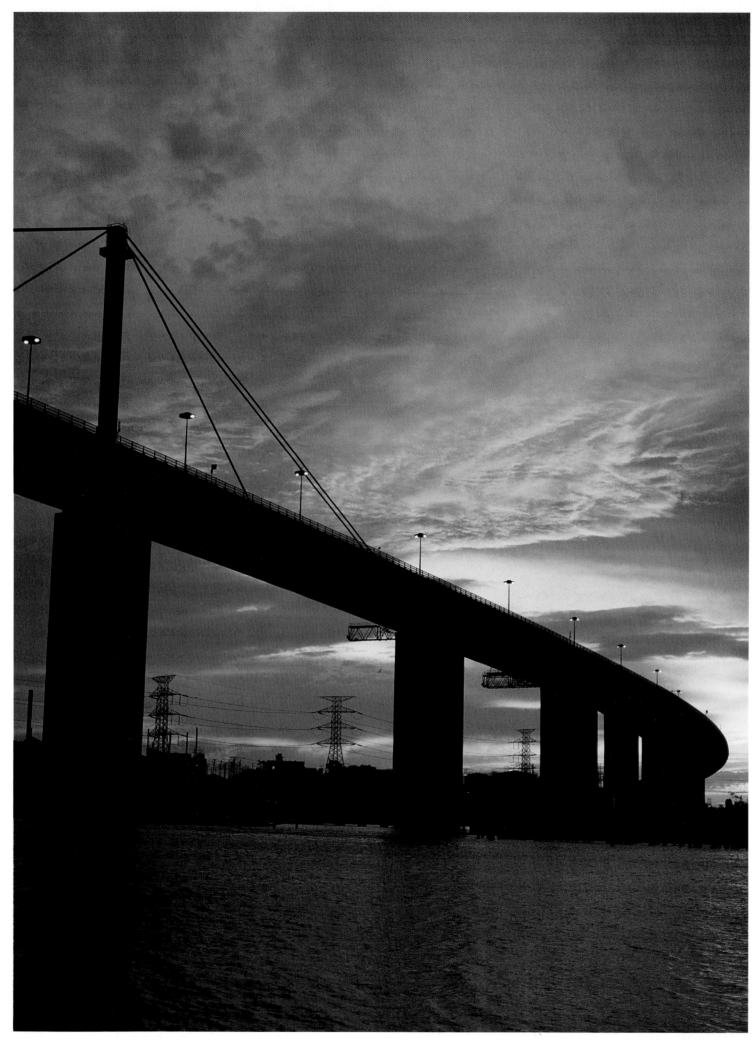

128    *Westgate Bridge spans the Yarra River, Melbourne.*

Above: *Enjoy international food, a scenic tour and the ambience of a historic wooden tram on Melbourne's Colonial Tramcar Restaurant.*

Above: *The two massive black Rialto towers loom over the historic Rialto Hotel, reflecting Melbourne's old wealth and modern-day prosperity.*

Below: *Melbourne's Exhibition Building—originally built for the Great Exhibition in 1880, this grandiose domed hall is still used for trade fair.*

Below: *The pyramid-style Shrine of Remembrance dominates Kings Domain, Melbourne.*

130 *The* Polly Woodside, *a restored square-rigged commercial sailing ship built in 1885, is now a maritime museum in Melbourne.*

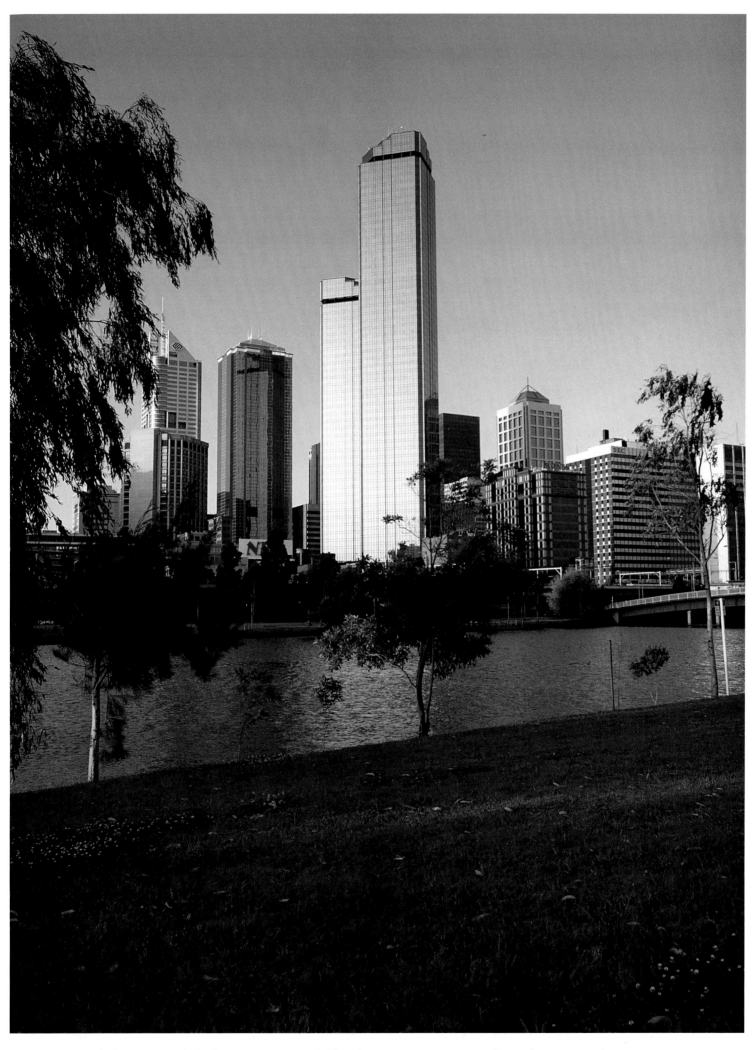

*Melbourne, capital of Victoria, overlooks the Yarra River. Founded by John Batman in 1835, it is today an elegant cosmopolitan city.*

Above: *On the hop—kangaroos in western Victoria.*

Below: *The wharf at the river city of Echuca, once Australia's largest inland port.*

Below: *Sovereign Hill, a reconstruction of a goldmining settlement, is a major tourist attraction just outside the centre of Ballarat.*

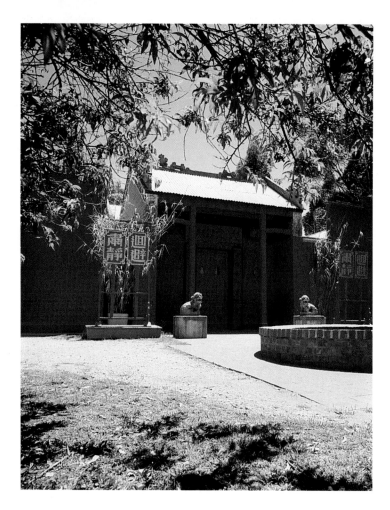

Above: *The Chinese Joss House, Bendigo, was built by the many Chinese miners who worked the gold diggings here.*

Below: *Paddlesteamers depart from Mildura wharf on trips up and down the Murray and Darling rivers.*

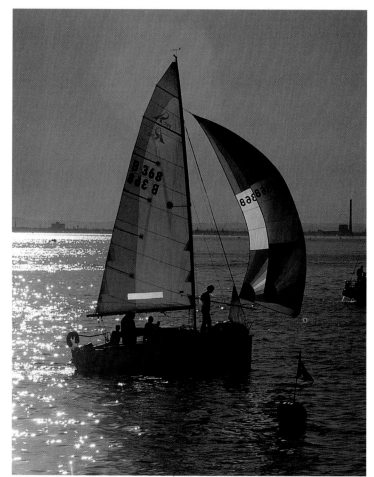

Above: *Sailing at Brighton on Port Phillip Bay.*

Opposite: *Skiers on the slopes of Mt Buller in the Victorian Alps.*

Below: *Open to the public—'Hymettus', a prize-winning cottage garden in Ballarat.*

Left: *The Organ Pipes—a series of hexagonal basalt columns that rise more than 20 metres above Jacksons Creek at Organ Pipes National Park. They were formed when lava cooled in an ancient river bed.*

Opposite: *Autumn colours in the 40-hectare Botanic Gardens at Ballarat.*

Below: *Fishing boats at the popular holiday town of Lakes Entrance at the eastern end of the Gippsland Lakes. Victoria's commercial fishing industry is dominated by scallop and abalone.*

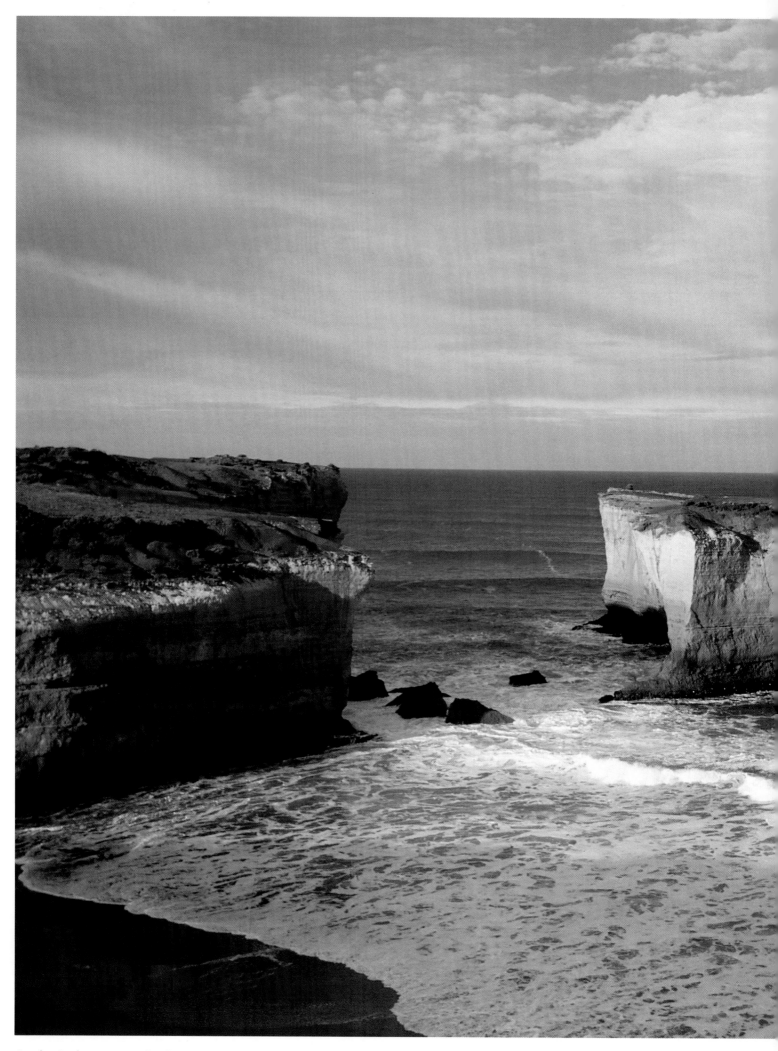

138   *London Bridge, an unusual rock structure sculpted out of soft limestone cliffs by the pounding sea at Port Campbell.*

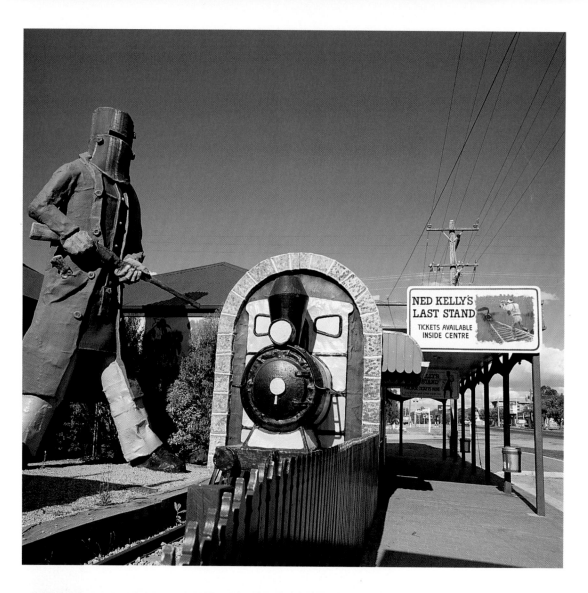

Left: *Famous bushranger Ned
Kelly's last stand at Glenrowan.
Ned was captured here after a
bloody gunfight and was
subsequently condemned and
hanged in Melbourne.*

Below: *Erskine Falls in the scenic
Otway Ranges behind the coastal
resort of Lorne.*

Right: *Wildflowers bloom near the Cathedral in Mt Buffalo National Park. More than 400 species of plants and flowers are found on this high granite plateau.*

Below: *Trout fishing in the Ovens River.*

Above: *Picking peaches near Swan Hill for the fresh fruit market.*

Opposite: *Victoria's most imposing national park, the Grampians, is a series of high weathered ridges forming the westernmost heights of the Great Dividing Range.*

Right: *Petrified forest at Cape Bridgewater near Portland.*

Above: *Crayfish catch at the holiday resort town Port Fairy, home to a large fishing fleet and once one of the biggest ports in Australia.*

Below: *Chateau Tahbilk, built in 1860, is one of the most picturesque wineries in the Goulburn River Valley.*

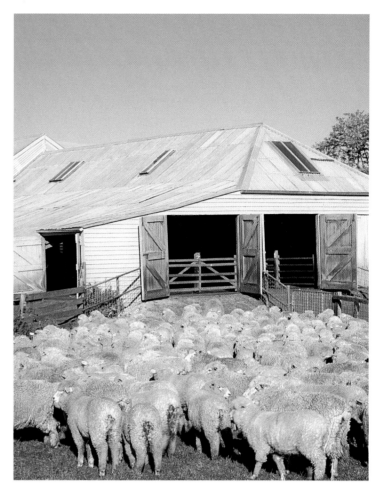

Above: *Ready for shearing at a property in the Western District, an area which supports one-third of Victoria's best sheep and cattle.*

Below: *Relaxation for an oldtimer at the Swan Hill Pioneer Settlement, a reconstruction of the days when paddlesteamers were the Murray Valley's main form of transport.*

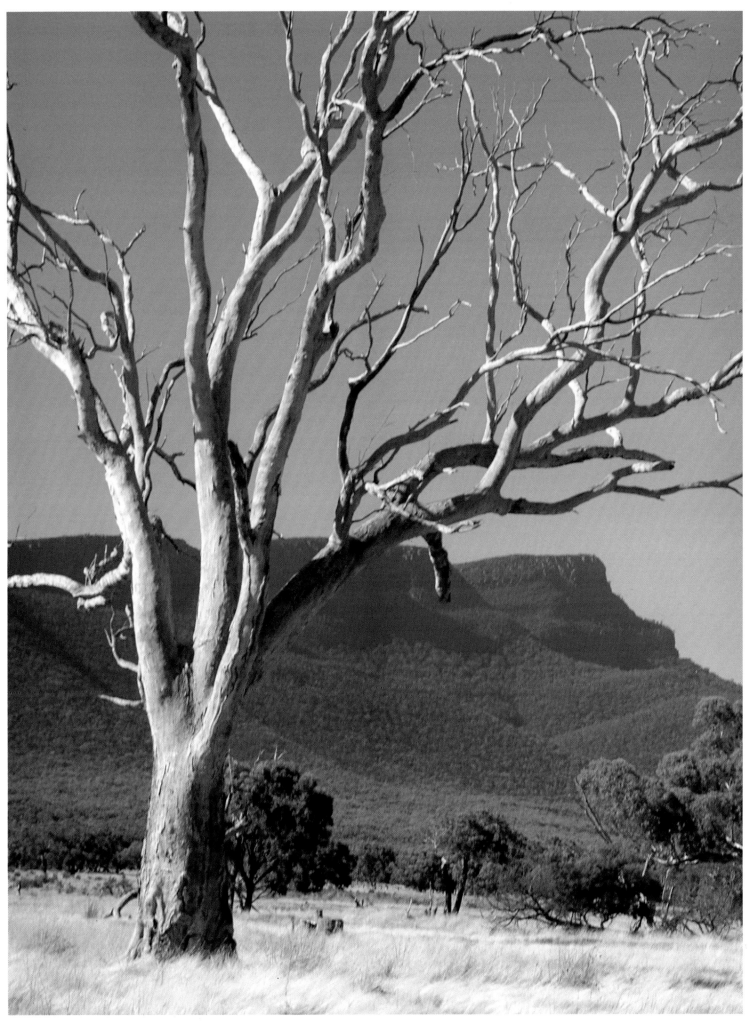

*Mount William, the highest peak in the Grampians, was climbed by Major Mitchell in 1836. He named the ranges after the Grampians in his native Scotland.*

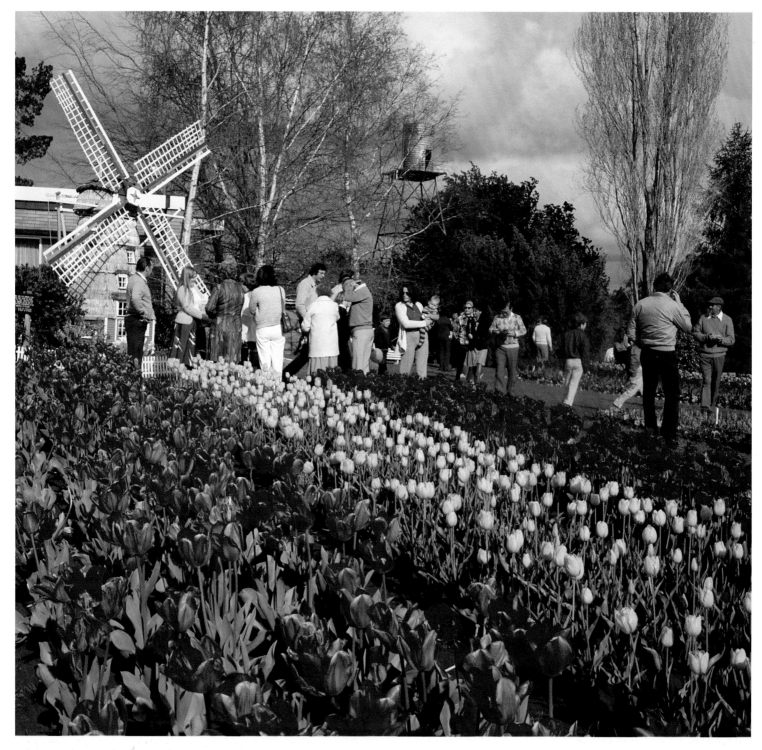

Above: *Glowing tulip beds at commercial gardens in the Dandenongs'
town of Silvan.*

Opposite: *Surf fishing on the beautiful Ninety Mile Beach which
separates the lakes from the ocean in the Gippsland region.*

Above: *Tidal River flows into Norman Bay, a popular camping and swimming area on Wilsons Promontory.*

Opposite: *The spectacularly eroded coastline of Port Campbell, scene of many shipwrecks in the late nineteenth century.*

Below: *Eucalyptus forest surrounds the Glenelg River on its journey from the Grampians to the Southern Ocean.*

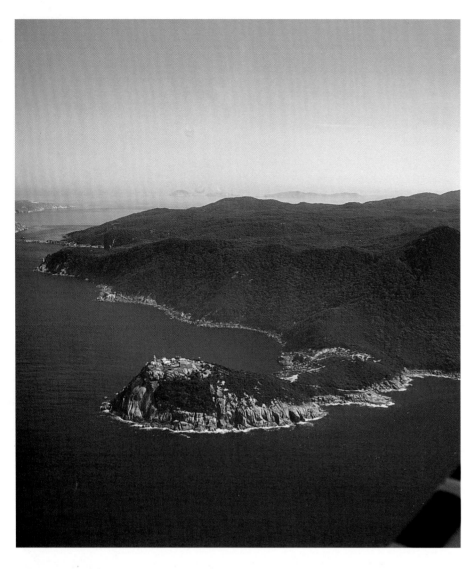

Left: *South East Point, on the tip of the rugged, densely vegetated Wilsons Promontory.*

Opposite: *Sweeping views over the Grampians range from the 'Jaws of Death'*

Below: *The many English and European trees bring spectacular autumn colours to the town of Bright in the heart of the beautiful Ovens Valley.*

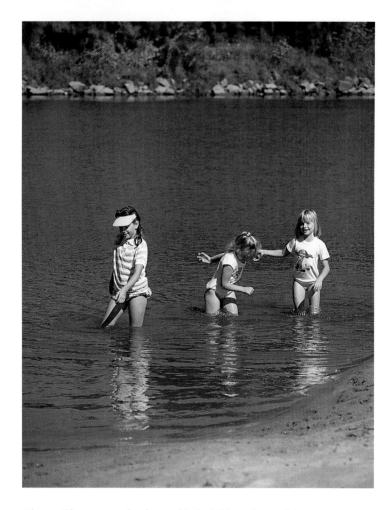

Above: *Playtime on the shores of Lake Eildon, the state's largest man-made lake and a popular resort area.*

Below: *Fog softens the man-made Lake Wendouree at Ballarat.*

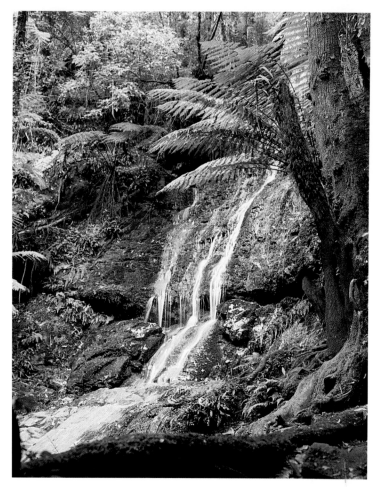

Above: *Waterfalls, ferny rainforest and walking tracks are features of Tarra Valley National Park near Morwell.*

Below: *Harvesting grain in the Wimmera region, the granary of the state, where wheatfields stretch as far as the eye can see.*

Above: *Rocky reflections at Whisky Beach, Wilsons Promontory, at the southernmost tip of the Australian mainland.*

Right: *Temperate rainforest in the charming Lilly Pilly Gully in Wilsons Promontory National Park.*

Above: *At work on a fishing net at Portland, the only deep-water port between Melbourne and Adelaide.*

Below: *Gathering seed on a flower farm at Leopold on the Bellarine Peninsula.*

Above: *Time out for shearers on a sheep station in western Victoria.*

Above: *Thompson's seedless grapes—grown for export and fresh fruit markets. Victoria's main grape-growing area is centred around Rutherglen and extends down into the Ovens and Goulburn Valleys.*

Above: *The annual vintage farm display at Nhill, a small wheat town halfway between Melbourne and Adelaide.*

Below: *Dramatic coastal scenery near Peterborough.*

156    *Bird's eye view of the fishing township of Mallacoota on the Gippsland coast.*

Above: *Charming old buildings are testament to the prosperity of the gold boom era in Ballarat.*

Opposite: *Futuristic architecture of the Daimaru complex in Melbourne.*

Above: *Bottle-lined cellars in a winery at the small town of Great Western which has given its name to many fine wines.*

Below: *A riot of colour in the Warrnambool Gardens.*

*Triathlon at the flourishing coastal resort of Warrnambool.*

# ANNUAL EVENTS—VICTORIA

The following list is a general guide only. Precise information may be obtained from Tourism Victoria.

## JANUARY–MARCH

**Abbotsford** Vietnamese Lunar Festival
**Ballarat** Begonia Festival
**Buninyong** Gold King Festival
**Camperdown** Leura Festival
**Craigieburn** Festival
**Croydon** Festival
**Eltham** Montsalvat Jazz Festival
**Geelong** Highland Gathering
**Geelong** Pako Festa
**Glenlyon** New Year's Day Sports
**Hanging Rock** Harvest Picnic
**Keilor** Australian Stock Car Championships
**Kinglake** Rasberry Fair
**Korumburra** Twilight Music Festival
**Mansfield** Festival
**Melbourne** Antipodes (Greek) Festival
**Melbourne** Australian Open Tennis Championships
**Melbourne** Food and Wine Festival
**Melbourne** Ford Australian Open
**Melbourne** International Dragon Boat Festival
**Melbourne** International Motor Show
**Melbourne** Irish Festival
**Melbourne** Moomba Festival
**Melbourne** Music Festival
**Metung** Regatta
**Port Fairy** Folk Festival
**Port Melbourne** Blessing of the Waters
**St Kilda** Festival
**South Oakleigh** Australian Masters Golf Tournament
**Springvale** Holland Festival
**Sunbury** Fair
**Tolmie** Sports Day
**Yarra Valley** Grape Grazing Festival

## APRIL–JUNE

**Beachworth** Harvest Celebration
**Bells Beach** Rip Curl Pro
**Bendigo** Easter Fair
**Bright** Autumn Festival
**Geelong** Heritage Fair
**Gladysdale** Apple Festival
**Keilor** Australian Stock Car Championship
**Maldon** Easter Fair
**Mangalore** Air Show
**Melbourne** International Comedy Festival
**Melbourne** International Film Festival
**Melbourne** Marathon
**Mornington Peninsula** Heritage Festival
**Mount Helen** Eureka Jazz Festival
**Mount Macedon** Autumn Floral Display and Gardens Open Day
**Omeo** Rodeo
**St Kilda** Film Festival
**Stawell** Gift
**Warrnambool** May Racing Carnival
**Yarram** Tarra Festival

## JULY–SEPTEMBER

**Ballarat** Royal South Street Society Eisteddfod
**Hamilton** Sheep Vention Sheep Show
**Kyneton** Daffodil and Arts Festival
**Melbourne** AFL Finals Series
**Melbourne** Chinatown Autumn Moon Lantern Festival
**Melbourne** Exhibition of Victorian Winemakers
**Melbourne** Royal Melbourne Show
**Melbourne** Sheep and Woolcraft Show
**Mildura** Country Music Week
**Red Hill** Spring Flower Festival
**Rutherglen** Wine Show
**Silvan** Tesselaar's Tulip Festival

## OCTOBER–DECEMBER

**Avoca** Wool and Wine Festival
**Belarine Peninsula** Wellington Strawberry Fair
**Carlton** Lygon Street Festa Weekend
**Daylesford** and District Agricultural Show
**Daylesford** Highland Gathering
**Daylesford** New Year's Eve Gala
**Dimboola** Agricultural Show
**Dimboola** Rowing Regatta
**Echuca** Rich River Festival
**Elmore** Field Days
**Kialla West** Strawberry Fest
**Maldon** Folk Festival
**Mansfield** Mountain Country Festival
**Melbourne** Carols by Candlelight
**Melbourne** Caulfield Cup
**Melbourne** Cup
**Melbourne** International Festival of the Arts
**Melbourne** Spring Racing Carnival
**Melton** Djerriwarrh Festival
**Mildura** Sunraysia Jazz and Wine Festival
**Mornington** Tea Tree Festival
**Mornington Peninsula** Carnival of Wines
**Myrtleford** Golden Spurs Rodeo
**Nariel Creek** Folk Festival
**Port Fairy** Moyneyana Festival
**Wangaratta** Festival of Jazz
**Warrnambool** Agricultural Show
**Yarrawonga** ICI-Red Cross Murray Marathon

# *Tasmania:*
## THE HERITAGE

Tasmania's history is one of hardship and struggle on a tiny, isolated island at the end of the world. It is so totally different from the rest of Australia that there have been times when mainlanders have ignored its existence.

Tasmania is wet and cold where the mainland is predominantly hot and dry. It is intimate and undulating; the mainland is flat and expansive. It is European in its style; the mainland is aggressively Australian and post-colonial.

Over and over again Tasmania's history has run counter to the events which were unfolding on the mainland. When Sydney Town was thriving, the settlement at Hobart Town was struggling. When pastoralists were opening up the vast grazing lands of eastern Australia, Tasmanians were struggling with small acreages between Hobart and George Town.

When eastern Australia was gripped by gold fever, Tasmania was dealing with both a depression and a political crisis. Even today Tasmania operates with a different set of values. In the 1990s when the largest festival in Australia is Sydney's Gay & Lesbian Mardi Gras, Tasmania still has statutes against homosexuality. In the 1980s when the world was rapidly embracing environmental concerns, Tasmania was still committed to drowning wilderness areas for hydro-electricity dams and felling forests for wood chip and paper manufacture.

There is no easy answer to why Tasmania is so different from the rest of Australia. The combination of Bass Strait (which is a formidable barrier), a history of hardship, a small population and a fragile economic base has resulted in a deep conservatism produced by a perception that Tasmania is permanently in danger of economic collapse.

It is believed that Aborigines first arrived in Tasmania about 30–40 000 years ago. Between 10 000 and 6500 years ago the sea level between Tasmania and the mainland rose. This meant that the people trapped on the island were isolated from all contact until the arrival of European explorers in the seventeenth and eighteenth centuries.

The first European to reach Tasmania was the Dutch navigator and explorer, Abel Tasman. Sailing from Batavia he landed on the east coast of Tasmania in 1642 and, not knowing he was on an island, took possession of the land naming it in honour of Anthony Van Diemen, the Governor-General of the Dutch East Indies.

No further exploration of the island took place for the next 130 years. Then, at the end of the eighteenth century, in quick succession, the island was visited by Marion du Fresne (1772) Furneaux (1773), Cook (1777), Bligh (1788), J. H. Cox (1789), Bruni d'Entrecasteaux and Huon de Kermadec (1792–93) and John Hayes (1793). It wasn't until 1798–99 that Bass and Flinders circumnavigated the island.

The too-frequent visits by French explorers concerned the British authorities in both Sydney and London. In 1803 it was decided that a colony should be established on the island to secure British territorial claims. Although this was the first formal European settlement it was the culmination of over a decade of random exploitation and plunder by whalers and sealers who had already established a pattern of maltreatment of the local Aboriginal population. It was common for sealers to enslave Aboriginal women and to use them for both sexual purposes and hunting.

Between March 1803 and June 1804 convicts, soldiers and free settlers arrived at Risdon Cove and Sullivans Cove on the Derwent River. The settlement was named Hobart Town. The early history of the settlement was characterised by extreme hardship and constant skirmishes with the local Aborigines.

Later in 1804 a settlement was established at George Town at the mouth of the Esk River. Two years later it moved inland to the present site of Launceston. It wasn't until 1812 that the independent settlements at Hobart and Launceston were brought together under a single administration.

In the early years of settlement free settlers were encouraged in spite of the difficulties presented by the land and the island's infant economy. By 1820 the island's European population was 5468 of whom 2588 had arrived as convicts.

The life of convicts transported to Van Diemen's

*Macquarie Street, Hobart, in the 1880s.*

Land was impossibly difficult. Those sent to Macquarie Harbour, on the island's west coast, were expected to row up to 20 miles a day from the penal camp at Sarah Island to the Gordon River where they felled huon pine for the construction of ships. At Port Arthur the line between 'convict labour' and 'slavery' blurred when convicts were used to power a huge 24-man treadmill—surely one of the most demeaning and arduous forms of punishment ever invented.

The most important work done by convict gangs in the early nineteenth century centred on the establishment of a series of elegant stone villages (including some particularly impressive bridges and churches) along the route from Hobart to Launceston. Today villages like Richmond and Ross bear witness to this work.

In 1825 Van Diemen's Land became a separate colony. The early governors—Arthur (1824–36), Franklin (1837–43), Eardley-Wilmot (1843–46) and Denison (1847–55)—struggled to manage a colony which was expanding rapidly. Thirteen thousand convicts arrived on the island between 1817 and 1830. Most were assigned to the new landowners.

During this period Aborigines were hunted and killed like animals. It is probable that some kind of undeclared warfare—more a series of skirmishes between settlers and Aborigines—broke out.

The island's fragile economy became a continuing nemesis. In the 1830s, when the economy was relatively stable, settlers still had to grapple with high interest rates and a shortage of currency. A sudden boom in land prices in the late 1830s led to a depression in the 1840s which was exacerbated by too much spare convict labour.

The situation became so bad that Lieutenant-Governor Franklin was recalled to England in 1843 and his successor, Eardley-Wilmot, was confronted with horrendous economic problems as a result of the British government's refusal to pay for the police or the gaols.

Tasmanians have often looked for scapegoats. In the 1840s the island's economic problems were blamed on transportation. Although the economy began to improve in the latter part of the decade it was not enough to slow down a burgeoning anti-transportation movement lead by the preacher and historian, John West. The Governor of the time, William Thomas Denison, resisted the anti-transportation moves but by 1852 the island had a representative council and the British parliament agreed that transportation would cease the following year.

In spite of these changes (and a change of name from Van Diemen's Land to Tasmania in 1855) the island's economic woes persisted. The economy was almost continuously depressed from 1856 to 1872. Wages fell, crops failed and labourers left to try their luck on the Victorian goldfields. The economy of the island was barely surviving on exports of whale oil and fruit.

Tasmania's saviour went by the unlikely name of 'Philosopher' Smith. For twenty-five years he had been prospecting along the island's west coast. In 1871 he discovered tin at Mount Bischoff and, although the west coast has some of the harshest weather conditions in Australia, the prospect of riches attracted men to the area where subsequently gold was found along the Pieman River, silver was found at Waratah, Zeehan, Dundas and Farrell, copper was mined at Mount Lyell and tin at Renison Bell.

In twenty years (1871–91) the island's population rose from 99 000 to 146 000. The mining boom flowed on to other industries. Fruit found a larger mainland market and wool established itself as the island's most significant export.

Unfortunately, this brief flurry of economic activity could not be sustained. World War I drew men away from the island and the short postwar boom was not accompanied by any significant increase in prosperity or population. The population was 218 316 in the census of 1921 and this had only increased to 227 000 by 1931.

Surprisingly, since World War II Tasmania's population has grown. In 1992 it was 471 118. Although the state still has high unemployment levels it has been seen by many people as an alternative to the increasing Americanisation and modernisation of the mainland centres.

The forces at work in contemporary Tasmania are complex and unusual. They seem to be the result of a conflict between deeply conservative rural communities and radical, free-thinking new settlers who advocate modern moral and social reforms.

This conflict can be seen in such contemporary issues as the environment—in the 1989 Federal elections five Tasmanian seats were won by Greens—and homosexual law reform.

'This is a confused and complex society in crisis,' Peter Hay, a political scientist at the University of Tasmania has observed. 'It isn't sure where it's going. It's had an uncomplicated modern history; it was sure of itself. Everyone believed in a small number of clichéd truths, but in the last twenty years that has all been thrown out the window.'

# WHERE TO GO AND WHAT TO SEE

**Tasmania**

## Hobart and Environs

Anglesea Barracks,
   Davey Street,
   Hobart

Battery Point
Botanic Gardens,
   Lower Domain Road,
   North Hobart

Cadbury's Chocolate Factory
Cascade Brewery
Cat and Fiddle Arcade,
   Murray–Elizabeth Streets,
   Hobart
Constitution Dock

Folk Museum

Government House,
   Lower Domain Road,
   Hobart

Maritime Museum,
   46 Bayfield Street,
   Bellerive
Model Tudor Village
Mount Wellington
Museum and Art Gallery,
   5 Argyle Street,
   Hobart

Narryna Folk Museum

Parliament House, Hobart
Post Office Museum,
   19 Castray Esplanade,
   Hobart

Risdon Cove Historical Site
Runnymeade—restored colonial
   house

Salamanca Place, Hobart
Shot Tower, Taroona

Tasmanian Maritime Museum,
   46 Bayfield Street,
   Bellarive
Tasmanian Museum and Art Gallery,
   5 Argyle Street,
   Hobart
Town Hall,
   Macquarie Street,
   Hobart
Transport Museum


University of Tasmania,
   Churchill Avenue,
   Sandy Bay
Wrest Point Casino,
   410 Sandy Bay Road,
   Sandy Bay

## Beyond Hobart

Asbestos National Park

Ben Lomond National Park

Bridestowe Lavender Farm, Nabowla
(flowers January only)
Bruny Island
Burnie

Callington Mill, Oatlands
Cape Barren Island
Cataract Gorge, Launceston
Clarendon House—historic house,
near Nuile
Copper Mine, Queenstown
Cradle Mountain–Lake St Clair
National Park

Derwent River Power Development
Scheme—public viewing galleries
at power stations at Liapootah,
Tarraleah, Tungatinah and
Trevallyn
Devils Gate Dam
Douglas Apsley National Park

Eaglehawk Neck
Entally House—colonial restoration,
Hadspen

Flinders Island
Franklin House—historic house,
South Launceston

Frenchmans Cap National Park
Freycinet National Park

Gordon River State Reserve

Hartz Mountains National Park
Home Hill—historic house,
Devonport
Huon Valley

King Island
Lake Barrington
Lake Gordon
Lake Pedder
Limestone Caves, Hastings
Longford Wildlife Park

Maria Island National Park/Mersey-
Forth Power Scheme Development
Montezuma Falls
Mount Lyell Copper Mine,
Queenstown

Oatlands—historic town
Old Colony Inn—historic house,
New Norfolk

Penny Royal World, Launceston
Poatina Underground Power Station

Port Arthur National Park

Queen Victoria Museum and Art
Gallery,
Wellington Street,
Launceston
Richmond—historic village
Rocky Cape National Park
Ross—historic township

Salmon Ponds, New Norfolk
South West National Park
Stanley—historic township

Tasmanian Wildlife Park and
Noctarium, near Chudleigh
Tasmanian Wool Centre, Ross
The Nut—rock outcrop, Stanley
Thermal Pool, Hastings

West Coast Pioneers Memorial
Museum, Zeehan
White House—Museum and Bakery,
Village Green, Westbury
Woolmers and Brickendon Estates—
Brickendon, Woolmers Lane,
Longford

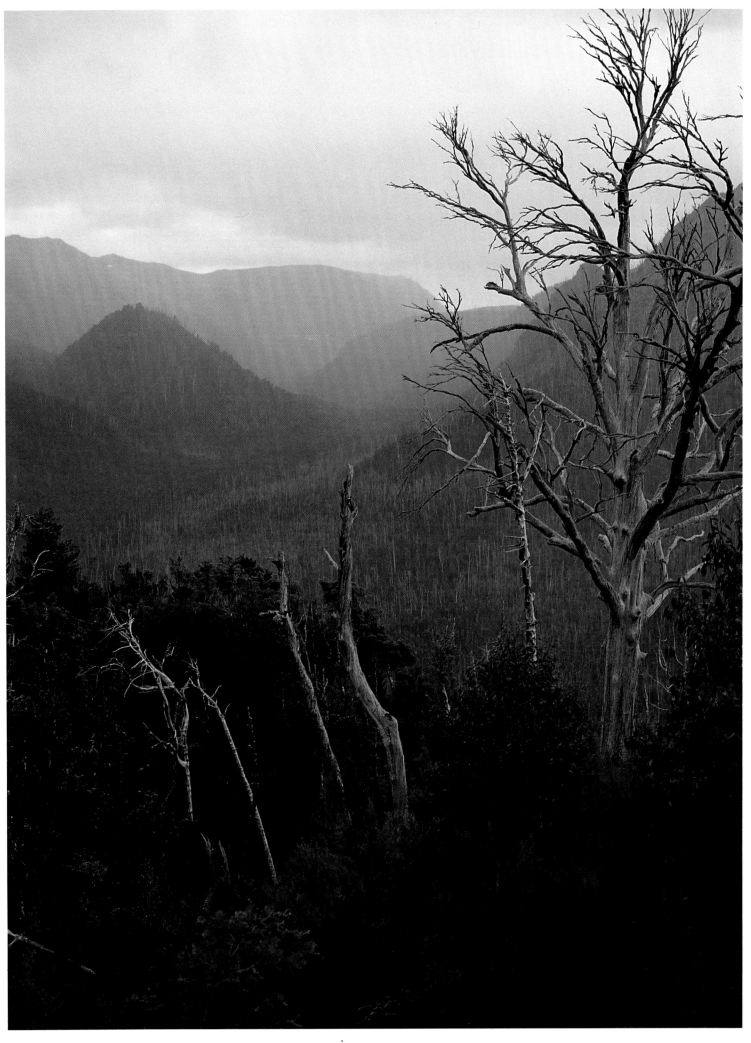

*The sheer cliffs of Frenchmans Cap rise into the swirling mists of Tasmania's south-western naturelands.*

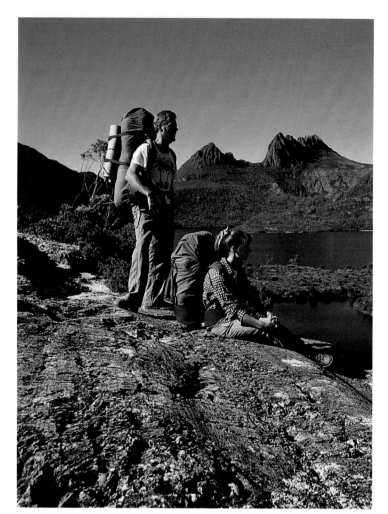

Above: *The tide laps across the geometric patterns of the Tessellated Pavement, formed by wave erosion on the eastern side of Eaglehawk Neck.*

Below: *Walkers enjoy the mossy forests and extensive tracks at Lake St Clair, one of the most famous hiking areas in Tasmania.*

Above: *Enjoying breathtaking views across the blue waters of Lake Dove to the jagged silhouette of Cradle Mountain in the northern end of the magnificent Cradle Mountain–Lake St Clair National Park.*

Opposite: *Rugged coastline at Sleepy Bay on the Freycinet Peninsula.*

Below: *The highlands of Tasmania are home to the Tasmanian Devil* (Sarcophyllus harisii), *Australia's largest marsupial predator.*

170 *Silhouettes of dead trees rise from the waters of Lake Pedder, an extensive man-made lake and focal point of the South-west National Park.*

Above: *One of Australia's most famous historic sites—the Port Arthur convict settlement. About 12 500 men and boys were transported here.*

Below: *Wrest Point Casino, Australia's first hotel/casino and Tasmania's most renowned venue for sophisticated nightlife.*

Opposite: *Colourful open-air craft markets at Salamanca Place, Hobart, where fine examples of early merchant warehouses can be seen.*

Below: *A very heavy game of chess at Franklin Square, Hobart.*

174   *Hobart, seen here from the Mt Nelson lookout, is Australia's second oldest and most southerly city.*

Left: *Hobart is memorable for its deep-water harbour on the estuary of the Derwent River, its mellow early colonial sandstone buildings and the backdrop of majestic Mt Wellington*

Opposite: *New Norfolk, on the banks of the Derwent River, is a classified historic town nestled among English trees and hop fields.*

Below: *A suspension bridge straddles the South Esk River at Cataract Gorge, Launceston.*

Above: *Tasmania's rivers provide great opportunities for exhilarating jet boat rides.*

Below: *Pennyfarthing races at the small unspoilt township of Evandale, where buildings date from as early as 1809.*

Below: *One of Launceston's best-known tourist attractions, the Penny Royal Watermill complex, which includes a museum, working cornmill and a windmill.*

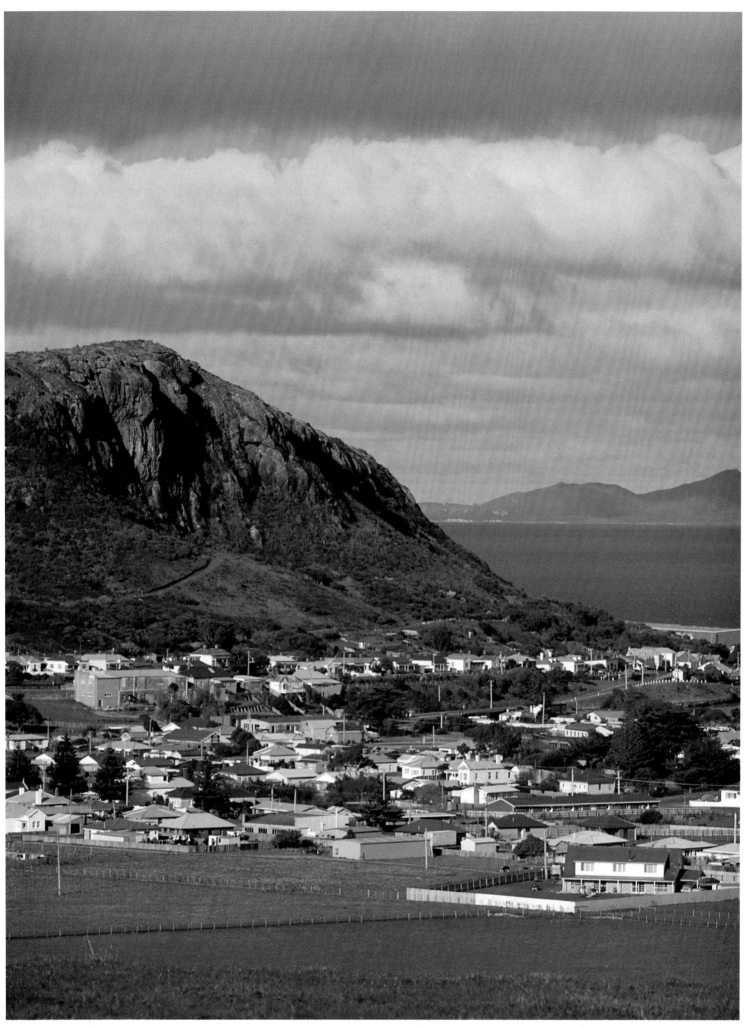

*The quaint township of Stanley nestles under a massive rocky outcrop known as The Nut. Old whalers and sailing ships used to berth at the wharf here, nowadays the wharf handles crayfish and shark fishing fleets.*

179

Above: *Winterscape in the Cradle Mountain–Lake St Clair National Park.*

Left: *Cascading falls and moss covered vegetation are features of the water-dominated south-west coast.*

Below: *Tasmania's majestic, untamed west coast is indented by wild rivers meeting the sea.*

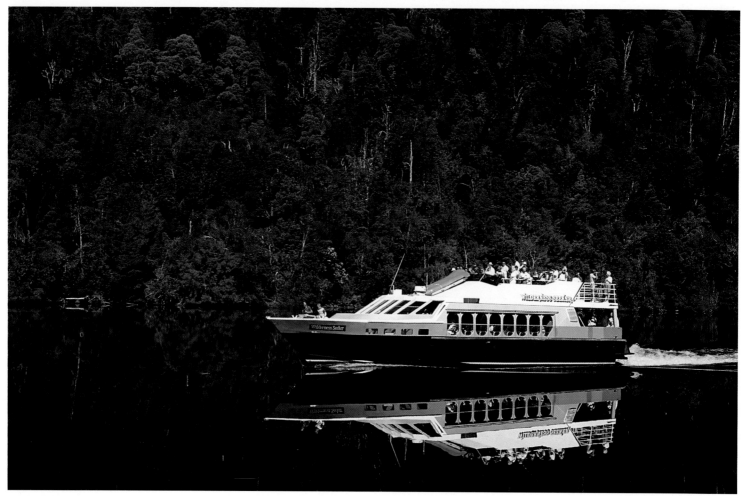

Above: *The* Wilderness Seeker *carries sightseers down the magnificent Gordon River in south-west Tasmania, one of the last great temperate wilderness areas in the world.*

Below: *Waves froth against the rocky coastline on Tasmania's west coast.*

Opposite: *The dark cliffs of Cape Pillar and Tasman Island rise up from the deep blue of the Tasman Sea.*

Below: *Winter sports on the snowfields at Ben Lomond National Park in north-eastern Tasmania.*

Left: *Winter light on the War Memorial at Queenstown, an old mining town carved out of the surrounding mountains.*

Below: *Richmond Bridge, the oldest bridge in Australia, is one of the many attractions in the historic town of Richmond.*

Opposite, top: *The lush countryside near Deloraine is used mainly for dairying and mixed farming.*

Opposite, bottom: *Picturesque Strahan, the only port on the rugged west coast of Tasmania.*

185

Above: *Autumn colours the hop fields at Bushy Park near New Norfolk.*

Below: *The largest lavender farm outside Europe is found at Nabowla, a farming township in north-east Tasmania.*

Below: *Surf, rock, spear and estuary fishing are all available at the popular holiday resort of Bicheno on the east coast.*

# ANNUAL EVENTS—TASMANIA

The following list is a general guide only. Precise information may be obtained from the Tasmanian Tourist Centre.

## JANUARY–MARCH
**Brighton** Craft Fair
**Burnie** Athletics Carnival
**Bushy Park** Agricultural Show
**Bushy Park** New Norfolk Hop Festival
**Claremont** Lily and Summer Flower Show
**Cradle Mountain** Overland Run
**Derwent** Brighton Craft Fair
**Derwent** Garden Week and Tasmanian Fine Food Fair
**Devonport** Cup
**Devonport** Food and Wine Fun Fiesta
**Devonport** Great Tasmanian Bike Ride
**Evandale** National Penny Farthing Championships
**Fingal Valley** Coal Shovelling Festival
**Hobart** Cup Carnival
**Hobart** King of the Derwent Yacht Race
**Hobart** Royal Hobart Regatta
**Hobart** Tasmanian Pacing Championship
**Hobart** Vintage Classic Yacht Race
**Hobart** Women's International Tennis Open
**King Island** Art and Craft Competition
**King Island** Show
**King Island** Surfing Carnival
**Kingborough** Festival
**Launceston** Annual Craft Bazaar and Working with Wood Exhibition
**Launceston** Cup
**Meander** Tasmanian Mountain Cattlemen's Championships
**New Norfolk** Hop Festival
**Port Arthur** Beating Retreat
**Port Arthur** Historic Ghost Tours (all year)
**Port Cygnet** Huon Valley Folk Festival
**Sheffield** Steamfest
**Triabunna** Spring Bay Crayfish Derby

## APRIL–JUNE
**Beauty Point** Three Peaks Race
**Eaglehawk Neck** Tasmanian Bluefin Tuna Championships
**Hobart** Autumn Rose Show
**Hobart** International Winter Fest and Oyster Festival
**Launceston** National Exhibition of Tasmanian Aboriginal Art
**Launceston** Targafest
**Port Arthur** Isle of the Dead Remembrance Day
**St Helens** Suncoast Jazz Festival
**Ulverstone** Craft Fair

## JULY–SEPTEMBER
**Ben Lomond** Descent
**Burnie** Adidas Ten Foot Race
**Burnie** Festival
**Burnie** St George's Floral Festival
**Circular Head** Garden Club Spring Flower Show
**Derwent** Rotary Club of Brighton Working Craft Fair
**Hobart** Daffodil and Camellia Show
**Hobart** Folk and Decorative Arts Society of Tasmania Exhibition
**Hobart** Orchid Show
**Hobart** Rotary Travel and Leisure Show
**Hobart** Tasmanian Tulip Festival
**Hobart** TFL Grand Final
**Launceston** Garden Festival
**Mt Field** Forestry Tasmania Winter Challenge
**Richmond** Southern Cross Marathon and Half Marathon
**Sheffield** Daffodil Show
**Somerset** Wynyard Garden Club Daffodil Show
**Swansea** Show
**Tasmazia** Open Day

## OCTOBER–DECEMBER
**Bruny Island** 'Social and Serious' Solo and Relay Run
**Burnie** Christmas Festival
**Burnie** Melbourne to Burnie Yacht Race
**Burnie** Orchid Festival
**Burnie** Show
**Burnie** Tasmanian Art and Pottery Exhibition
**Campbell Town** Country Music festival
**Deloraine** Tasmanian Cottage Industry Exhibition and Craft Fair
**Derby** Day
**Evandale** Railex (railway exhibition)
**Flinders Island** Show
**Glenorchy** Tasmanian Pacing Championship
**Hobart** Carols by Candlelight
**Hobart** Christmas Pageant
**Hobart** City to Summit Half Marathon and Walk
**Hobart** Konica Women's 10km Classic and 5km Fun Run
**Hobart** Melbourne–Hobart Yacht Race
**Hobart** Rhododendron Show
**Hobart** Rose and Iris Show
**Hobart** Summer Festival and Taste of Tasmania
**Hobart** Sydney–Hobart Yacht Race
**Huon Valley** Show
**Kangaroo Bay** Christmas Fun Fair
**Kingston** Oliebollen Fair
**Latrobe** Wheel and Latrobe Gift (foot and cycle race)
**Launceston** Carols by Candlelight
**Longford** Village Green Garden Fair
**New Norfolk** Regatta
**New Norfolk** Truck Show
**New Norfolk** Tulip Time
**North Hobart** Fiesta
**Port Arthur** Boxing Day Woodchopping Carnival
**Port Arthur** Irish Festival
**Richmond** Village Fair
**Strahan** Strahan to Zeehan Miners Marathon
**Swansea** Fun Fish
**Swansea** The Great Oyster Bay Festival
**Ulverstone** Show
**Westbury** Garden Day
**Wynyard** Tulip Festival

# South Australia:
# THE HERITAGE

In 1627 the Dutch ship, *Gulden Zeepaard*, sailed along the southern coast of New Holland and reached the area around Ceduna in South Australia before turning back and making its way north to Batavia. This was the first recorded sighting of South Australia by Europeans.

The coastline remained unexplored until 1792 when the French explorer, Bruni d'Entrecasteaux, sailed and up into the Great Australian Bight. He was followed in 1800 by Lieutenant James Grant and in 1802 by Matthew Flinders who, during his circumnavigation of Australia, chartered much of the future state's coastline. These explorers did little to encourage settlers to the area. Their reports of a difficult coastline with a dry, harsh hinterland were not designed to create a rush of interest. In fact in 1804 a government survey ship sailed along the coast of Kangaroo Island and concluded that it was unsuitable for human habitation.

The eventual settlement of South Australia by Europeans was the result of an experiment in social engineering. In the early part of the nineteenth century, with people pouring into the overcrowded cities of England, social reform became increasingly important.

Against this background the tireless social reformer, Edward Gibbon Wakefield, developed a theory of systematic colonisation. He rejected the notion of colonies being a dumping ground for Britain's prison overflow and advanced a scheme where the money raised from the sale of crown land could be invested in the cost of shipping labourers to work on the newly privatised land. Here was a plan for the development of Australia which did not rely on convict labour.

In the early stages it seemed that bureaucracy would conspire to ensure that it failed. However, in May 1835 ten commissioners were appointed to oversee the sale of land in the new colony of South Australia. Before the colony could become a reality they needed to sell land to the value of £35 000. This was achieved in seven months.

In rapid succession Captain John Hindmarsh was appointed Governor of the new colony, William Light was appointed Surveyor-General, James Hurtle Fisher was appointed Resident Commissioner and eight ships sailed from England bound for the shores of South Australia.

By March 1837 William Light had surveyed the site of Adelaide and land had been allotted. It looked as though the colony would be an unqualified success. Livestock and settlers were pouring into South Australia and there was a sense of entrepreneurial enthusiasm in the air. Unfortunately most of the new settlers seemed more interested in land speculation than in clearing land, growing crops and trying to make their allotments economically viable.

Acrimony between the Governor and Resident Commissioner resulted in their recall to England and the appointment of Colonel George Gawler to both positions. Gawler tried to control what was rapidly becoming an uncomfortable free-for-all. By 1840 there were 14 000 people in the colony and the government were effectively bankrupt. Money had been poorly spent, only 7500 labourers had been sent to the colony, and there were accusations of serious financial mismanagement.

By 1842 the British government had deemed the experiment a failure and South Australia had reverted to an ordinary Crown colony. In spite of this turnaround the experiment did eventually work. Two years later under the governorship of Captain George Grey, the colony had resolved its financial problems and the farmers (landowners who, in many instances, had been persuaded to go and work their land) were actually producing more wheat than the colony could use.

The colony's economic base expanded during the 1840s when silver was discovered near Adelaide and huge copper deposits were located near Kapunda. This mining activity, when added to the successes in the rural sector, attracted new immigrants and by 1850 the population of South Australia had grown to 64 000.

The discovery of gold the following year saw the colony's population drop by 25 per cent as men rushed to the goldfields. In a particularly astute move the colony's parliament passed the Bullion Act which offered a range of incentives to miners to return to South Australia with their wealth. So successful was the legislation (which offered high local prices for gold and regular gold escorts) that more than £2 million returned to Adelaide in two years.

The miners who returned wanted a more democratic political process and in the mid-1850s they successfully petitioned Britain to establish two elected houses of parliament to administer the colony. In this they reflected the political radicalism which was sweeping Australia at the time.

The result was a new constitution for South Australia which was widely regarded as the most forward-looking and democratic in the British Empire. Unfortunately the constitution was not accompanied by the establishment of political parties and, with independents dominating, the power base changed no fewer than thirty-seven times in the next thirty-three years.

The most important reform brought about during this volatile period was the establishment of the Torrens Title system of registering land. This piece of legislation, introduced by Sir Robert Torrens in 1858, eventually would be adopted throughout Australia.

By the 1860s the economic success of the goldrushes had given way to a period of economic

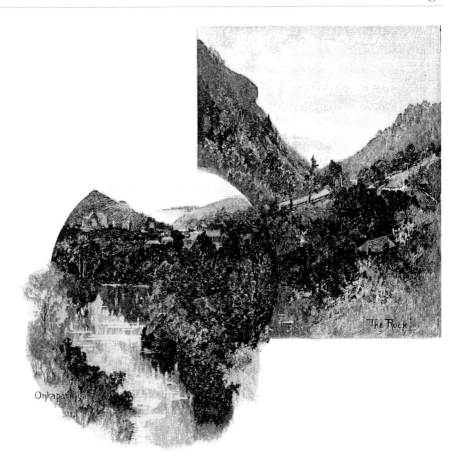

*Onkaparinka and the Rock in the Adelaide Hills, South Australia, in the 1880s.*

hardship. In spite of this the state prospered. John McDouall Stuart became the first person to cross the continent from south to north. In the process he opened up valuable grazing lands in the north of the state. Huge copper reserves were found at Moonta. South Australia gained control of the Northern Territory in 1863 and the state's sheep and human populations nearly doubled in the decade. This prosperity and success continued until the depression of the 1880s.

The boom of the 1860s collapsed in the 1880s when the state's population growth slowed and its agricultural productivity, hit by drought, was greatly reduced. This was to become a pattern for future decades. The problem was that so much of the state was marginal land. The slightest change in climatic or economic conditions had the consequence of decimating what had previously been valuable and economically viable.

As with the depression of the 1860s the state's economic fortunes were saved by the discovery of silver, lead and zinc at Broken Hill. Although the mine was in New South Wales the economic benefits flowed into South Australia where huge

*Port Adelaide in 1840.*

treatment works were constructed at Port Pirie, bringing work and prosperity to the area.

Combined with this windfall the state committed itself to expanding arable agricultural land through the use of superphosphates, the clearing of marginal swamp land and the establishment of communities along the Murray River.

During the 1890s the United Labor Party, a party formed by the local trade union movement, saw South Australia at the forefront of political reform. In 1891 free education was introduced and in 1894 the state granted full suffrage to women. The state also pioneered compulsory industrial arbitration during this period.

Economic prosperity was maintained through to the Great Depression. Iron ore was discovered to the west of Port Augusta at Iron Knob, a steelworks was built at Whyalla, the state's approach to land management and agricultural productivity was forward looking, and a strong secondary industry base was established during the first two decades of the twentieth century. After World War I the state actively settled returned soldiers on the Murray River floodplains and Adelaide grew rapidly.

The Depression decimated the state's economy.

By 1931, 12 per cent of the state's population (24 per cent of its workforce) was unemployed. In 1933 the Labor government was defeated. It would not regain power until 1965. During this period the state's conservative forces, led from 1938 by Thomas (later Sir Thomas) Playford, would push the state's economy to new levels of success. This success was fuelled firstly be the manufacturing demands of World War II and secondly by the stable, and booming, economy which emerged in the postwar years. The list of achievements during this period is impressive. The Morgan–Whyalla pipeline was completed. The huge Whyalla steelworks and ship building yard were constructed. The Mannum pipeline bringing water from the Murray River to Adelaide was built. The city of Elizabeth, named after the Queen, was created in 1955. Oil refineries, cheap electricity, munitions factories and successful mining operations all helped to boost the state's economy. Although this was an enviable economic base it was still vulnerable to international forces.

Sir Thomas Playford's government was defeated by Labor in 1965. Playford had been state premier for twenty-eight years. It was the end of the state's political stability. The Labor Party ruled until 1968 when Steele Hall regained power for the Liberal Party. He was swept from office in 1970 when Don Dunstan became premier. In turn the Liberals regained power in 1979 under David Tonkin. They lost it in 1982 to John Bannon who, forced from office by a scandal involving the gross mismanagement of the state bank, was duly replaced by the Liberal Party in the early 1990s.

Today South Australia has a reputation as a forward-looking, modern and innovative state. In the eyes of most Australians it is seen as the home of the country's wine industry and the Adelaide Festival, an arts festival of international repute.

# WHERE TO GO AND WHAT TO SEE

## South Australia

### Adelaide and Environs

Adelaide Casino
Adelaide Hills
Art Gallery of South Australia,
  North Terrace,
  Adelaide
Athelstone Wildflower Garden
Ayers House—historic house,
  288 North Terrace,
  Adelaide

Black Hill Wildflower Garden

Constitutional Museum,
  North Terrace,
  Adelaide

Electrical Transport Museum

Festival Centre,
  King William Road,
  Adelaide

Fisherman's Wharf Market (Sundays
  and Monday public holidays)
Fort Glanville, Semaphore

Glenelg Beach
Government House,
  North Terrace,
  Adelaide

Horsnell Gully Conservation Park

Lake Torrens
Lights Vision,
  Montefiore Hill,
  North Adelaide

Maritime Museum, Port Adelaide
Migration and Settlement Museum,
  Adelaide
Morialta Conservation Park

Old Adelaide Gaol

Parliament House, North Terrace,
  Adelaide
Pennington Gardens

St Francis Xavier's Cathedral,
  Wakefield Street,
  Adelaide
St Peter's Cathedral,
  King William Road,
  Adelaide
South Australian Historical Museum,
  North Terrace,
  Adelaide
Sturt's Cottage—historic house

Tandanya Aboriginal Cultural
  Institute
Telecommunications Museum,
  131 King William Street,
  Adelaide
Town Hall,
  King William Street,
  Adelaide

University of Adelaide,
North Terrace,
Adelaide

Victoria Square, Adelaide

Windy Point Lookout

Zoological Gardens,
Victoria Drive,
Adelaide

## Beyond Adelaide

Alligator Gorge
Andamooka Opal Mines

Barossa Kiddypark, Tanunda
Barossa Valley
Birdwood Mill Museum
Blue Lake, Mount Gambier
Bool Lagoon National Park
Browne Lake

Canundra National Park
Cape Labatt Recreation Park
Ceduna
Cleland Conservation Park
Cockatoo Valley
Coffin Bay National Park
Coober Pedy Opal Mines
Coorong National Park

Dangali Conservation Park

Eyre Peninsula

Fairy Penguins, Penneshaw, Kangaroo
Island
Fleurieu Peninsula

Flinders Chase National Park
Flinders Ranges National Park

Gammon Ranges National Park
Gawler Folk Museum
Gawler Ranges
Glacier Rock, Inman Valley
Granite Island
Great Australian Bight
Greenhills Adventure Park, Victor
Harbor

Hahndorf Academy Gallery and
Museum, Hahndorf
Hincks Recreation Park
Hot Air Ballooning, Tanunda

Innes National Park
Iron Knob Iron Ore Quarries

Jip Jip Conservation Park

Kangaroo Island
Kapunda
Kellidie Bay Park
Koorungle Park Wildlife Reserve

Lake Albert
Lake Alexandria
Lake Eyre
Lake Frome
Lake George
Lake Gillies Recreation Park
Leg of Mutton Lake
Leigh Creek Coal Fields
Lincoln National Park
Luhrs  Pioneer German Cottage,
Nuriootpa
Lyndoch Mechanical Music Museum

Marree (Birdsville Track)
Moonta

Mount Gambier
Mount Lofty
Mount Remarkable National Park
Mount Rescue Conservation Park
Murray Bridge
Myponga Conservation Park

Naracoorte Caves

Parlana Hot Springs
Pioneer Village, Morphett Vale
Pitchi Ritchi Railway, Quorn
Pooginook Conservation Park
Port Pirie

Renmark
Riverland District

St Marys Peak, Wilpena Pound
Springmount Conservation Park
Story Book Cottage and Whacky
Wood, Tanunda
Streaky Bay

Valley Lake
Victor Harbor

Whale Watching, Great Australian
Bight
Whites Dam Conservation Park
Wilpena Pound
Wineries and Vineyards—Barossa
Valley, Clare Valley, Riverland
District Southern Vales
Woomera
Whyalla Steel Works

Yatco Lagoon
Yorke Peninsula

*Comfortable underground living at the opal-mining town of Coober Pedy where most of the population live in dugouts as protection from the severe temperatures.*

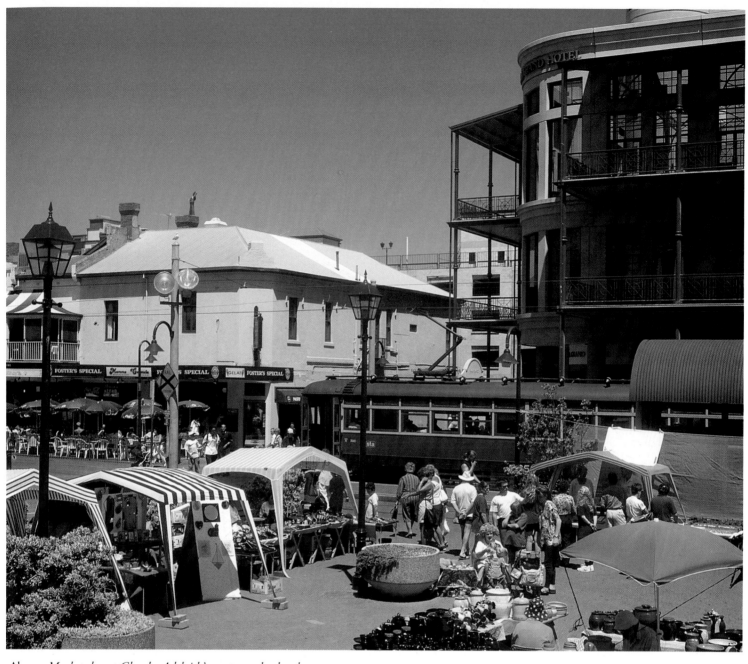

Above: *Market day at Glenelg, Adelaide's most popular beach.*

Below: *'Dingley Dell' home of the poet Adam Lindsay Gordon, now a museum in Port MacDonnell.*

Below: *Port Adelaide has many imposing buildings, a reminder of the port's heyday in the 1880s.*

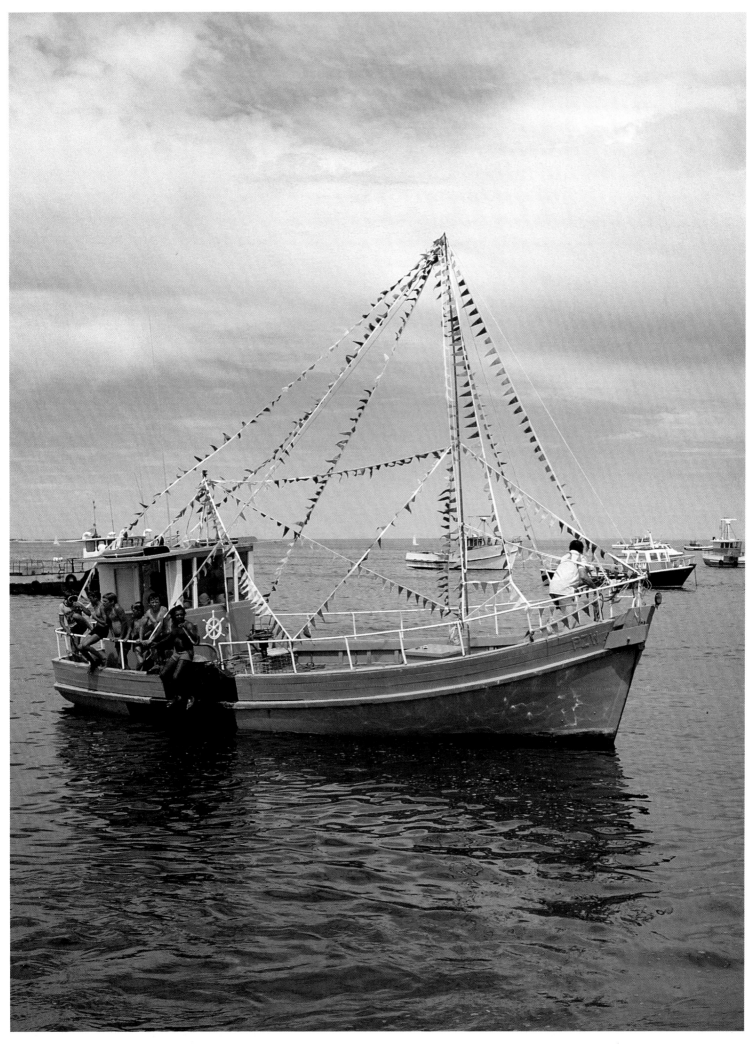

*All dressed up for the Blessing of the Fleet at Port MacDonnell, home to the largest rock lobster fishing fleet in South Australia.*

Above: *The Casino, Adelaide.*

Left: *The spacious, well-planned city of Adelaide is situated on the Torrens River on a narrow coastal plain between the blue waters of St Vincents Gulf and the rolling hills of the Mt Lofty Ranges. The Festival Theatre is in the foreground.*

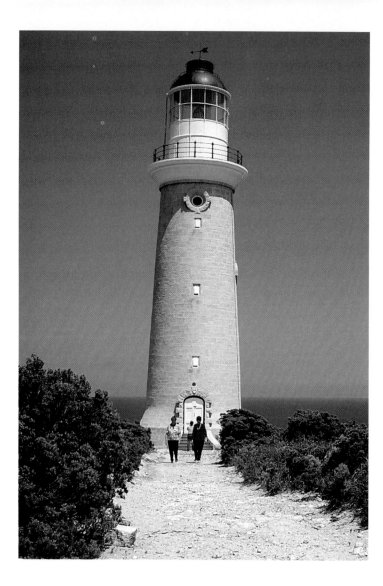

Left: *The picturesque Cape du Couedic lighthouse, one of the old landmarks in the Flinders Chase National Park on Kangaroo Island.*

Opposite: *Twilight on the Torrens, Adelaide.*

Below: *The 197 metre deep Blue Lake near Mt Gambier changes from a dull grey to a vivid blue each November.*

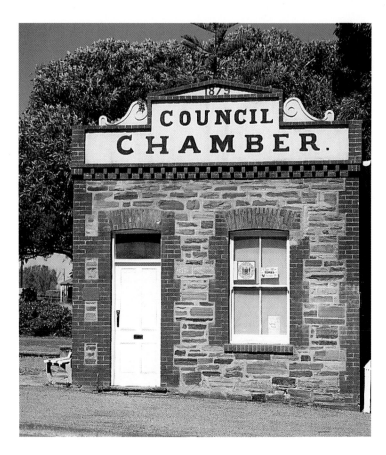

Above: *Council Chamber at Port Elliot, a quiet coastal town and the first port established on Encounter Bay.*

Below: *The Shell Garden, an unusual display at Millicent.*

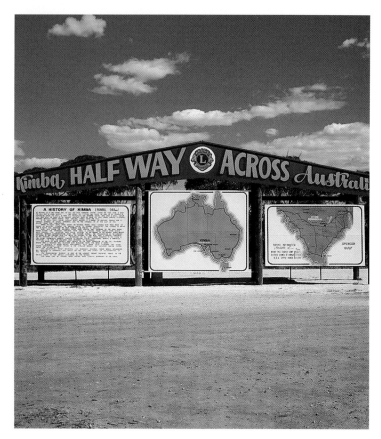

Above: *Halfway mark at the small township of Kimba at the edge of South Australia's outback.*

Opposite: *The Murray River flows through the Riverland district near Renmark. It is one of the most picturesque areas along the length of the river.*

Below: *Wool is one of the main agricultural crops of South Australia.*

Above: *Farm landscape in a valley near Quorn in the Flinders Ranges.*

Below: *Twilight on the walls of Wilpena Pound and the Cazneaux Tree—named after photographer Harold Cazneaux who first photographed the tree in 1937.*

Above: *Many creeks wind their way through the valleys of the ancient Flinders Ranges.*

Opposite: *An unbroken wall of cliffs borders the edge of the Nullarbor Plain on the Great Australian Bight.*

Left: *A series of saltwater lagoons, fed by the waters of the Murray and divided from the sea by the massive white sandhills of the Younghusband Peninsula, the Coorong area is one of the last natural bird sanctuaries in Australia.*

Below: *The colourful Yarwondutta Rocks near Minnipa on the Eyre Peninsula.*

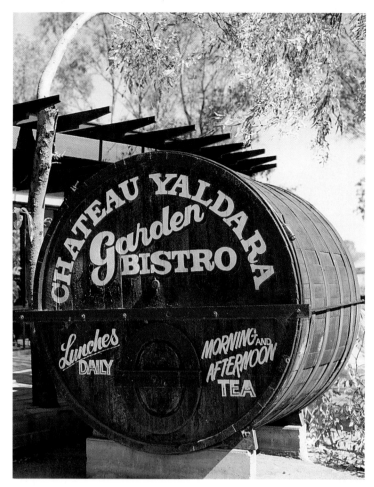

Above: *Chateau Yaldara, near Lyndoch in the Barossa Valley, offers wine-tasting and sales.*

Below: *The Barossa Valley, Australia's premier wine-producing region.*

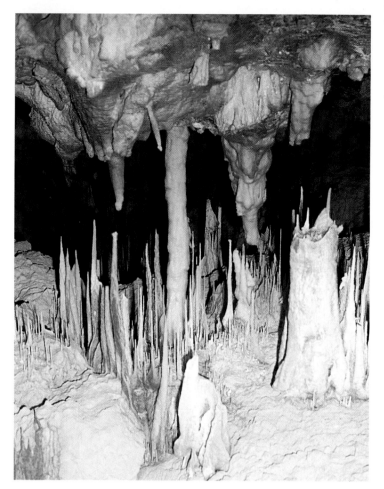

Above: *Fascinating limestone formations at Kelly Hill Cave Conservation Park on Kangaroo Island.*

Opposite: *Wilpena Pound in the Flinders Ranges, an immense elevated basin covering about 50 square kilometres and encircled by rock cliffs that rise more than 1000 metres from the surrounding plains.*

Below: *The waters of the Torrens River froth through the Torrens Gorge near Adelaide.*

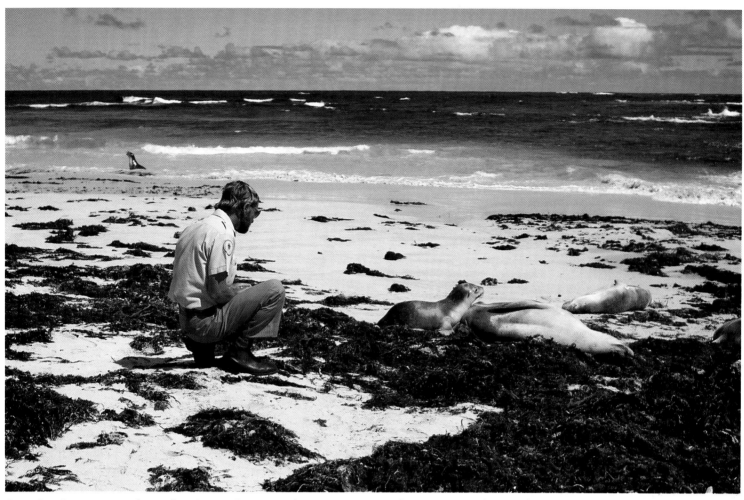

Opposite: *Pretty countryside seen from Norton Summit in the Mount Lofty Ranges behind Adelaide.*

Above: *A National Park Ranger checks Australian sea lions at Seal Bay on Kangaroo Island.*

Below: *Early settlers' well in the South Australian outback near Marree.*

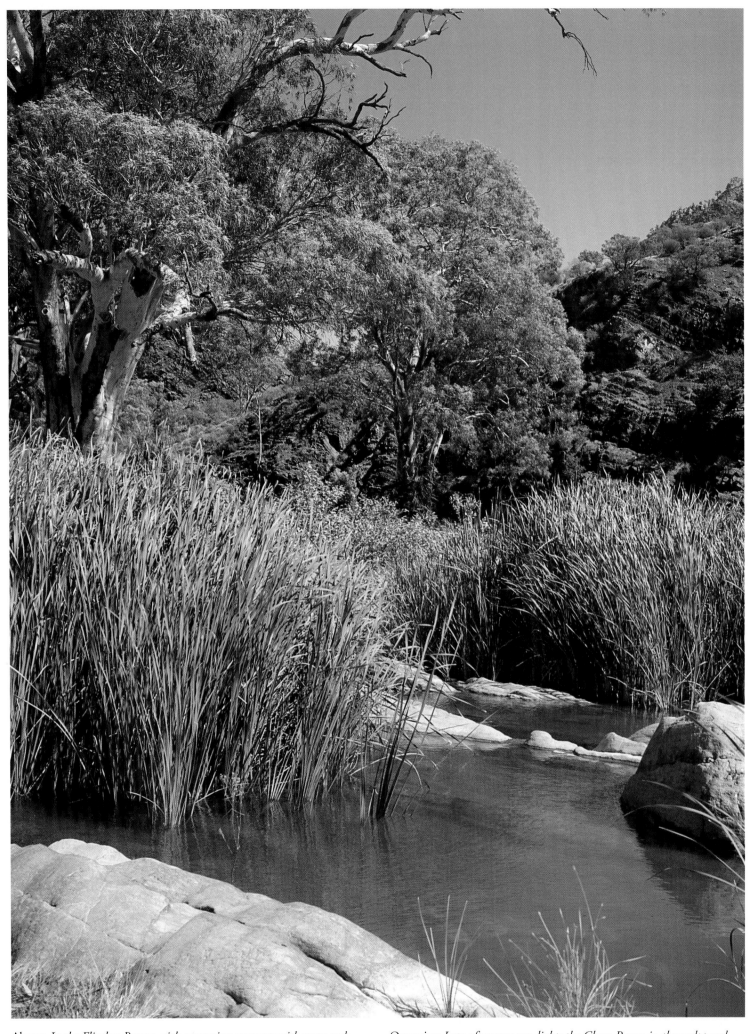

Above: *In the Flinders Ranges, rich vegetation contrasts with stony rock faces at Brachina Gorge.*

Opposite: *Late afternoon sun lights the Chase Range in the sculptured Flinders Ranges.*

*Left: The Pitchi Ritchi steam locomotive takes passengers on a round trip from Quorn, through the Pitchi Ritchi Pass.*

*Opposite: The Sir Joseph Banks Group of Islands Conservation Park, off Tumby Bay on the east coast of the Eyre Peninsula.*

*Below: St Peter's Cathedral, Adelaide, one of Australia's finest cathedrals.*

Above: *The 'Remarkable Rocks' in Flinders Chase National Park on Kangaroo Island.*

Below: *South Australia is both the nation's wine capital and her festival state—here the two combine at the biennial Barossa Valley Vintage Festival, a thanksgiving celebration for a successful harvest.*

Opposite: *The remains of the wreck of the* Ethel *at Ethel Beach in Innes National Park.*

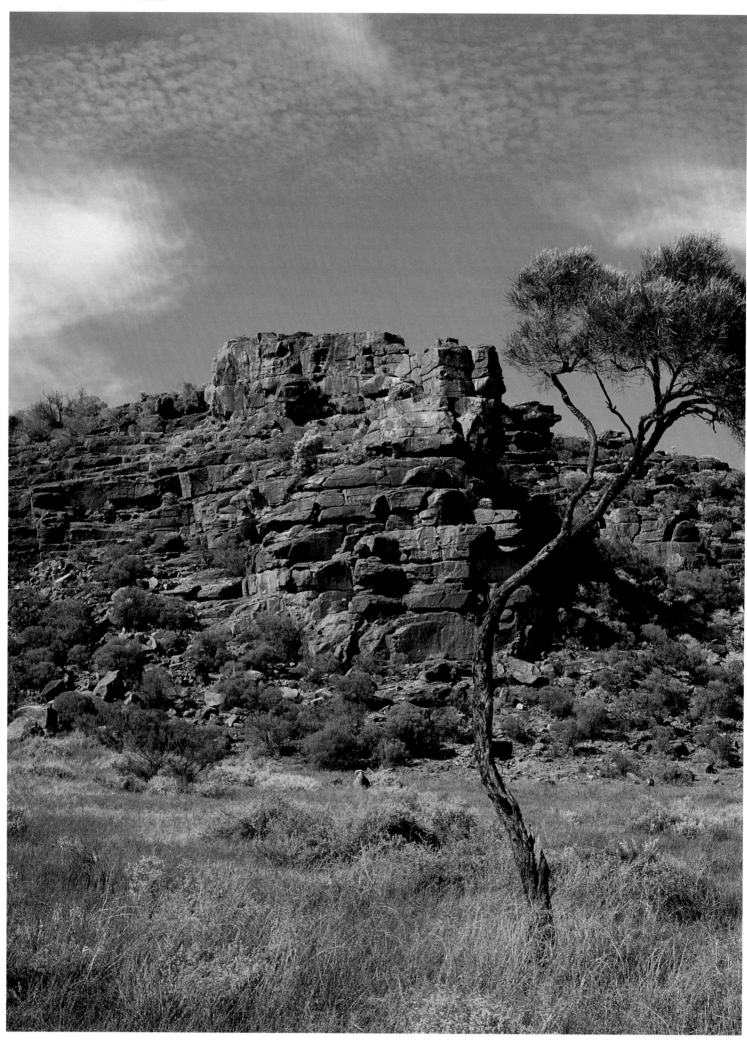

216　*Wild Dog Hill in the Whyalla Conservation Park in the heart of iron-ore mining country.*

# ANNUAL EVENTS—SOUTH AUSTRALIA

The following list is a general guide only. Precise information may be obtained from the South Australian Tourist Centre.

## JANUARY–MARCH
Adelaide World Music Festival
Adelaide The Come Out Youth Arts Festival
Adelaide Hills Harvest Festival
Angaston Two Day Show
Barossa Valley Oompah Fest
Booleroo Steam and Tractor Preservation Society Steam Rally
Hahndorf German Festival
Kangaroo Island Produce Fair
Kangaroo Island Racing Carnival
Mount Compass Cup Cow Race
Port Lincoln Tunarama Festival
Strathalbyn Penny Farthing Challenge and Street Fair
Thebarton Glendi Greek Festival
Tanunda Essenfest

## APRIL–JUNE
Adelaide Cup
Adelaide Heritage Week
Adelaide Rose Festival
Aldgate Autumn Leaves Festival
Barmera South Australian Country Music Awards
Barossa Valley Balloon Regatta
Barossa Valley Vintage Festival (alternate [odd] years)
Clare Gourmet Weekend
Coober Pedy Opal Festival
Gawler 3-Day Equestrian Event
Kadina Kernewck Lowcndcr Festival
Kangaroo Island Food Fair
Kapunta Celtic Folk Festival
Laura Folk Fair
Mount Gambier Generations in Jazz
Mount Lofty Autumn Leaves Festival
Oatbank Easter Racing Carnival
Seppeltsfield Balloon Regatta
Tanunda Melodienacht
William Creek Picnic Races

## JULY–SEPTEMBER
Adelaide Hills Affare Food and Wine Festival
Adelaide Music Fiesta
Adelaide Royal Show
Aldgate Camellia Festival
Barossa Valley Classic Gourmet Weekend
Barossa Valley Music Festival
Kangaroo Island Settlement Day
Port Pirie Blessing of the Fleet
Port Pirie Festival of Country Music
Victor Harbor Folk and Music Festival
Willunga Almond Blossom Festival

## OCTOBER–DECEMBER
Adelaide John Martins State Bank Christmas Pageant
Andamooka Opal Festival
Barossa Valley Music Festival
Forest Range Apple Blossom Festival
Hahndorf German Festival
Hahndorf St Nicholas Night
Kapunda Copper Festival
McLaren Vale Bushing Festival
Marrabel Rodeo
Mount Gambier Blue Lake Festival
Murray River Big River Challenge
Port Pirie Christmas Pageant

# *Western Australia:* THE HERITAGE

Although Western Australia covers nearly one-third of the Australian continent (it is 2 525 500 square kilometres) most of it is harsh, uninhabitable desert. In spite of its vast size Western Australia has a population of only 1 662 777 of whom 1.2 million live in Perth. Its economy is driven by mining, wool and wheat and yet only 15 per cent of the state's population live in rural areas.

The history of the state, in many ways, has been a continuous battle against the harshness of the vast deserts. So harsh is life beyond the narrow southern coastal strip that, in recent times, both Aborigines and white Australians have died of dehydration and exhaustion when they have lost their way or when their cars have broken down.

When, in 1699, William Dampier sailed down the coast of Western Australia, he noted the lack of water. His description of Shark Bay in *A Voyage to New Holland* expresses his frustration 'Twas the 7th of August when we came into Shark's Bay; in which we Anchor'd at three several Places, and stay'd at the first of them (on the W. side of the Bay) till the 11th. During which time we searched about, as I said, for fresh Water, digging Wells, but to no purpose.'

Australia's first inhabitants probably arrived on the coast of north-west Western Australia some 50 000 years ago. Over the next 20 000 years they slowly moved southward and eastward across the landmass. Certainly Aborigines were well established throughout Western Australia by the time the Dutch ships started bumping into the coast in the early seventeenth century. In fact there is considerable evidence that the obvious poverty of the coastal Aborigines, who were trying to eke out a living from near-desert, did much to discourage serious exploration of the coast.

After Henderik Brouwer and Dirk Hartog, the Dutch sailor Willem de Vlamingh reached the island in 1697 and, finding Hartog's pewter plate still in its original position, removed it and replaced it with another. The original was

returned to Holland where it still is kept in the Rijksmuseum.

De Vlamingh's replacement plate had an even less interesting inscription than Hartog's. After getting the date wrong he listed all the important sailors on the voyage and concluded with 'Our fleet set sail from here to continue exploring the Southern Land, on the way to Batavia.'

In 1818 the French explorer Louis de Freycinet, while exploring the coast, came across de Vlamingh's plate and removed it to France. The plate was eventually returned to Australia in 1947 and is currently housed in the Maritime Museum in Fremantle.

In the early nineteenth century the British became concerned about the possibility of a French colony being established on the coast of Western Australia and thus, in 1826, the New South Wales Governor Ralph Darling was instructed to establish a colony at King George Sound with a view to establishing a permanent penal colony in the area. The 'penal colony' (24 convicts and a detachment of soldiers) was short-lived. By 1831 it had closed and a new, and more permanent, colony had been established on the Swan River 500 kilometres to the north.

The founding father of modern Western Australia was Captain James Stirling who, in 1827, explored the Swan River area in the HMS *Success*. As a result of his explorations attempts to establish a new colony in the west were renewed and on 2 May 1829 Captain Charles Fremantle claimed Western Australia for Britain. A month later a party of free settlers, accompanied by free workers (the plan was to establish the colony without convict labour) arrived under the control of Captain Sterling and a colony was established near the mouth of the Swan River.

By 1831 the population of the colony had reached 1500 but the difficulties of clearing the land and growing crops were so great that by 1850 the population had only increased to 5886. This population settled around the south-western coastline at Bunbury, Augusta and Albany and slowly moved inland looking for pastures for their flocks, cutting down the hardwoods and grubbing out sandalwood for export to Asia.

In spite of this relative success the colony could not resist the temptation of convict labour and on 1 June 1850 the first boatload of convicts arrived. Western Australia was becoming a convict state at a time when the eastern states, largely due to the goldrushes, were abandoning convict labour. Between 1850 and 1868, when transportation stopped, a total of 9718 convicts arrived. Their effect on the colony's economy was considerable and by 1869 the population had increased to 22 915.

The harshness of the climate and the marginal nature of the land ensured that Western Australia would never be densely populated. Even Perth, which was to grow into a particularly beautiful modern city, struggled with its population. By 1849, 1148 were living in the city and by 1891 this had only grown to 8447. Even in 1911 it was just a medium-sized country town with a population of 31 300. The arrival of the Trans-Australian Railway in 1917 and the early success of the gold-mining towns pushed the population to 272 528 in 1947 and the subsequent immigration from Britain meant that by 1990, 1 193 100 people were living in Perth and its suburbs. In this sense it is probably the only Australian capital city which is almost totally dependent on the economic well-being of the state.

In his novel *City of Men* Gavin Casey astutely observes: 'When the crop fails the city fails. Townies who ask how the wheat-belt is looking aren't just making conversation. They want to know. It's a wheat-growing city, if you can understand the term. It doesn't make anything. It just buys and sells things, and the only places to which it can sell anything except the wheat and wool and gold are the goldfields, the wheat-belt and the grazing areas.'

Until the 1870s the economy of the state was based on wheat, meat and wool. The early explorers opened up the inland but they were not followed by eager developers because all they found was desert. Major Peter Egerton Warburton made the perilous journey from Alice Springs to the Western Australian coast. A. C. and F. T. Gregory in the 1840s and 1850s carried out extensive explorations along the continent's western coastline and hinterland. Ernest Giles twice traversed the Gibson Desert.

The real change in the state's fortunes occurred in the 1880s when gold was discovered and prospectors by the tens of thousands swarmed across the land in a desperate attempt to discover new goldfields. Paddy Hannan's discovery at Kalgoorlie, and the early discoveries at Coolgardie, sparked true gold fever.

In 1891 the rush to the Murchison goldfields began when Tom Cue discovered gold at the town which now bears his name. In the years that followed dozens of gold towns—Day Dawn, Meekatharra, Nannine, Peak Hill, Garden Gully, Dead Finish, Pinnicles, Austin Island and Austin Mainland—grew up only to die when the seams were exhausted and the gold fever moved on.

As a result of this sudden influx of miners, and the wealth which they brought with them, the state was granted responsible government in 1890.

The wealth generated from gold soon disappeared and by the early years of the twentieth century the economy was once again dependent on wool and wheat. This dependency meant that a dramatic fall in wool and wheat prices in the late 1920s to early 1930s saw the state's economy collapse. It was not to recover until after World War II when the Federal government's postwar immigration policy saw a huge influx of migrants, nearly all of them from Britain, in the period 1947 to 1970.

In the early 1980s the state boasted the remarkable population profile of having 1.3 million people of whom 72 per cent were native-born Australians and 15 per cent were British-born immigrants.

Symbolic of these new immigrants was Alan Bond who, along with Robert Holmes à Court, Laurie Connell, Brian Burke, and a large number of high-flying entrepreneurs, put Western Australia very firmly back on the Australian map during the 1980s.

Bond was symptomatic of the times—high profile and prepared to do anything to draw attention to the state. His coup was the winning of the elusive America's Cup. He had four attempts at the Cup before he was successful.

Bond was matched for audacity by Robert Holmes à Court whose Bell Group made a bid for Australia's biggest company, BHP. The bid was repulsed but not before Holmes à Court made it clear that he had $2.5 billion credit available for future takeovers.

In tandem with these dealings the premier, Brian Burke, did everything in his power to nurture the entrepreneurs. Such was the government's involvement that the term 'WA Inc' was coined to describe its entrepreneurial enthusiasm.

By the mid-1980s Western Australia was the land of opportunity. It was the state where everyone could get rich quickly. However, the stockmarket crash of 1987 put an end to all these dreams. Today Western Australia is still a gigantic and very successful mineral bin with huge deposits of iron ore, gold and diamonds but the entrepreneurs have all fallen from grace and the state is retreating into a new conservatism and nurturing a sense of separateness which looks with disdain on the decadent lifestyle of those who live on the continent's east coast.

*Howick Street, Perth.*

## Western Australia

### Perth and Environs

Adventure World, Bibra Lake

Art Gallery of Western Australia,
  Perth Cultural Centre

Barracks Archway, Perth

Botanic Gardens

Burswood Resort Casino, Perth

Cables Water Ski Park, Spearwood

Cameleer Camel Park, Wanneroo

Caversham Wildlife Park and Zoo.
  West Swan

Concert Hall,
  St Georges Terrace,
  Perth

Creative Native Aboriginal Art
  Gallery,
  32 King Street,
  Perth

Fremantle Art Gallery, 6 Short Street

Fremantle Arts Centre, 1 Finnerty
  Street

Fremantle Crocodile Park

Fremantle Gaol, Kings Square

Fremantle Historic Boat Museum

Fremantle Maritime Museum, Cliff
  Street

Fremantle Markets, South Terrace
  (Friday/Saturday/Sunday)

Fremantle Old Customs House

Fremantle Port Authority Building

Fremantle Prison Museum

Fremantle Round House

Fremantle St John's Church

Fremantle Town Hall, William Street

Gosnells Railway Markets,
  Albany Highway and Fremantle
  Road,
  Gosnells

Government House,
  St Georges Terrace,
  Perth

Hyde Park

Kalamunda History Village

Kings Park

London Court

Music Shell,
  Barrack Street,
  Perth

Old Courthouse,
  Barrack Street,
  Perth

Old Gaol,
  Museum Street,
  Perth

Old Mill,
  Mill Point Road,
  South Perth

Parliament House,
  Harvest Terrace,
  Perth

Perth Mint,
  310 Hay Street,
  Perth

Pioneer Village, Armadale

Queens Gardens

St George's Cathedral,
 St Georges Terrace,
 Perth
St Mary's Cathedral,
 Victoria Square,
 Perth
Scarborough Fair Markets,
 Scarborough (Fridays and Sundays)
Scitech Discovery Centre, West Perth
State Library,
 James Street,
 Perth
Stirling Gardens
Town Hall,
 St Georges Terrace,
 Perth

Underwater World, Hillarys Boat
 Harbour
University of Western Australia,
 Mounts Bay Road,
 Crawley

Western Australian Museum,
 Francis Street,
 Perth
Whale Watching Cruises, Perth and
 Fremantle (October/November)
Wildflower Tours, Perth
 (July–November)

Zoological Gardens,
 Labouchere Road,
 South Perth

## Beyond Perth
Abrolhos Islands
Albany Coastline Reserve
Argyle Downs Homestead—historic
 house, Ord River
Avon Valley National Park

Batavia Coast
Bay of Isles (Recherche Archipelago)
Beedelup National Park
Benedictine Abbey, New Norcia

Brockman National Park
Broome—former pearling centre

Cape Leeuwin
Cape Leeuwin–Naturaliste National
 Park
Cape Le Grand National Park
Cape Range National Park
Chichester Range National Park
China Wall, near Halls Creek
Coral Coast

Darling Range
Dryandra State Forest
Drysdale River National Park
Fitzgerald River National Park
Fortescue Falls

Geike Gorge National Park
Golden Mile—
 Coolgardie/Kalgoorlie/Boulder
 gold mining area
Goldfields Museum, Coolgardie

Hamersley Range
Hamersley Range National Park
Houtman Abrolhos Islands National
 Park

John Forrest National Park

Kalbarri National Park
Kalgoorlie Goldfields
Kimberley Region
Kwinana Industrial Complex

Lake Argyle

Marble Bar
Meekatharra Gold Mine
Millstream Station
Monkey Mia, Shark Bay (swim with
 the dolphins)
Mount Augustus National Park
Mullewa
Mundaring Weir

Nambung National Park

New Norcia Museum and Art Gallery
Ningaloo Marine Park
Nullarbor Plain

Ord River Irrigation Area
Overseas Telecommunications
 Commission Base, Carnarvon
Pemberton National Park
Pilbara Region
Pinnacle Desert, Namburg National
 Park
Porongarup National Park
Prospect Villa—historic house,
 Busselton

Recherche Archipelago (Bay of
 Islands)
River and Vineyard Cruises, Swan
 Valley
Rottnest Island

Scott National Park
Stirling Range National Park
Swan Valley

Timber Museum, Manjimup
Toodyay—historic town
Two People Bay Flora and Fauna
 Reserve

Valley of the Giants—forest near
 Walpole

Walpole–Nornalup National Park
Warren National Park
Wave Rock, near Hyden
Wellington Dam, Collie River
 Irrigation Scheme
Windjana Gorge
Wineries and vineyards, Swan Valley
Wolf Creek Meteorite Crater
Woodbridge—historic house,
 Guildford

Yalgoorup National Park
Yallengup Caves
Yanchep National Park
York

222   *Perth, the capital of Western Australia, is situated on the banks of the clear blue Swan River.*

Above: *Burswood Island Casino, Perth.*

Opposite, top: *St Francis Xavier Cathedral, Geraldton.*

Opposite, bottom left: *The passing parade at Hay Street Mall, in the centre of Perth's shopping district.*

Opposite, bottom right: *New Norcia Cathedral. This settlement had its origins in a mission established by Spanish Benedictine monks in 1846.*

Above: *Gardens at the resort town of Yanchep, north of Perth.*

Right: *The spring-flowering Albany cat's paw* (Anigozanthos preissi) *is native to the south-western part of the state.*

Opposite: *A carpet of wildflowers sets the countryside south of Perth ablaze every spring.*

Opposite, top: *Carnarvon's prawn fleet lines up at the jetty.*

Opposite, bottom left: *Goldrush relics are displayed at the Goldfields Museum in Coolgardie, one of the best known ghost towns in Australia.*

Opposite, bottom right: *Sand patterns on Babbage Island, Carnarvon.*

Above: *Reflections at the former goldmining town of Mount Magnet.*

Below, left: *Intricate formations decorate Lake Cave in the Leeuwin-Naturaliste National Park.*

Below: *Lake Argyle, created by the Ord River Dam, is ideal for boating and fishing.*

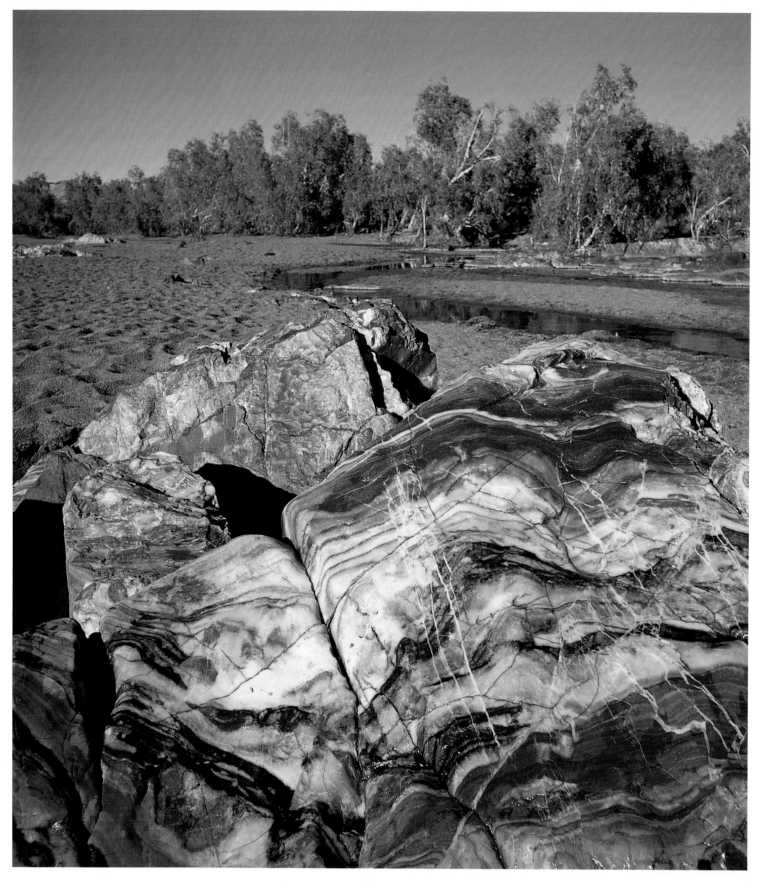

Above: *Marble Bar, reputedly the hottest place in Australia, takes its name from the bar of red-coloured jasper which crosses the Coongnan River.*

Opposite: *Palm trees frame Echidna Gorge in the Bungle Bungle National Park.*

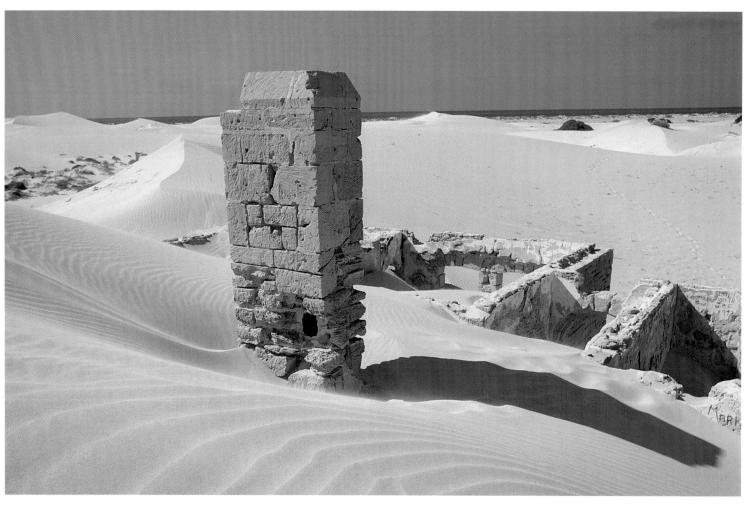

Above: *Ruins of the Old Telegraph Station at Eucla, once one of the busiest in Australia, are gradually being covered by sand.*

Below: *The rugged peaks of the Stirling Range rise abruptly above countryside rich in native vegetation.*

Above: *The boiling white foam of the Southern Ocean pounds against jagged rock formations at East Mylies Beach at Fitzgerald River National Park.*

Below: *The steep-sided multi-coloured walls of Geikie Gorge rise some 60 metres above the water.*

Opposite: *White sandy bays and granite headlands at Thistle Cove in the Cape Le Grand National Park near Esperance.*

Above: *Cheynes Beach Whaling Station Museum near Albany. The whaling fleet once based here used to harpoon about 700 whales per year.*

Below: *Stopover at the National Hotel in the tiny settlement of Sandstone off the Great Northern Highway.*

236 Above: *Sunset over the Gibson Desert.*

Opposite: *Solitude at Cable Beach, Broome.*

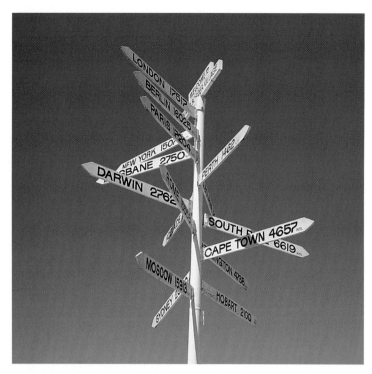

Left: *Signpost on the Western Australia/South Australia border.*

Opposite: *Hamersley Gorge, in the heart of Australia's great western mountain chain.*

Below: *Pearl luggers and fishing boats at Streeters Wharf, Broome.*

Above: *The Hamersley Range stretches more than 300 kilometres through the mineral-rich Pilbara region.*

Below: *Intrepid travelling on the Gunbarrel Highway in the Gibson Desert.*

Above: *Deep River flows into the Nornalup inlet, a broad expanse of water surrounded by the Walpole-Nornalup National Park.*

Below: *Estimated to be 2700 million years old, the remarkable 15 metre high Wave Rock in Hyden has been naturally sculpted out of granite.*

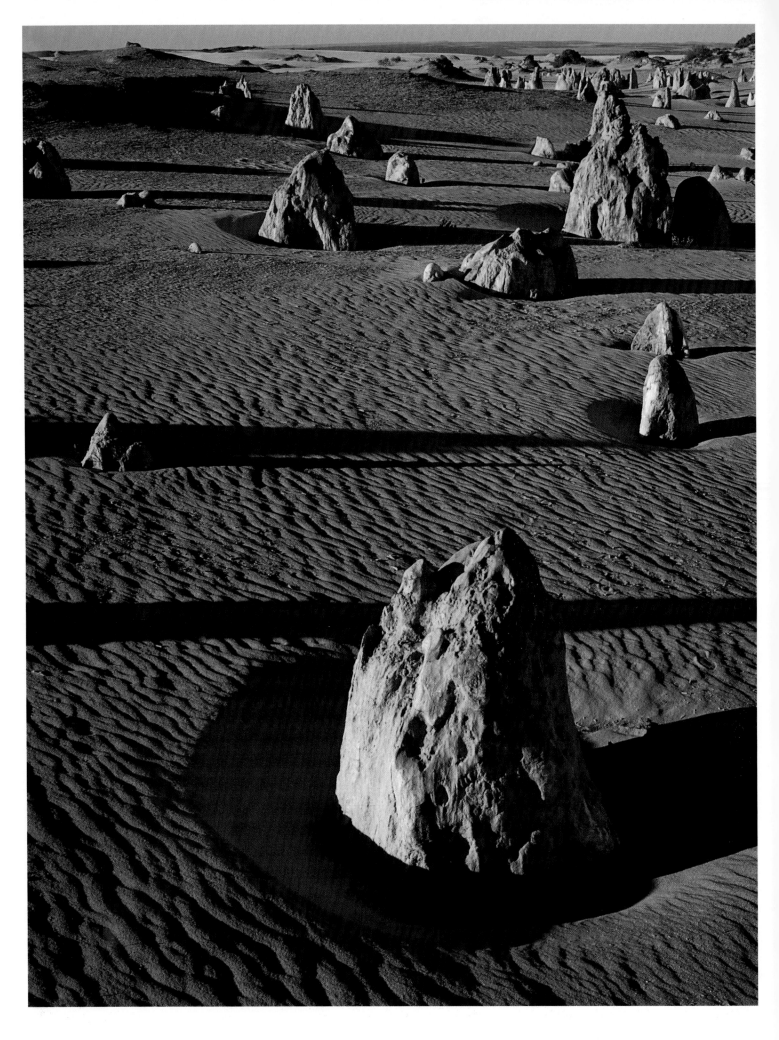

Above: *The Pinnacle Desert, unusual limestone rock formations in the*
242 *Nambung National Park.*

Opposite: *Rugged coloured hills surround the Ord River near Kununurra, Aboriginal for 'big water'.*

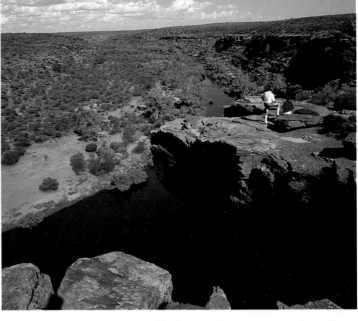

Above: *Shot Hole Canyon, near Exmouth in the arid Pilbara region, one of the most heavily mineralised areas in the world.*

Above: *Hawks Head Lookout affords magnificent views over the wild landscape of Kalbarri National Park, encompassing the lower reaches of the Murchison River.*

Below: *Fresh fish at Fremantle, the largest port in the state.*

Opposite: *Yardie Creek, imprisoned between vertical cliffs, is the only permanent water in the rugged Cape Range National Park.*

# ANNUAL EVENTS—WESTERN AUSTRALIA

The following list is a general guide only. Precise information may be obtained from Tourism Western Australia.

## JANUARY-MARCH

**Albany** Rainbow Coast Air Show
**Broome** Locals Chinatown Street Party
**Busselton** Beach Festival
**Busselton** Collectors Exhibition and Antique Fair
**Geraldton** Australia Day Festival
**Harvey** National Slalom and Wild Water Canoeing Championships
**Lancelin Beach** Bundaberg Rum Ocean Classic
**Margaret River** Wine and Food Festival
**Morawa** Bikes, Band and Brute Force Weekend
**Nannup** South West Music Festival
**Northam** Avon Valley Vintage and Classic Fair
**Perth** Australia Day Sky Show
**Perth** Festival of Perth
**Perth** Healthway Perth Cup
**Perth** Hopman Cup
**Perth** Kyana Aboriginal Culture Festival
**Perth** National Sailing Championships
**Perth** Vines Golf Classic
**Pinjarra** Fairbridge Music Festival
**Porongurup** Great Southern Wines Festival
**Rottnest Island** Festival

## APRIL-JUNE

**Bunbury** Marathon and Half Marathon
**Donnybrook** Apple Festival
**Fremantle** Artcraft Expo
**Fremantle** Medieval Festival
**Fremantle** Rythm and Blues Festival
**Geraldton** *Batavia* Festival
**Guilderton** Fine Arts and Crafts Group Exhibition
**Guilderton** King of the River Regatta
**Kalgoorlie-Boulder** Goldfields Timber Week
**Karrratha** Festival
**Perth** National Boomerang Championships
**Swan Valley** Queen Sirikit Cup
**Western Australia Week** (statewide)
**York** Earthcare Festival

## JULY-SEPTEMBER

**Albany** Wildflower Festival
**Badgingarra** Quilty Camp Draft
**Bencubbin** Agricultural Show
**Beverley** Agricultural Show
**Boulder** Back to Boulder Week
**Broome** Aboriginal Culture and Arts Festival
**Broome** Pearl Festival
**Carnarvon** Sandhurst Run
**Dalwallinu** Agricultural Show
**Dampier** Dampier Classic
**Denmark** Winter Festival
**Derby** Boab Festival
**Derby** Country Music Festival
**Esperance** Agricultural Show
**Fitzroy Creek** Rodeo
**Harvey** Country Music Spectacular
**Kellerberrin** Agricultural Show
**Kojonup** Wildflower Festival
**Kununurra** Agricultural Show
**Moora** Central Midlands Agricultural Show
**Mullewa** Wildflower Show
**Newman** Fortesque Festival
**Northam** Agricultural Show
**Pernejori** Agricultural Show
**Perth** People's Marathon
**Perth** Wildflower Show

**Pingelly** Agricultural Show
**Pingelly** Art and Tulip Festival
**Port Hedland** Beerfest
**Port Hedland** Spinifex Spree Festival
**Quairadin** Agricultural Show
**Roebourne** Royal Show

## OCTOBER-DECEMBER

**Albany** Agricultural Show
**Beverley** Dorcas Rose Show
**Bindoon** Agricultural Show
**Broome** Mango Festival
**Brunswick Junction** Agricultural Show
**Busselton** Agricultural Show
**Busselton** Wildflower and Craft Exhibition
**Collie** Agricultural Show
**Coolgardie** Camel races
**Dongara** Blessing of the Fleet
**Donnybrook** Agricultural Show
**Dumbleyung** Gymkhana
**Fremantle** Festival
**Goomalling** Harvest festival
**Harvey** Agricultural Show
**Jerramungup** Agricultural Show
**Kalgoorlie** International Land Sailing Championships
**Katanning** Agricultural Show
**Kojonup** Agricultural Show
**Koorda** Agricultural Show
**Margaret River** Agricultural Show
**Mount Barker** Agricultural Show
**Mount Barker** Mardi Gras
**Narrogin** Agricultural Show
**Nyabing** Agricultural Show
**Perth** Artrage Festival
**Poringurup** Spring Festival
**Swan Valley** Spring in the Valley
**Tambellup** Agricultural Show
**Toodyay** Show. Hotham Valley Steam Train
**Waroona** Agricultural Show
**Wiluna** Gymkhana

# Northern Territory:
## THE HERITAGE

The Northern Territory of Australia is large in area and small in population. Covering 1 346 200 square kilometres (only Western Australia and Queensland are larger), it is larger than France, Germany and the United Kingdom combined. Yet the territory's population in 1992 was only 168 643. It is a vast wilderness of desert, scrub, savanna grassland and mangrove swamps. Its economy is driven by mining, cattle and tourism. It is, in a very real sense, Australia's last frontier.

There is little doubt that the territory's 6200 kilometre coastline has been the site of most of the continent's significant sightings and arrivals. Available evidence suggests that some 50 000 years ago the ancestors of Aborigines arrived in the Northern Territory travelling overland from the north.

It is probable that the first non-Aborigine to sight the coast was the Chinese explorer Cheng Ho, who in the early years of the fifteenth century ventured into the Indian Ocean. It is quite likely that a statue found near the present-day site of Darwin in 1879 was left by Cheng Ho.

The first confirmed European contact with Australia occurred when Willem Janszoon explored Cape York in 1606. Seventeen years later Jan Carstensz, commanding the Dutch East India ships the *Pera* and *Arnhem* sailing east from the trading port of Batavia, explored the south coast of New Guinea and discovered and named the Gulf of Carpentaria and Arnhem Land.

The entire coastline was explored and chartered by Abel Tasman in 1644 and in 1803, during his circumnavigation of Australia, Matthew Flinders chartered the coast although he did not recognise Melville Island as being separate from the mainland, that was left to Phillip Parker King in 1818.

King found to his surprise that the Aborigines knew some Portuguese words suggesting that they had made contact with Portuguese sailors and that a Portuguese ship had possibly been wrecked nearby. King named the island after Viscount Melville.

Early attempts to settle the coast of the Northern Territory can best be described as tragic disasters. The British, fearing that the explorations of Frenchmen like Nicolas Baudin would lead to the establishment of a French colony, decided that it was necessary to establish a fort or an outpost on the coast.

The first attempt occurred in 1824 when the British government sent three vessels, under the leadership of Captain J. J. G. Bremer. The ships arrived at Port Essington and, determined to lay claim to the area, declared that the north coast of Australia from 129° to 135° east was a British colony.

On 26 September 1824 the party landed at King Cove and over the next month a settlement was built. On 21 October it was named Fort Dundas.

There was no reason, beyond a vague notion that the French or Dutch may lay claim to the region, to settle the area. This became very obvious when sickness, attacks from the local Aborigines and pirates, and dissension over policies caused pressures in the community. By 1826 the post was being wound down and it was officially closed in 1829.

In 1826, after unsatisfactory reports of the settlement at Fort Dundas had filtered through to the Colonial Office in London, it was decided to set up a second military outpost at Raffles Bay. The outpost was to be known as Fort Wellington. The 'settlers' consisted of some convicts and some members of the 39th Regiment. They arrived at Raffles Bay on 17 June 1827.

The settlement suffered the inevitable problems of disease, pestilence, tropical lethargy, attacks from unfriendly Aborigines, and isolation. In 1828, with the arrival of Collet Barker, it looked as though the settlement might succeed. Barker established good relations with the Aborigines and started encouraging settlement from the East Indies. However the settlement was closed down in 1829.

Port Essington was the third attempt to settle the northern coastline. Because the settlement lasted for over a decade, and because it was the site of Ludwig Leichhardt's greatest triumph, it is perhaps more widely known than the other less successful attempts at Raffles Bay and Fort Dundas.

Port Essington was actually chosen as the site of the first settlement but when the settlement party arrived in 1824 they found that there was no fresh water and so, after three days, they moved to Fort Dundas.

On 26 October 1838 Captain J. J. Gordon Bremer (who, by this time, must have been convinced that he was really out of luck when it came to leading expeditions) arrived at Port Essington. It was a military outpost and for the next eleven years was manned almost exclusively by Royal Marines. The population never exceeded seventy-eight and the conditions were harsh.

In June 1839 Bremer had the good fortune to be posted to China to be part of the British forces during the Canton uprising. He never returned to the settlement which was smitten with fever and the problems which had beset the other settlements in the area. The settlement was abandoned in 1849 and it wasn't until twenty years later that the successful settlement at Palmerston (the modern-day site of Darwin) was established.

It is worth remembering that Thomas Huxley passed through the settlement just before it closed down in 1849 and left a graphic description of the sheer awfulness of Port Essington describing it as 'the most wretched, the climate the most unhealthy, the human beings the most uncomfortable and houses in a condition most decayed and rotten.'

The history of permanent white settlement in the territory really started in 1861–62 when John McDouall Stuart, after two previously unsuccessful attempts, crossed the country from south to north. This was much more than just a successful expedition. The subsequent route for the Overland Telegraph Line was worked out by using Stuart's maps and journals. In turn the repeater stations which were established at Port Darwin, Yam Creek (Pine Creek), Daly Waters, Powells Creek, Tennant Creek, Barrow Creek, Alice Springs and Charlotte Waters along the Overland Telegraph route became the first communities in the Territory.

The pastoralists compounded this by using the Telegraph Line as a stock route. To improve the water supply along the track bores were sunk and often where these bores were sunk a small community developed.

In the wake of all these people moving into the Territory it was inevitable that certain minerals were discovered and these mineral deposits also produced settlements.

Although John McDouall Stuart had passed through the Barkly Tablelands in 1862, the area's first explorers were Ludwig Leichhardt, who journeyed overland from Queensland in 1844, and Augustus Gregory who trekked south and east from the Victoria River in 1855. It was partly as a result of the rather exaggerated reports of Leichhardt and Gregory that the area was settled soon after the Overland Telegraph Line was built. Both explorers had returned with glowing reports of the grazing potential and this was enough to encourage adventurers to overland cattle into the area in the hope of making a quick fortune.

In 1863 the entire Northern Territory was annexed to South Australia and on 28 June 1864 Boyle Travers Finniss established a fourth coastal colony at Escape Cliffs. Like all the previous attempts it failed. It was abandoned two and a half years later.

The determination to settle the Territory remained undiminished. In 1869 George Goyder, the Surveyor-General of South Australia, arrived at Port Darwin. By 23 February he had surveyed the site of Darwin which was to be known as Palmerston. The timing was right. The Overland Telegraph had opened up the inland and by 1874 Palmerston had a population of 600 whites and 180 Chinese and Malays. The town had its own newspaper and there were eleven stores.

By the 1880s the northern coast was sparsely settled but, like so much of the Territory, all that was required was a good drought to drive even the most committed pastoralist back to the milder and easier climates of the southern states.

The Barkly Tablelands to the south of Darwin were opened up by the famous stockman Nat Buchanan who travelled from Rocklands Station in Queensland across the tablelands to the Overland Telegraph Line in 1877. The trip was not very successful because by the time Buchanan arrived at the Telegraph Line speculators had already claimed, sight unseen, most of the land on the tablelands. The resulting invasion of sheep, which were totally unsuited to the ecology of the area, resulted in surveys being carried out in 1879 to determine ownership. By 1884 there were over 100 000 sheep in the area. In the 1890s the area became legendary as the great herds of beef cattle were driven across the semi–desert areas from the fertile Kimberleys into north Queensland.

During the war, with the aid of US funds, the Barkly Highway was built from just north of Tennant Creek across to Cloncurry via Mount Isa. It was subsequently upgraded so that today it is the main artery for all transportation through the area.

Independence for the Territory came slowly. In 1890 it elected two members to the South Australian House of Assembly and, with federation, the territory became part of the huge electorate of Grey.

In 1911 the Commonwealth government took over the administration of the territory. It was around this time that the Palmerston became known as Darwin.

The Northern Territory probably changed from being perceived as a wild, tropical outpost to being an integral part of Australia during World War II. Fears of a possible Japanese invasion occurred shortly after the attack on Pearl Harbor in December 1941. Women and children were evacuated from Darwin and early in 1942 a number of American troops joined Australian forces. On 19 February 1942, 188 Japanese aircraft attacked Darwin. The official casualties numbered 243 dead and approximately 350 wounded.

Between 19 February 1942 and 12 November 1943, Darwin sustained 64 air attacks resulting in 261 deaths and 410 injured. It was impossible for people in the rest of Australia to pretend that the Northern Territory was a distant outpost. If Darwin was being attacked, Australia was being attacked.

After the war the Commonwealth government drew up plans to redevelop Darwin. The rebuilding of the city started in the early 1950s and by the mid-1970s it was expanding rapidly. This progress was halted on Christmas Day 1974 when Cyclone Tracy destroyed 90 per cent of the buildings and killed fifty people. The rebuilding of Darwin for the second time started at the end of 1975 and was completed in 1978. On 1 July 1978 the Territory was granted full self-government.

Today the Territory has become one of Australia's premier tourist destinations. The beauties of the Kakadu National Park (which is now part of the World Heritage listings), the magic of Uluru and the dry, dramatic scenery around Alice Springs attract vast numbers of visitors to the region. The population may still be small but the attractions are considerable.

## Northern Territory

### Darwin and Environs

Aquascene,
  28 Doctors Gully Road,
  Darwin
Aviation Museum,
  Stuart Highway,
  Winnellie

Banyan Junction Markets, Mitchell
  Street (every night)
Big Flea Market, Rapid Creek
  (Sundays only)
Botanic Gardens,
  Gardens Road,
  Darwin

Catholic Cathedral,
  90 Smith Street,
  Darwin
Civic Centre,
  Henry Chan Avenue,
  Darwin

Chinese Temple,
  Woods Street,
  Darwin
Christchurch Cathedral,
  2 Smith Street,
  Darwin

Darwin Harbour

East Point Military Museum, East
  Point

Fannie Bay Gaol Museum, Fannie
  Bay

Government House,
  Government House Esplanade,
  Darwin

Leichhardt Memorial,
  The Esplanade,
  Darwin

Museum and Art Gallery,
  Mitchell Street,
  Darwin
Music Bowl,
  Botanic Gardens,
  Darwin

Northern Territory Museum of Arts
  and Sciences, Fannie Bay

Olympic Pool,
  Ross Smith Avenue,
  Fannie Bay

Palmerston Night Market (Fridays
  only)
Parap Markets (Saturdays only)

Pearling Exhibition,
  The Wharf Precinct,
  Darwin

Public Library,
   The Esplanade,
   Darwin

Ross Smith Memorial,
   Ross Smith Avenue,
   Fannie Bay

Smith Street Mall Markets
   (Friday–Wednesday nights)

Wharf Precinct,
   Stokes Hill Wharf,
   Darwin

## Beyond Darwin

Adelaide River
Alice Springs
Arltunga Historical Reserve, near
   Alice Springs
Arnhem Land Aboriginal Reserve

Bathurst Island
Berry Springs Nature Park
Butterfly Gorge Nature Park

Crocodile Farm, Noonamah
Cutta Cutta and Tindal Caves

Daly River

Daly Waters
Devils Marbles, near Wauchope
Devils Pebbles, near Tennant Creek
Douglas Hot Springs Nature Park

Ewaninga Rock Carvings

Finke River Gorge National Park
Fogg Dam Reserve

Glen Helen Gorge
Gove Peninsula

Henbury Meteorite Craters
Hermannsburg Mission
Hot Air Ballooning, Alice Springs
Howard Springs Nature Park

Jumping Crocodiles, Adelaide River

Kakadu National Park
Katherine
Katherine Gorge National Park
Kimberley
Kings Canyon

Lake Bennett
Lakes Tourist Resort, Berry Springs
Litchfield National Park

MacDonnell Ranges
Manton Dam
Marrakai Plains

Mataranka Museum of the Never
   Never
Mataranka Thermal Pool Reserve

Nobles Nob open cut gold mine

Okiri Rock
Olgas, The
Organ Pipes, Finke River
Ormiston National Park

Palm Valley
Pine Creek
Pitchi Ritchi Sanctuary and Museum,
   Alice Springs

Ross River Homestead

Simpsons Gap National Park
Springvale Homestead—historic
   house, near Katherine
Standley Chasm

Telegraph Historical Reserve, Alice
   Springs
Tennant Creek
Territory Wildlife Park

Uluru National Park

West McDonnell Ranges National
   Park

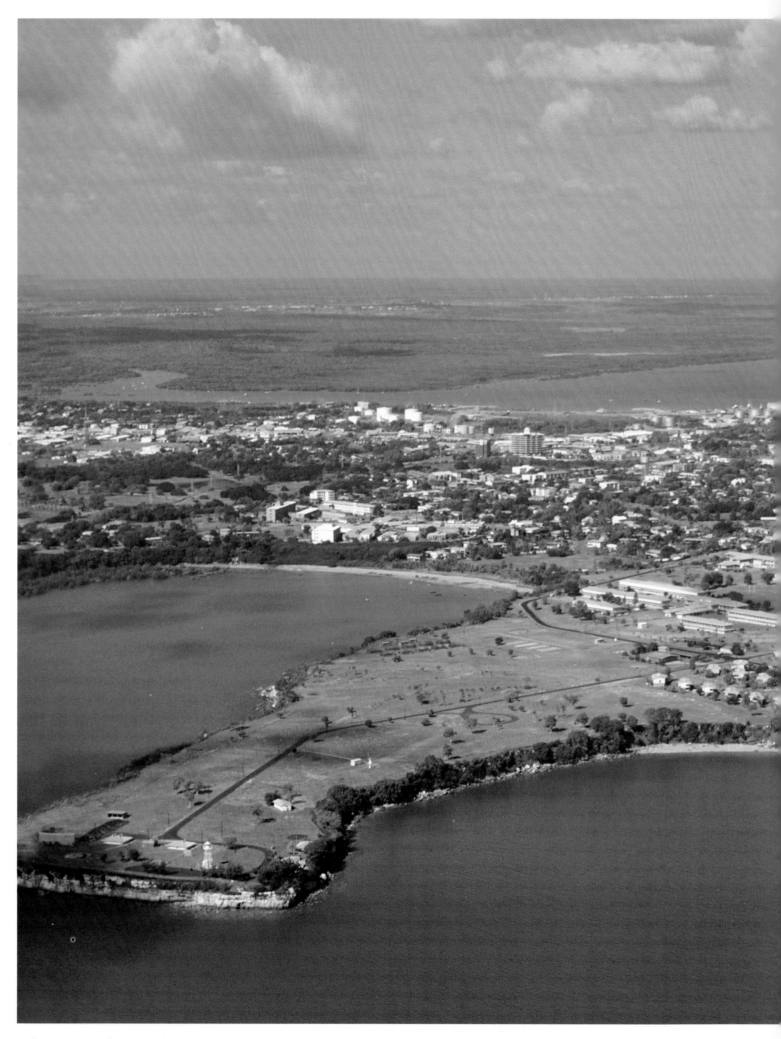

*The relaxed city of Darwin, despite extensive damage from Cyclone Tracy in 1974, has grown in prosperity, based largely on the mineral wealth of the*

252 *Northern Territory.*

Above: *Government House, Darwin, dates from 1870.*

Left: *One of Darwin's most historic hotels, The Old Victoria, has been restored and made into a modern shopping complex.*

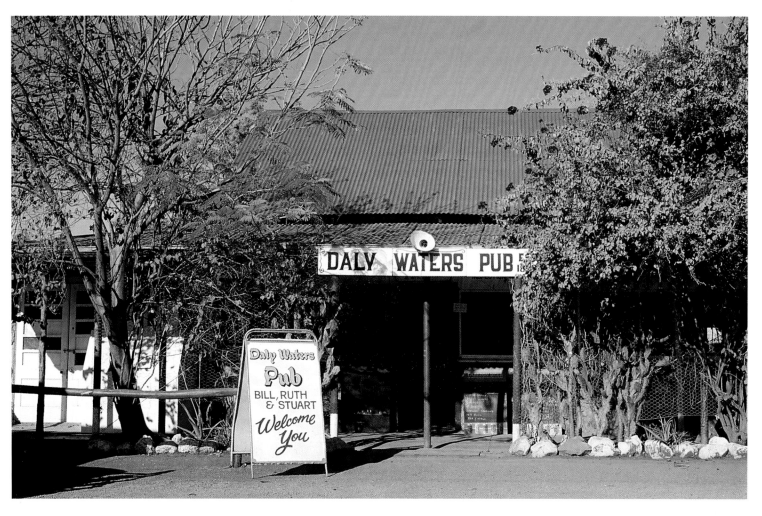

Above: *Watering hole at the tiny settlement of Daly Waters at the junction of the Stuart and Carpentaria Highways.*

Below: *The Mission Church at Daly River, a small township and Aboriginal Reserve on Joseph Bonaparte Gulf.*

Above: *The bakery at the settlement of Pine Creek, originally a goldmining centre.*

Opposite: *Twilight at Alice Springs in the heart of the Red Centre, almost 1000 kilometres from the nearest capital city.*

Left: *Sculptures by William Ricketts at Pitchi Ritchi open-air pioneer museum and bird and flower sanctuary at Alice Springs.*

Above: *Colours of the Red Centre on the road between Ayers Rock and the Olgas.*

Left: *Aboriginal children play on the East Alligator River in Arnhem Land, one of Australia's most fascinating wilderness areas.*

Opposite: *The Macdonnell Ranges curve in a great arc of parallel ridges across the very heart of Australia.*

Above: *Waterlilies float on Majela Creek in the magnificent Kakadu National Park in the remote tropical north.*

Opposite: *Sunset over Fannie Bay, Darwin.*

Below: *Kakadu National Park contains the most outstanding concentration of Aboriginal rock art in Australia.*

Below: *Dramatic rock patterns and formations, carved by ancient waterways, are a feature of King's Canyon National Park.*

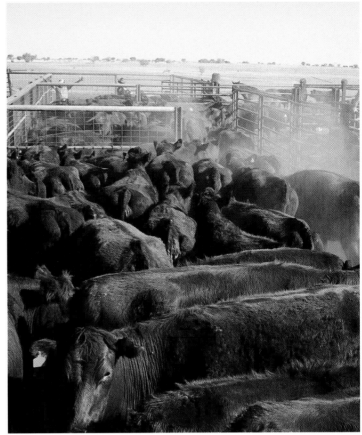

Above: *Heat rises and dust swirls at the outback cattle property of Mt Ebenezer near Alice Springs.*

Opposite: *Obiri Rock in Kakadu National Park is a remnant of the original plateau, now cut back by the East Alligator River.*

Below: *Huge road trains are a familiar sight in the Outback areas of the Northern Territory.*

Above: *The colours of Glen Helen Gorge, west of Alice Springs, have been captured by Aboriginal artist Albert Namatjira, and are today an inspiration to photographers.*

264

Opposite: *Apart from a couple of large waterholes Ormiston Creek shrinks to scattered shallow puddles in the dry season, bordered by the dark red rocks of Ormiston Gorge.*

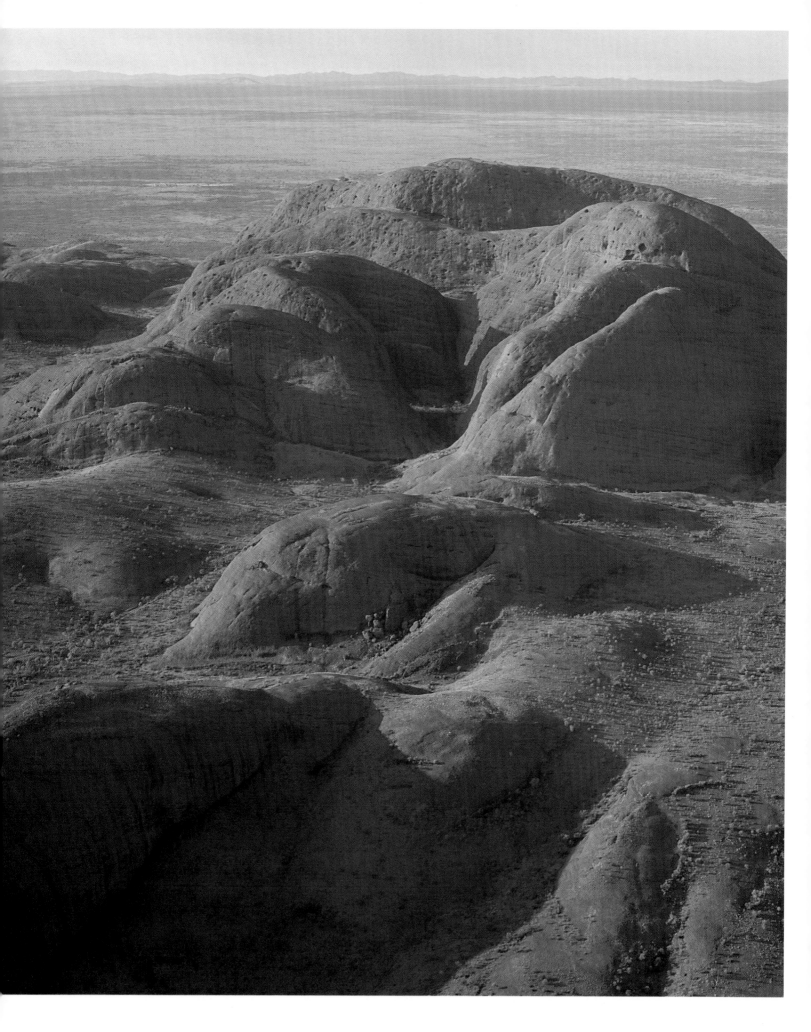

Above: *Katatjuta—the Olgas—rise steeply from the desert in the Red Centre. The thirty domes are separated by narrow vertical chasms and the highest point is 450 metres above the plain.*

Opposite: *White-trunked river gums contrast with dark red rock walls at Ellery Gorge in the Macdonnell Ranges, west of Alice Springs.*

266

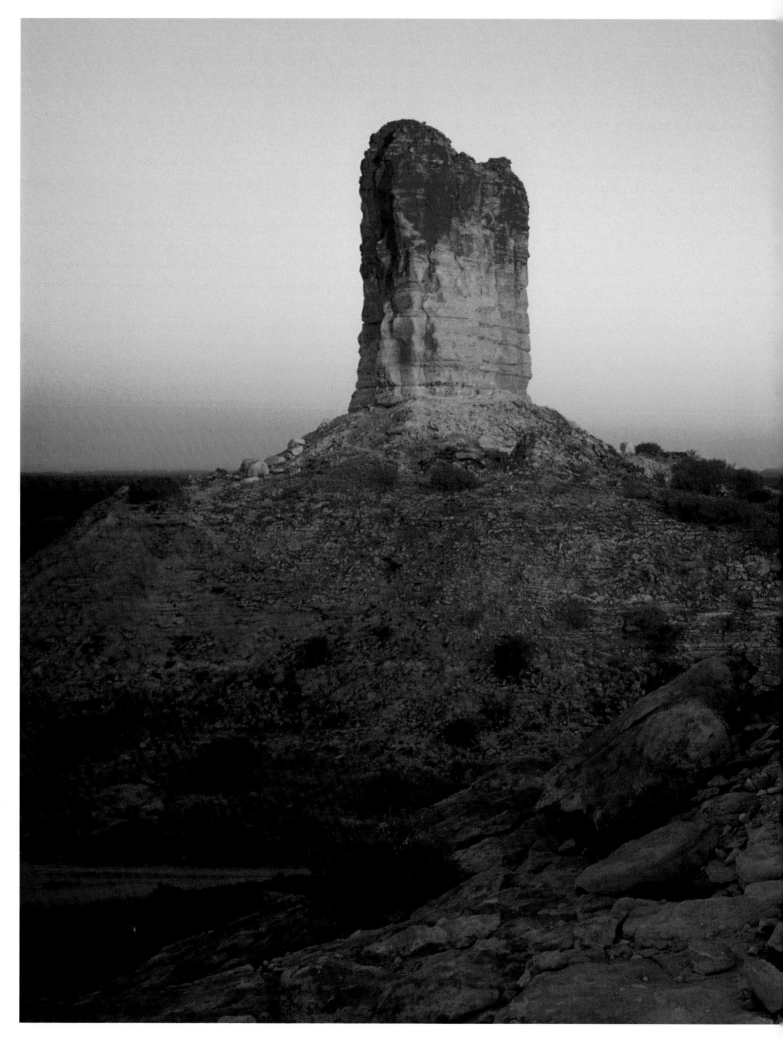

*The huge sandstone Chambers Pillar, south of Alice Springs, catches the last rays of sunlight to glow above the surrounding countryside. Many early explorers have carved their names on this monolith.*

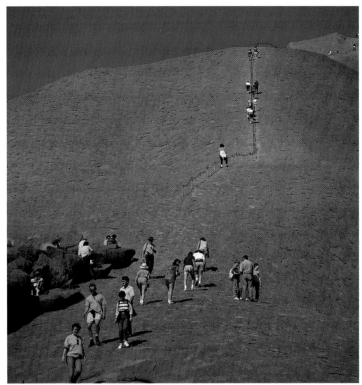

Above: *The 348 metre rope-assisted climb to the summit of Ayers Rock requires plenty of energy and a good head for heights.*

Left: *Ayers Rock, the world's largest monolith, is the Aboriginal people's sacred dreaming place. Caves around the 9 kilometre base contain elaborate and ancient Aboriginal rock paintings.*

Below: *Tourists take a boat trip down the Katherine River to enjoy some of Australia's most spectacular gorge country.*

271

Above: *The Finke River cuts through red sandstone walls in the Finke Gorge National Park.*

Right: *Treescape in the Simpson Desert.*

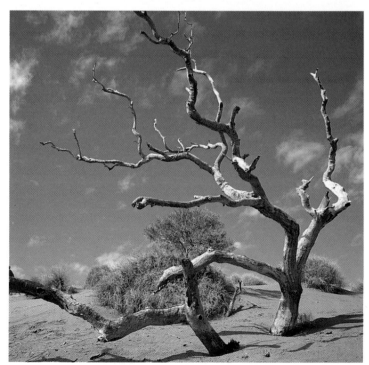

# ANNUAL EVENTS—NORTHERN TERRITORY

The following list is a general guide only. Precise information may be obtained from the Northern Territory Tourist Centre.

## JANUARY–MARCH

**Alice Springs** Crafts Council Open Day and Artists Market
**Darwin** NTFL Premiership Grand Final
**Darwin** Territory's Sevens Rugby Union Tournament
**Diamond Beach** Casino NTFL CUB Australia Cup Carnival
**Larrimah** 'Irish' Ashes
**Tiwi Island** Grand Final

## APRIL–JUNE

**Adelaide River** NT Country Music Talent Quest
**Adelaide River** Rodeo, Campdraft and Gymkhana
**Alice Springs** Alice Craft Acquisition
**Alice Springs** Amateur Open Golf Championships
**Alice Springs** Bangtail Muster
**Alice Springs** Central Australian Country Music Festival
**Alice Springs** Centralian Eisteddfod
**Alice Springs** Cup Carnival
**Alice Springs** Finke Desert Race
**Alice Springs** Heritage Week
**Alice Springs** Lasseters Hotel Casino Cup Carnival
**Alice Springs** Lions Camel Cup

**Alice Springs** National Dance Week
**Alice Springs** Outback Rugby Union Championships
**Arnhem Highway** Corroboree Park Challenge
**Daly Waters** Carry on Down the Daly
**Darwin** Barramundi Classic
**Darwin** Bougainvillea Festival
**Darwin** Cannonball Run
**Darwin** Freds Pass Rural Show
**Darwin** Greek Glendi
**Darwin** International Guitar Festival
**Darwin** Kampfari
**Darwin** Merrepen Arts Festival
**Darwin** National Dance Week
**Darwin** On the Beach
**Jabiru** Stormfront Festival
**Katherine** Barunga Festival
**Katherine** Red Cross Canoe Marathon
**Tennant Creek** Go-Kart Grand Prix
**Tennant Creek** National Dance Week
**Tennant Creek** Renner Springs Picnic Races
**Tennant Creek** RSARC Campdraft and Cutting Competition

## JULY–SEPTEMBER

**Alice Springs** Central Australian Aboriginal Art and Craft Exhibition
**Alice Springs** Harts Range Amateur Races
**Alice Springs** Lions Camel Cup
**Alice Springs** Marathon

**Alice Springs** NT Art Award
**Alice Springs** Old Timer's Fete
**Alice Springs** Rodeo
**Alice Springs** Show
**Barrow Creek** Races
**Daly Waters** Rodeo, Campdraft and Gymkhana
**Darwin** Barefoot Mudcrab Tying Championships
**Darwin** Beer Can Regatta
**Darwin** Bougainvillea Festival
**Darwin** Cup Carnival
**Darwin** National Aboriginal Art Award
**Darwin** Rodeo
**Darwin** Territory Rent-a-Car Variety Club Bash
**Harts Range** Races
**Jabiru** Wind Festival
**Katherine** Mataranka Rodeo
**Katherine** Red Cross Triathlon
**Katherine** Show
**Tennant Creek** CWA Annual Arts Award
**Tennant Creek** Rodeo
**Yuendumu** Sports Weekend

## OCTOBER–DECEMBER

**Alice Springs** Corkwood Festival
**Alice Springs** Henley-on-Todd
**Alice Springs** International Cultural Festival
**Alice Springs** Quilting Club Exhibition
**Tennant Creek** Goldrush Festival

# Queensland:
## THE HERITAGE

It is likely that the first contact with the Queensland coast made by Europeans occurred in 1606 when Captain Luis Vaez de Torres sailed south-west from the New Hebrides and probably came close to the reef near Cape York. The following year the Dutch sailor Willem Jansz made the first confirmed contact with the reefs in the Cape York area and in 1768 Bougainville heard the sound of waves crashing on the reef when he sailed as far south as the present site of Cooktown.

The first significant European contact occurred in 1770 when Captain James Cook sailed up the east coast of Australia charting and naming significant landmarks as he went. He saw Aborigines on the shore but made no attempt to explore the hinterland. Trying to chart his way through the Great Barrier Reef proved impossible and, as a result of the reef, Cook ran aground and was forced to drag his boat up for repairs in the estuary of the Endeavour River at the present-day site of Cooktown.

In 1799 Matthew Flinders sailed up the coast charting it as he went. He discovered rivers and bays which Cook's fairly superficial exploration had overlooked.

The reef was explored and surveyed between 1802 and 1850 by a variety of well-known adventurers and explorers amongst whom the most notable were Flinders, Philip King (1815) and Owen Stanley (1848).

The first explorer to travel by land into the area now known as Queensland was John Oxley who, in 1823, discovered the Tweed River and recommended Moreton Bay as a suitable location for a penal colony.

The establishment of a penal colony at Moreton Bay in 1824 prevented the further development of the area for nearly twenty years. The government decided to prevent any free settlers entering the area around the colony and this law remained until 1842 when Governor Gipps declared that 'all settlers and other free persons shall be at liberty to proceed to the Darling Downs in like manner as to any other part of the Colony.'

The settlement of Moreton Bay in 1824 led inevitably to a more serious assessment of the coast. Whaling boats and light craft sailed up the coast, the narrow strait between Fraser Island and the mainland was discovered, the Mary and Burnett Rivers were explored.

The character of the area changed dramatically when Queensland (at the time it was still part of New South Wales) was opened up to free settlers. Almost immediately settlers moved into the coastal area and crops of sugar cane were grown while dairy and beef cattle were raised in the hinterland.

Pastoralists from the south moved large flocks of sheep north to take advantage of the good soils. The graziers, with their substantial production of wool, hides and tallow, forced the opening up of a number of ports on the coast. Suddenly the colony was booming.

Although the Darling Downs had been discovered and explored by Europeans as early as the 1820s (Allan Cunningham passed through the area in 1823) it wasn't until the government allowed squatters and pastoralists to move onto the rich and fertile plains that the area was settled.

*Queen Street, Brisbane, near the Edward Street corner, in the 1880s.*

Consequently many of the towns on the Darling Downs date their origins to the establishment of a specific land holding in the early 1840s. A town like Dalby, for example, dates its origins to a river crossing where a solitary white man lived and where the itinerant rural workers would pause for a rest and a drink as they passed through to the properties which lay to the west.

In 1844 Jimbour Station was the furthest outpost of European settlement. Beyond it lay an unexplored wilderness. It was the last European settlement visited by Ludwig Leichhardt before he made his epic 5000 kilometre trek from the Darling Downs across to Port Essington.

Leichhardt had been in Australia for two years when he heard of plans for an expedition from Sydney to Port Essington—an outpost on the coast of the Northern Territory. The expedition was to be led by Sir Thomas Mitchell but the Governor of the time, Governor Gipps, declared that it was 'an expedition of so hazardous and expensive a nature, without the knowledge and consent of the Colonial Office.' Irritated by this delay Leichhardt organised

his own expedition. With a party of six he left Sydney on 13 August 1844. They were joined by another four people in Moreton Bay. They then rode to Jimbour and on 1 October headed west. For the next fifteen months they traversed western Queensland and the north-eastern section of the Northern Territory arriving at Port Essington, exhausted, on 17 December 1845. When they finally returned to Sydney on 25 March 1846 Leichhardt was greeted as a hero and hailed as the 'Prince of Explorers'.

As a result of Leichhardt's glowing reports on the land beyond Jimbour there was a push for settlement of the Dawson River area and the Central Western region of Queensland.

The settlers who followed Leichhardt's recommendations opened up the area to the north of the Darling Downs. This was a region of large land holdings which was hugely productive.

During the 1850s settlers pushed north into the Central Highlands where they met with strong resistance from the local Aborigines. The area around Taroom gained a reputation as one of the bloodiest killing fields in Australia. The local Aborigines, the Yeeman, fought for their land against the encroachment of European graziers. They fought with such determination that they were eventually wiped out. In the process a man named Billy Fraser almost certainly killed over one hundred members of the tribe making him the greatest mass murderer in Australian history.

Beyond the hills and valleys of the Great Dividing Range lay the vast, flat near-desert of the Gulf country and the Great Artesian Basin. This area was first explored by Burke and Wills who, in 1860, with a bizarre disregard for common sense and the rules of exploration, led an expedition from Melbourne to the Gulf of Carpentaria. The *Australian Dictionary of Biography* entry on Robert O'Hara Burke makes the observations that 'it took four months to do the 1500 miles. They walked from 5 am to 5 pm with only a single day of rest in the whole period...It was magnificent, but it was not exploration. Burke kept no journal; there was no time for scientific observation, and nothing useful was discovered...Indirectly, discovery was promoted because, although Burke's own journey was worthless as exploration, solid gains in geographical knowledge were made by the explorers Howitt, McKinlay and Landsborough, who led parties in search of him'.

The expeditions of William Landsborough, Frederick Walker and John McKinlay scoured the area for the ill-fated Burke and Wills and in the process discovered both the pastoral and mining potential of the Gulf. William Landsborough referred, somewhat inaccurately, to the area as the 'Plains of Promise', John McKinlay noted the presence of copper near the present-day site of Cloncurry, and Frederick Walker sent back glowing reports of the region's pastoral potential.

The first settler into the area was the remarkable Duncan McIntyre who followed Burke and Wills up the Darling River and settled in the area in 1865 at Dalgonally Station north of Julia Creek. He was followed in the 1870s and 1880s by what could reasonably be described as a 'land grab'. Pastoralists moved in and claimed huge areas of the land which they stocked with cattle.

This pastoral industry was the basis of Queensland's economic success for nearly a century. Beef cattle and the wool industry began to decline in importance in the 1960s when synthetic fibres and the establishment of the European Economic Community played havoc with traditional markets.

The next major development occurred when gold was discovered in Gympie, along the Palmer River and at various points on the Atherton Tablelands. This was in the 1860s and 1870s and did much to open up the ports on the colony's northern coastline.

The towns which began to appear on the coast were all built for one reason: to provide port access. At first it was port access for the mineral wealth which was being dug out of the hinterland. Townsville, Cardwell, Port Douglas, Cairns and Cooktown all started life as ports from which gold could be shipped out. Later it became sugar with towns like Innisfail, Ingham and Mourilyan springing up. It was to these towns in the late nineteenth century that Polynesian labour, known as 'kanakas', was brought to harvest the sugar.

The construction of the ports was no great challenge. The real challenge was finding routes from the tablelands down the steep escarpment. Not only were the early trail blazers—men like Christie Palmerston, John Atherton and Bill Smith—confronted with sheer cliffs but they also had to deal with dense rainforest and local Aborigines who were far from happy about the incursions made into their territory.

It was John Atherton, after whom the tablelands are named, who first brought cattle into the area. He realised that the miners needed to be fed and overlanded cattle to the Herberton fields. The result is that today the Atherton Tablelands are still a highly productive beef and dairy area.

Historically the coast was settled by farmers and fishermen. The ports grew to meet rural demands. Thus Cairns was originally created as a sugar and timber port. It became a meat exporting centre after World War II.

The result of this development is that Queensland's population distribution is dramatically different from that of other Australian states. Nearly half of the state's population lives in the greater Brisbane area. A further 34 per cent live in centres with populations of over 1000 people. In terms of its relatively small population Queensland has more cities over 20 000 than any other state. It has no fewer than eleven cities over 20 000 including Brisbane, Gold Coast, Townsville, Toowoomba, Rockhampton, Cairns, Mackay, Bundaberg, Mt Isa and Gladstone.

By the turn of the century the coastal areas were becoming a tourist mecca for Queenslanders and visitors from the southern states.

The modern Gold Coast was really the inspiration of one man—Jim Cavill. In 1933 Elston was renamed Surfers Paradise and Cavell built his famous hotel which had a small zoo and a huge garden. It began to attract tourists.

During World War II the hotel was used by servicemen who were so impressed by the area that they returned with their families in the early 1950s.

As beef and wool declined in importance the tourist potential of the coast grew. The coast had always attracted the adventurous traveller. In the 1940s big game fishermen from all over the world travelled to Cairns to try and catch marlin. The American western writer, Zane Gray, made a series of short movies of his fishing exploits off the coast of Cairns.

In the 1960s the area around Coolangatta began to grow and by the 1970s it was recognised as the premier beach resort on the east coast.

Modern-day Queensland has, at its heart, a great contradiction. Until thirty years ago it relied on beef, dairy products, wool and sugar cane for its wealth. It now relies on tourism, and preferably international tourism. The idea of farmers trying to develop one of the world's most beautiful coastlines and trying to match wits with aggressive developers is absurd yet it is precisely this absurdity which is the cornerstone of modern-day Queensland.

In recent times there has been a continuing argument about the utilisation of resources. In the case of the state's greatest treasure, the Great Barrier Reef, it is fair to say that since 1975, when the Federal Government enacted the Great Barrier Reef Marine Park Act, that it has been accepted that the reef must not be mined or damaged and that its

*Wharf at Rockhampton c. 1888.*

primary function must remain as an area of low-level tourism and scientific investigation. In 1981 it was accepted for World Heritage listing.

For most of this century Queensland's political life has been remarkably stable. The Labor Party held office from 1915 to 1957 (except for the period from 1929 to 1932) and then the Liberal–Country (later the National) Party held office until the Labor Party under Wayne Goss regained power. Today the state, although driven by its rural wealth, has a good future based on the desire of large numbers of people from New South Wales and Victoria to move north to retire—a situation which will continue until the next century. It also has a successful tourism industry with more than 60 per cent of people who visit Australia nominating Queensland as their prime destination.

## Brisbane and Environs

Anzac Memorial and Eternal Flame

Botanic Gardens, Mount Coot-tha
Botanic Gardens,
    George Street,
    Brisbane
Bunya Park

China Town, Fortitude Valley
City Hall,
    King George Square,
    Brisbane

Earlystreet Historical Village,
    Norman Park

Griffith University,
    Kessels Road,
    Nathan

*Kookaburra Queen* Cruises, Brisbane

Lone Pine Koala Sanctuary

McWhirters Market Place, Fortitude
    Valley
Moreton Bay Islands
Moreton Island
Mount Coot-tha

Newstead House—historic house,
    Breakfast Creek

Oasis Gardens
Observatory,
    Wickham Terrace,
    Brisbane
Old Government House (Institute of
    Technology),
    George Street,
    Brisbane
Old Windmill,
    Wickham Terrace,
    Brisbane

Parliament House,
    Alice Street,
    Brisbane

Queen Elizabeth II Jubilee Sports
    Centre, Nathan
Queen Street Mall
Queensland Art Gallery,
    160 Ann Street,
    Brisbane
Queensland Cultural Centre, South
    Bank

Queensland Museum,
    Gregory Terrace,
    Brisbane

Riverside Markets (Sundays only)

St John's Cathedral,
    Ann Street,
    Brisbane
St Stephen's Cathedral,
    Elizabeth Street,
    Brisbane
South Bank Parklands
Stradbroke Island

University of Queensland, St Lucia

## Beyond Brisbane

Aircraft Vintage Flights,
   Carrara Airport,
   Broadbeach
Atherton Tableland
Australian Sugar Museum, Mourilyan

Barakula State Forest
Barron Falls
Bellenden Ker National Park
Birdsville Track
Blackdown Tableland Forestry
   Reserve
Bookera Lagoon Wildlife Sanctuary
Bribie Island
Buderim Ginger Factory, Buderim
Bungee Downunder,
   Fishermans Wharf,
   Gold Coast
Bunya Mountains National Park
Burleigh Heads Fauna Reserve

Cable Ski World,
   Runaway Bay,
   Gold Coast
Callide Fish Hatchery
Callide Power Station
Cape York Peninsula
Captain Cook Memorial, Point
   Danger
Carnarvon National Park
Channel Country
Chillagoe Caves National Park
Chocolate Expo, Currumbin
Cooloola National Park
Cotton Ginnery, Blioela

Cunninghams Gap National Park
Currumbin Bird Sanctuary

Darling Downs
Dreamworld, Coomera, Gold Coast
Dunk Island

Eungella National Park

Fleay's Wildlife Park, Burleigh Heads
Fraser Island
Frassifern Valley National Park

Girraween National Park
Gladstone—mining, industrial and
   shipping centre
Glasshouse Mountains

Gold Coast
Gold Coast City Art Gallery
Great Barrier Reef
Gulf Country
Heron Island National Park
Hinchinbrook Island National Park

James Cook University, Townsville
Jupiter's Casino, Gold Coast

Lake Barrine National Park
Lake Eacham National Park
Lamington National Park
Lindeman Island National Park
Lizard Island National Park
McPherson Ranges
Mount Bartle Frere

Mount Glorious National Park
Mount Isa
Movieworld, Oxenford, Gold Coast
Mungana Caves
Mystery Craters, near Gin Gin

Noosa National Park
Nerada Tea Plantation

Offshore Islands

Palmerston National Park
Pioneer Plantation Wildlife Park, near
   Coolangatta
Pioneer Village, Laidley
Port Douglas

Santuary Cove
Sea World, Main Beach, Gold Coast
Snowy Mounts salt fields, near
   Rockhampton
Sunshine Coast

Tamborine Mountain National Park
Teewah Coloured Sands Cliffs
Thursday Island
Tinaroo Falls

Underwater World, Sunshine Coast

Wallaman National Park
Wet 'n' Wild Water Park, Gold Coast
Whitsunday Passage Islands
Winery, Romaville
Wivenhoe Dam

Yowel Opal Fields near Eulo

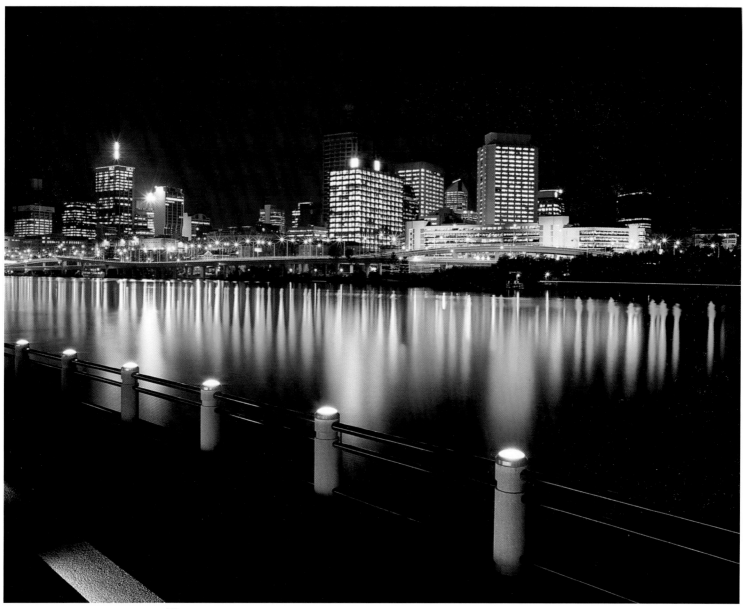

Opposite: *The city of Brisbane, on the banks of the Brisbane River, is the third largest city in Australia and the busiest river port.*

Below: *This man-made canal meanders through Brisbane's South Bank Parklands complex which was built on the Expo '88 site.*

Above: *Brisbane's colourful night lights throw shimmering reflections onto the Brisbane River.*

Below: *Luxury residences and pleasure craft at Sanctuary Cove, an exclusive complex on Hope Island.*

Opposite, top: *The William Jolly Bridge is one of several bridges spanning the Brisbane River to link the city with its spreading suburbs.*

Opposite, bottom: *Horse-drawn tours are a speciality in the township of Kuranda at the top of the Macalister Range. The station here is the destination point for the scenic rail trip from Cairns.*

Right: *Sunset lights the popular Sunshine Coast beach resort of Caloundra.*

Below: *The Tropical Display Dome, one of the features of the Mt Coot-tha Botanic Gardens, Brisbane.*

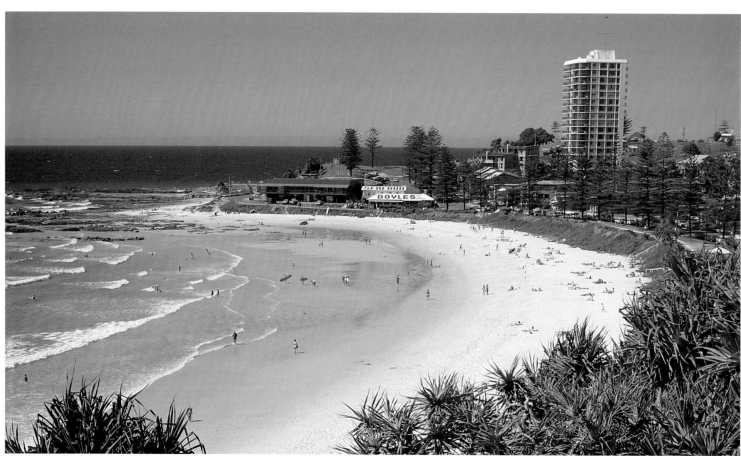

Opposite, top: *A Gold Coast landmark—Jupiters Casino at Broadbeach.*

Opposite, bottom: *Looking over an expanse of sand from the beach resort of Coolangatta to its sister city, Tweed Heads, across the border in New South Wales.*

Right: *Modern freeways skirt the Brisbane River in the city of Brisbane.*

Below: *Flower show in Laurel Bank Park in the garden city of Toowoomba. A Carnival of Flowers is held here every September.*

Opposite, top left: *Fishermen on the tranquil Maroochy River, Maroochydore, in the centre of the Sunshine Coast.*

Opposite, top right: *Windsurfing off Caloundra, one of the many very popular beach resorts on the Sunshine Coast.*

Opposite, middle left: *A gardener's delight—the historic and colourful railway station at Spring Bluff, near Toowoomba.*

Opposite, middle right: *Pineapples and tropical fruits are grown extensively on the coastal plains near Nambour, home of the Big Pineapple, a major tourist attraction.*

Opposite, bottom left: *Farmland is interspersed with lush rainforest in Brisbane's mountainous hinterland near Mt Glorious.*

Opposite, bottom right: *Burning the cane—the thick foliage is burnt off to prepare the cane for harvesting. Sugar growing is a major industry in north Queensland.*

Right: *Botanic gardens at the small town of Cooroy near Noosa Heads.*

Below: *Noosa—the most northerly of the sunshine coast resorts—has a unique combination of national park, beach, river and lake scenery.*

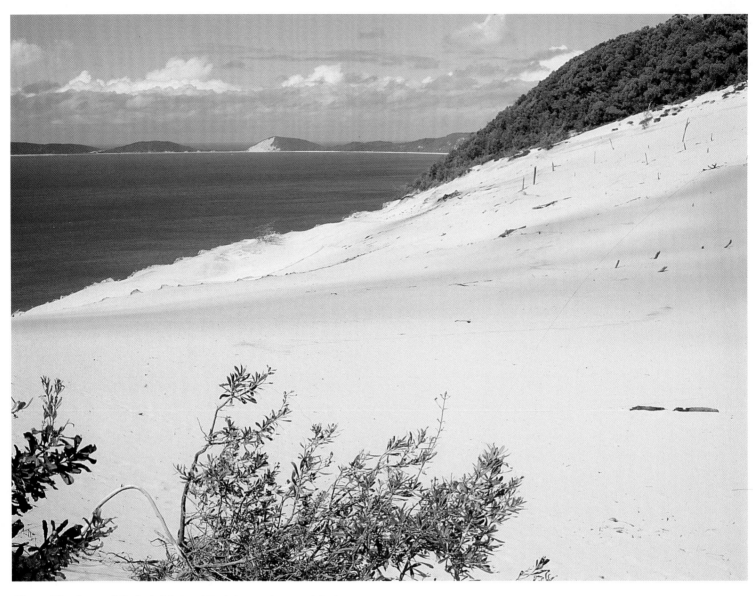

Above: *The dunes of Cooloola National Park in a region noted for its high dune formations, wind driven sandblows and multi-coloured sand cliffs.*

Below: *Enjoying the rock pools at Jourama Falls in Jourama National Park, north-west of Townsville.*

Below: *A river of white-water rapids, huge jumbled boulders and tumbling falls churns its way through Mossman Gorge National Park near Daintree.*

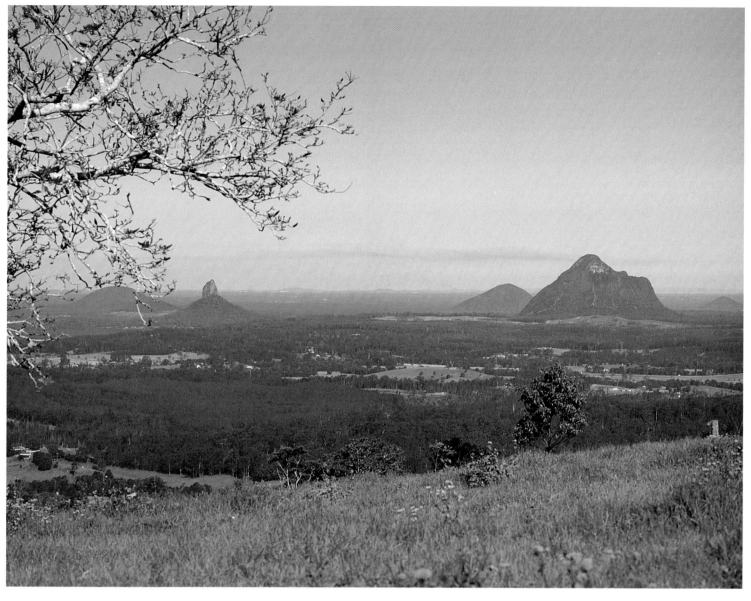

Above: *The rocky volcanic cores of the Glasshouse Mountains rise steeply out of the surrounding countryside. A rock climber's paradise, these mountains were named by Captain Cook in 1770.*

Below, left: *Building sandcastles on Mission Beach with Dunk Island on the horizon.*

Below: *The many hues of ochre, yellow, gold and brown in the coloured sands of Fraser Island, the world's largest sand island.*

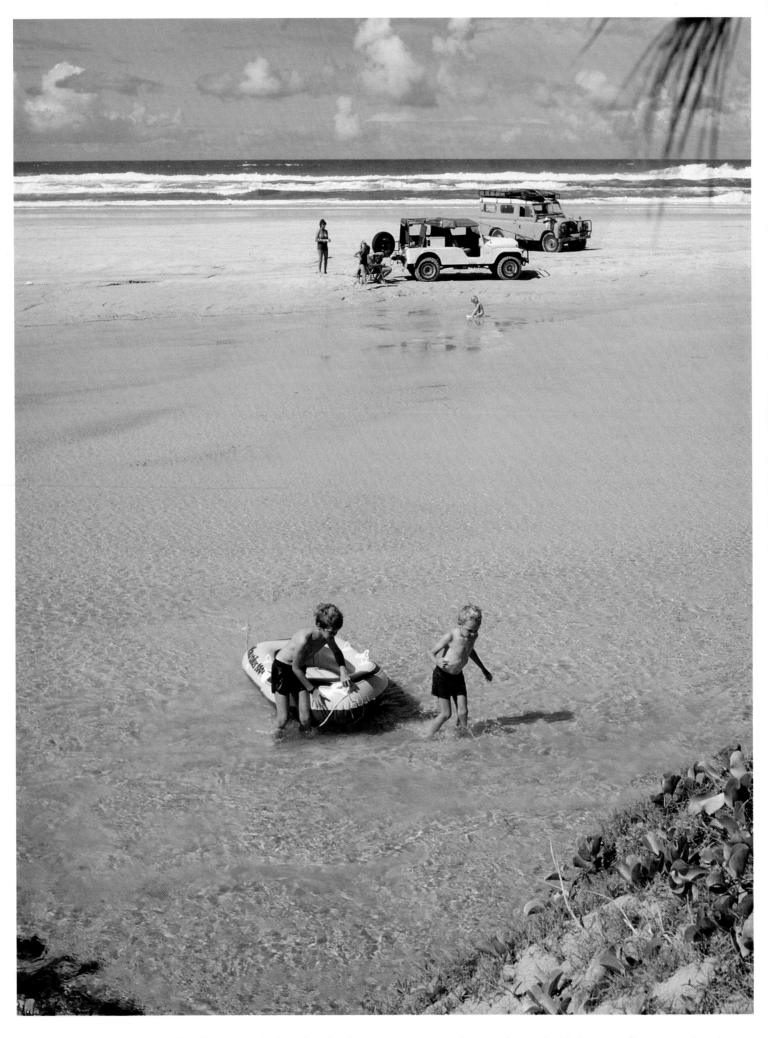

Above: *Four-wheel-drives and inflatable boats are both good modes of*
*transport near Eli Creek on Fraser Island.*

Opposite: *Shute Harbour—the ideal setting-off point to explore the many tropical islands in the beautiful Whitsunday waters.*

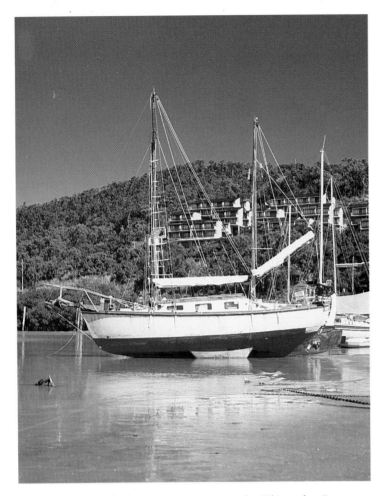

Above: *Airlie Beach, the main resort town on the Whitsunday Coast.*

Below: *Low tide brings interesting sand patterns at Yule Point, north of Cairns.*

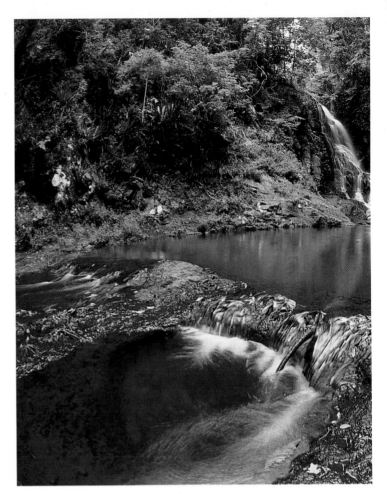

Above: *Elebana Falls, one of the many exquisite waterfalls in the Lamington National Park on the Gold Coast hinterland.*

Opposite: *Once a goldrush port, Port Douglas is now a popular resort offering tropical holidays on long beaches fringed with palms.*

Below: *Harvest time at Australia's only commercial tea plantation at Nerada, west of Innisfail.*

Opposite: *Windblown palms line the Johnstone River at Innisfail, south of Cairns.*

Above: *Sunrise reflections on the Diamantina River, near Birdsville.*

Above: *The Birdsville Hotel, about 100 years old, is the perfect overnight stop for tourists travelling down the infamous Birdsville track into South Australia.*

Opposite: *Lady Elliot Island at the southern tip of the Great Barrier Reef is a true reef island, a sand cay surrounded by coral reefs.*

Below: *Aboriginal rock paintings of sacred and ceremonial significance are a feature of the breathtakingly scenic Carnarvon National Park.*

Left: *A twentieth-century carving of Robert O'Hara Burke at Cooper Creek, just inside the Queensland border. This was the site of the last camp made by Burke and Wills on their tragic overland journey from Melbourne to the Gulf of Carpentaria.*

Below: *Pleasure craft moored at the peaceful seaside town of Port Douglas.*

Opposite. top: *The Birdsville water bore—the most isolated settlement in Queensland's town water supply.*

Opposite, bottom: *The railway station at Normanton, the main town of the Gulf Country, is a monument to the goldrush days.*

*Four-wheel drivers cross the dry and harsh Simpson Desert.*

Overleaf: *Tangalooma, a pleasant tourist resort nestled in among the wilderness on Moreton Island, is a popular base for big-game fishing.*

Above: *Aboriginal dancers at Laura on the Cape York Peninsula.*

Below: *Young locals line up to be photographed for posterity at Cunnamulla, a friendly sheep town on the Warrego River north of the New South Wales border.*

Opposite: *Reputedly Australia's widest waterfall, Millstream Falls is situated in eucalypt woodlands on the eastern slopes of the Atherton Tableland.*

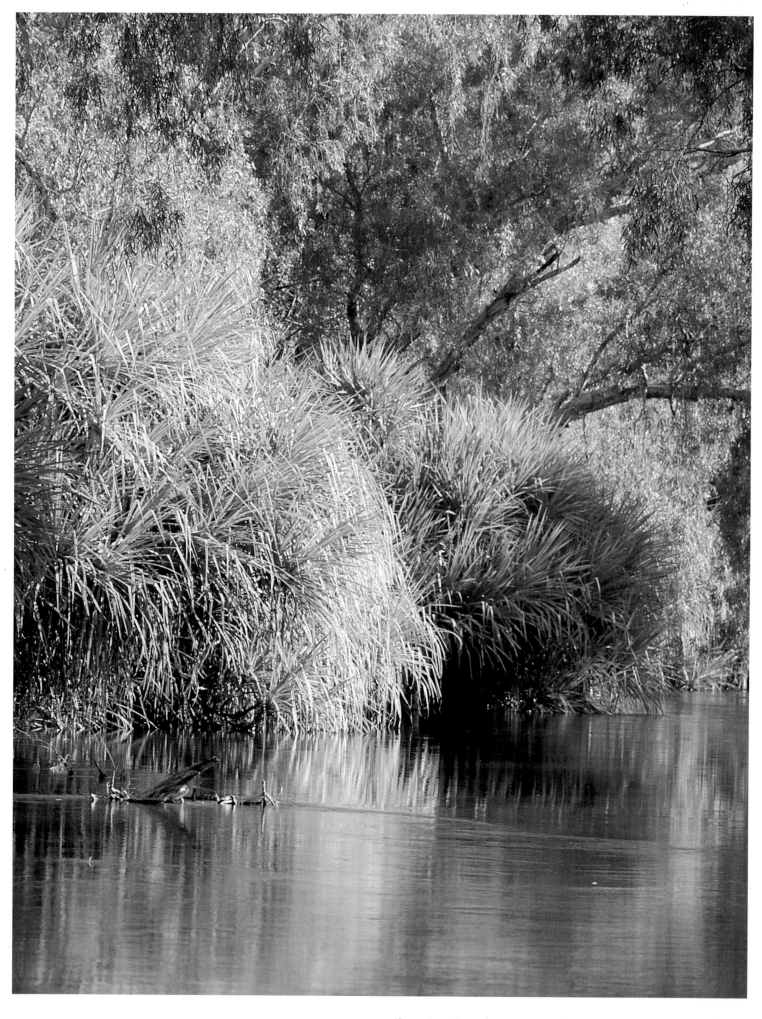

Above: *Cool greens colour the Gregory River near Gregory Downs in the Gulf Country—a vast, remote region that has more rivers than roads.*

Opposite: *Tropical vegetation and sheer red, orange and grey cliffs line the Lawn Hill Creek which snakes through the Constance Range on its way to the Gulf of Carpentaria.*

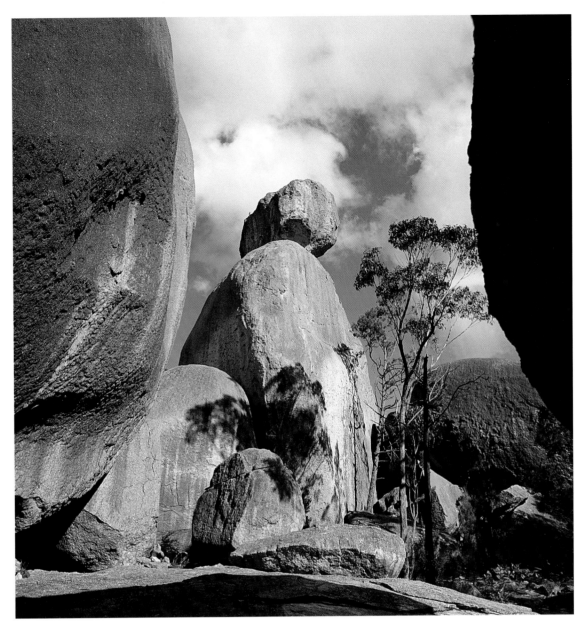

Above: *The Sphinx, a granite outcrop in Girraween National Park, on one of the highest parts of the Great Dividing Range.*

Left: *Enjoying the Murray Falls and rockpools near Cardwell.*

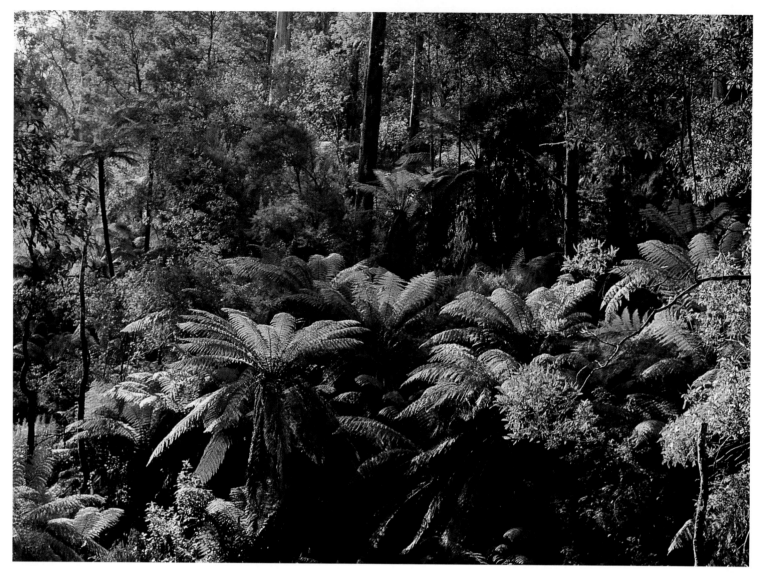

Above: *Cool and luxuriant vegetation at the Crater National Park, near Atherton. This small park is an important remnant of the upland type of rainforest, at an altitude of about 1000 metres.*

Below: *The local butcher shop at the former goldmining town of Croydon. Many of the town's buildings have been classified by the National Trust.*

Opposite: *Patterned sand dunes in the the Simpson Desert.*

Below: *The Pyramid stands sentinel over sugarcane country near Ravenshoe on the Evelyn Tableland.*

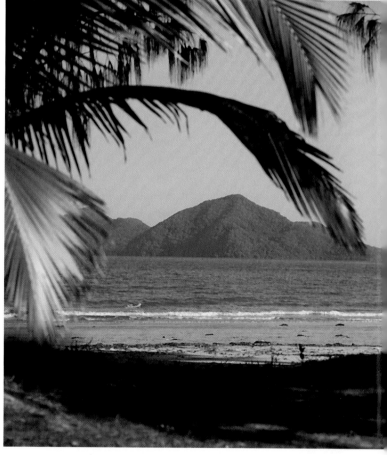

Above: *Wallaman Falls, where Storm Creek plunges 278 metres down sheer dark cliffs onto boulders and rainforest below. Situated in Wallaman Falls National Park, close to Ingham, these falls are the third longest in the world.*

Top: *The fast-flowing Broken River passes through rugged mountain terrain and luxuriant rainforest in the Eungella National Park on the central coast.*

Above: *Grassland and rainforest clothe the hilly resort island of South Molle in the middle of the Whitsunday Passage.*

Above: *High-rise development at Surfers Paradise, the brightest star on the commercialised Gold Coast.*

Below: *Photogenic koala at Lone Pine Sanctuary, just outside Brisbane.*

Below: *Fishing trawlers in the sheltered waters off Bribie Island. Commercial fishing plays an important role in Queensland's economy.*

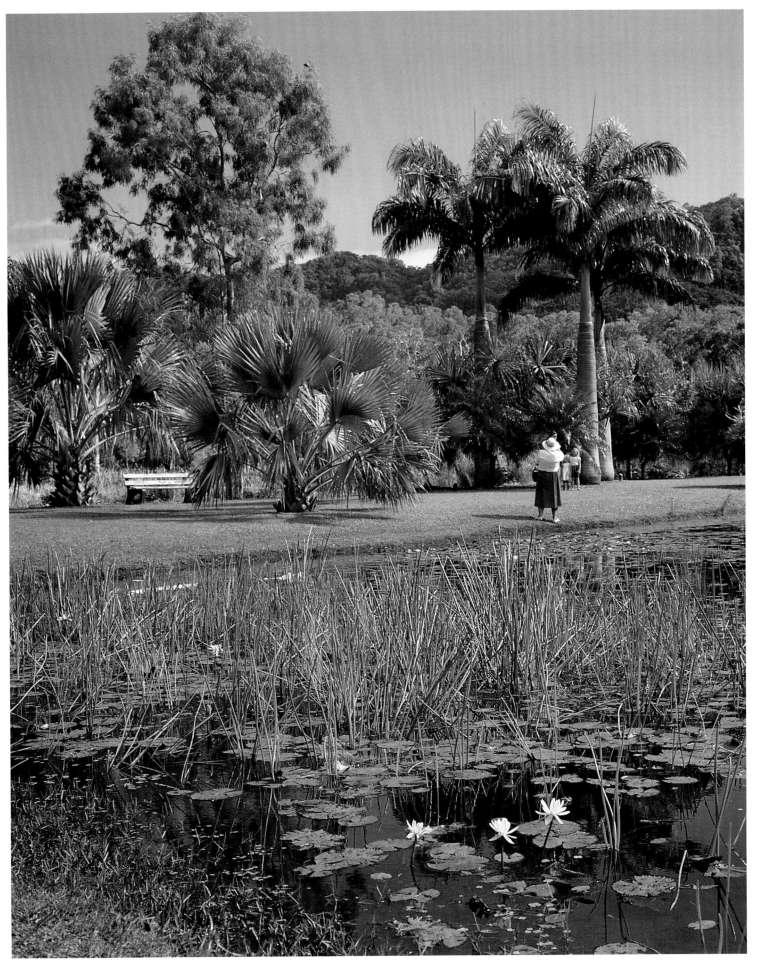

Opposite, top left: *The scarlet flowers of the* Poinciana pulcherrima *are a common sight in Queensland.*

Opposite, top right: *Hides Hotel at Cairns, the colourful 'capital' of tropical, far-north Queensland.*

Above: *Tropical plants are seen at their best in the Cairns Botanic Gardens.*

Opposite, bottom: *Rockhampton's Customs House (1901) is one of many fine stone public buildings to be found in the 'beef capital' of Australia.*

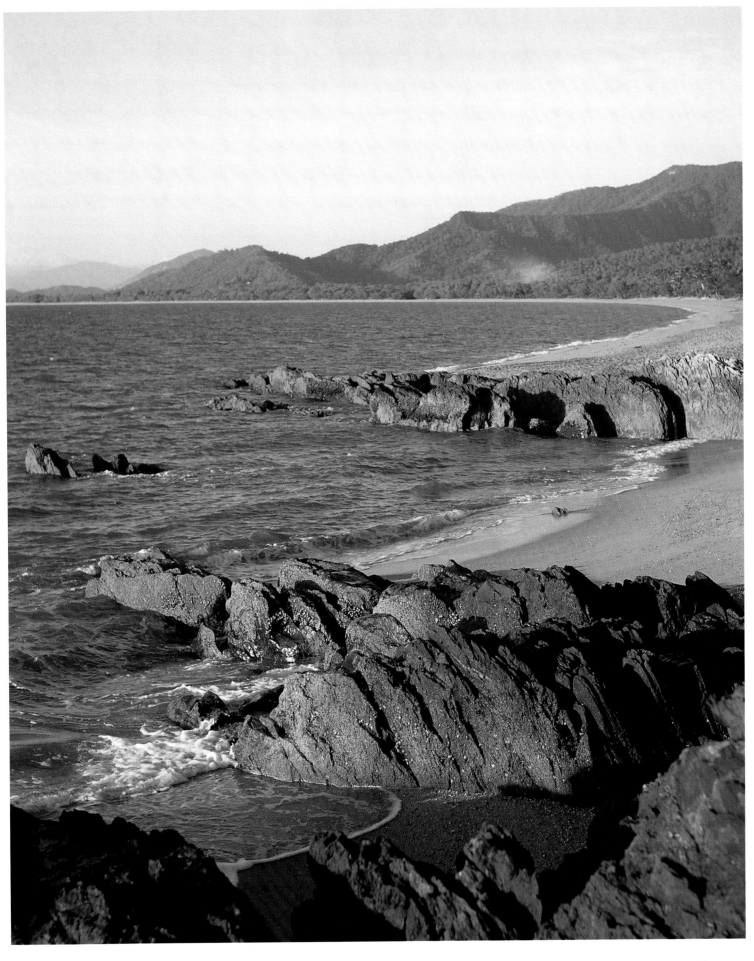

Opposite, top left: *Exotic Brahman cattle have been cross-bred with English shorthorns and Herefords to create top-quality disease-resistant herds. Beef-cattle raising is the major industry of the Rockhampton area.*

Opposite, top right: *Harvesting sugarcane in the Nambour area.*

Above: *Palm Cove, one of the unspoilt stretches of coastline north of Cairns.*

Opposite bottom: *Shady verandahs provide a welcome respite from the tropical heat at the Criterion Hotel in Townsville, the administrative, commercial and manufacturing capital of northern Queensland.*

# ANNUAL EVENTS—QUEENSLAND

The following list is a general guide only. Precise information may be obtained from the Queensland Tourist Centre.

## JANUARY–MARCH

**Brisbane** Australia Day Cockroach Races
**Caloundra** Kabbi Cook Festival
**Chinchilla** Canaga Cow Cockies Cutting Carnival
**Chinchilla** Melon Festival
**Fitzroy Island** Yacht Race
**Gin Gin** Wild Scotchman Celebrations
**Gold Coast** Indycarnival
**Gold Coast** Magic Millions Summer Carnival
**Gold Coast** Queensland Surf Life Saving Championships
**Jondaryan** Australia Day Activities
**Kingaroy** Peanut Festival
**Noosa** Malibu Classic
**Stanthorpe** Rodeo
**Toowoomba** Romance and Arts Festival
**Woodford** Maleny Folk Festival

## APRIL–JUNE

**Brisbane** Marathon and Half Marathon
**Brisbane** Paniyiri
**Brisbane** Winter Solstice Festival
**Buderim** Craft Cottage Easter Market
**Bundaberg** Food and Wine Festival
**Cairns** Jazz in June
**Charters Towers** Country Music Festival

**Cooktown** Discovery Festival
**Gayndah** Orange Festival
**Gladstone** Harbour Festival
**Gold Coast** Australian Surf Life Saving and Masters Championships
**Gold Coast** International Jazz and Blues Festival
**Ingham** Australian–Italian Festival
**Jondaryan** Woolshed Championship Shearing Competition
**Kingaroy** Show
**Longreach** The Outback Muster
**Noosa** Festival of Arts
**Queensland** Winter Racing Festival
**Rubyvale** Wheel Barrow Derby
**Surfers Paradise** International Triathlon

## JULY–SEPTEMBER

**Anakie** Festival of Gems
**Birdsville** Races
**Brisbane** International Film Festival
**Brisbane** Warana Festival
**Bundaberg** Bundy in Bloom
**Gold Coast** International Marathon, Half Marathon and 10km Walk
**Gold Coast** Men's Winter Bowls Carnival
**Hervey Bay** Whale Festival
**Longreach** Diamond Shears and South Pacific Shearing Championships
**Mackay** Festival of the Arts
**Miles** Back to the Bush Weekend
**Mount Isa** Rotary Rodeo and Mardi Gras
**Noosa** Jazz Party
**Redland** Strawberry Festival

**Toowoomba** Carnival of Flowers
**Townsville** Festival of Chamber Music
**Townsville** Winter Racing Carnival
**Yeppoon** World and Australian Cooee Championships

## OCTOBER–DECEMBER

**Brisbane** Fashion Design Awards
**Brisbane** South Bank Parlands Christmas Festival
**Brisbane Valley** 100 Canoe Race
**Cairns** Fun in the Sun
**Crows Nest** Day
**Crows Nest** Worm Races
**Dalby** Harvest Festival
**Gold Coast** Summer Lights
**Gold Coast** Tropicarnival
**Goondiwindi** Christmas Eve Celebrations
**Goondiwindi** Spring Festival
**Hamilton Island** Billfish Bonanza
**Jondaryan** New Year's Eve Bush Dance
**Karumba** Barra Ball
**Lamington National Park** Birdwatching Week
**Mooloolaba** Jazz on the Beach
**Noosa** Triathlon Weekend
**Ravenshoe** Torimba Festival
**Rockhampton** Summer Solstice
**Roma** Cup
**Townsville** Contempofest
**Townsville** Pacific Festival
**Warwick** Rodeo and Campdraft

# Index

Numerals in *italics* refer to illustrations